AMERICAN RITUAL DRAMAS

Social Rules and Cultural Meanings

MARY JO DEEGAN

CONTRIBUTIONS IN SOCIOLOGY, NUMBER 76

Greenwood Press
NEW YORK • WESTPORT, CONNECTICUT • LONDON

Library of Congress Cataloging-in-Publication Data

Deegan, Mary Jo, 1946–
   American ritual dramas : social rules and cultural meanings / Mary
Jo Deegan.
     p. cm.—(Contributions in sociology, ISSN 0084–9278 ; no.
76)
   Bibliography: p.
   Includes index.
   ISBN 0-313-26337-X (lib. bdg. : alk. paper)
   1. United States—Social conditions—1980– 2. United States—
Social life and customs—1971– 3. Social interaction—United
States. 4. Symbolic interactionism. I. Title. II. Series.
HN59.2.D44   1989
306'.0973—dc19   88–17772

British Library Cataloguing in Publication Data is available.

Library of Congress Catalog Card Number: 88–17772
ISBN: 0–313–26337–X
ISSN: 0084–9278

First published in 1989

Greenwood Press, Inc.
88 Post Road West, Westport, Connecticut 06881

Printed in the United States of America

The paper used in this book complies with the
Permanent Paper Standard issued by the National
Information Standards Organization (Z39.48–1984).

10 9 8 7 6 5 4 3 2 1

To Michael Hill

My Partner and Colleague

Contents

PART IV.   CONCLUSION

Tables

Preface

This book is about "good times" and the ambiguous contexts they generate. It is a product of many experiences, studies, and conversations that have occurred throughout my life. The major intellectual antecedents to the book can be summarized, however, succinctly.

Erving Goffman was a brutally clear observer of American life. His analysis of the role of stigma, or discrediting attributes, in everyday life opened new doors of understanding to me as a beginning graduate student in sociology. Since I was recovering from a visible physical handicap, his description of the process of being unacceptable in America clarified to me what I was experiencing. His bitterness and cynicism revealed our shared pain—a pain I had naïvely thought that only I experienced. His work has been a thread throughout my life since that first compassionate reading in 1969. I had the opportunity to correspond and meet briefly with Goffman before his death and found him to be as exasperating and charismatic as I had anticipated.

Victor Turner has a vastly different relation to my ideas and experience of the world. In his seminars on comparative symbology in 1972–73, memories of past celebrations were evoked. The seminar format was intellectually stimulating, the possibilities of human caring and sharing were elaborated and re-lived. Ironically, the Watergate investigation was occurring at this time and the press of modern life contrasted starkly with the oasis of thought and celebration generated by Edith and Victor Turner. Their openness to ideas, and the openness they created in others, revealed a side of life that healed me in a way very different from Goffman's shared laugh on human foibles and destructiveness.

Finally, T. R. Young has created a niche within sociology for understanding the role of critical analysis within an American experience and understanding of everyday life. He has pointed to a way to do sociology, to think about the world, and to engage in intellectual analysis that helps to jump the tremendous gaps between the work of Goffman and Turner. His writings and conversations with me over the past decade have expanded my understanding of critical thought.

I also owe thanks to the many people who have read portions of this manuscript: Valerie Malhotra, Helen Moore, Terry Nygren, Julia Penelope, and T. R. Young. I particularly thank Michael Stein for his years of conversations concerning the work of Goffman. His fascination with Goffman continually pushed me into positions of agreeing or disagreeing and thereby enabled me to grow as a person and theorist. Michael Stein also coauthored an earlier paper on Nebraska football that was used extensively in chapter 6 here. In a very concrete way, Norbert Wiley gave me the idea to write this book when he suggested I stop writing so many articles and start connecting them into a book. Baja Stack, Inge Worth, Laurie Eells, and Judy McCubbin helped to type many drafts of this book. The Women's Studies Program at the University of Michigan provided me with a "room of my own" in the winter of 1987 to work on this. The staff at Greenwood Press has been generous with their skills and time, as well, especially Loomis Mayer, Penny Sippel, and Mary Sive.

Michael R. Hill was a major supporter throughout the writing of this book. One of the most important ways he did this was through his concern that my theoretical work may have been suffering due to too many other commitments. He also read early drafts, listened to my working-through ideas, coauthored an earlier paper on fat-letter postcards, and understands why I try to do projects like this. This book and many of the times of celebration that it studies would be impoverished without his presence.

Finally, I owe a debt to my many cocelebrants and alienated others who have experienced American rituals with me. We are bound in a network of community and anomie, but we are not forced to continue in our ways of oppression. I hope this volume will give us all a thread to follow on the path of freedom.

PART I

INTRODUCTION

1

A Theory of American Drama and Ritual: Critical Dramaturgy

Everyday life is generated by the way we think, feel, work, and play. This living process is created through our use of a complex web of social rules and cultural meanings. In this book I explore the social construction of American life by analyzing community rules for ritual celebration. Through the use of the dramatic metaphor I examine the roles we play, the language we use, and the rules we follow when we are having fun. Critical inquiry into the social rituals of "fun" and "good times" reveals that they are paradoxically liberating and restrictive at the same time. The detailed data presented in this book explicate the points of structural weakness in our present ritual patterns so we may re-create our rituals and discover alternative patterns to generate far greater community playfulness and meaning than we now enjoy.

ON STRATEGY AND THE ORGANIZATION OF THIS BOOK

Writing a book about the vitality, drama, and spontaneity of everyday life presents a series of strategic problems. Writing captures something from the ongoing stream of everyday reality, reflecting on it in fixed paragraphs and chapters. This does great violence to reality, but it is no greater a distortion than selecting a "slice of the action," naming it, framing it, and discussing it in a cafeteria or a classroom. Books, like coffee breaks, radio shows, and academic lectures (Goffman, 1981), have their own structure and conventions.

The standard convention in social scientific studies provides the reader with an overarching, introductory logical structure into which the remaining chapters fall sequentially like posts in a fence encircling a topic, letting nothing important escape or anything extraneous enter uninvited. This expository formula wrenches loose the processual "logic-in-use" that led by twists and turns, up blind alleys and happenstance, to the researcher's discoveries and recasts it as an omnipotent, all-seeing "reconstructed logic" (Kaplan, 1964). Shulamit Reinharz (1984) observes:

Logic-in-use is dynamic and unsure of the future; it is becoming and creating knowledge. Reconstructions account for past behavior and order the past to inexorably yield the present. Logic-in-use attends to extralogical factors, such as inspiration, intuition, and coincidence. (p. 28)

My strategy combines logic-in-use and reconstructed logic. Thus there are theoretical insights in the following chapters that are not presented in this introduction. For example, chapter 6 employs Freudian concepts to elaborate and expand on ideas in prior chapters. The conclusion to this study (chapter 8) is derived from and dependent on the empirical journey reported in this book. The finale suggests ways to create emancipatory rituals that do not rest on my introductory points alone, or on any single ritual investigation, but on the whole adventure from singles bars (chapter 2) to the Emerald City of Oz (chapter 7).

Having said this, I do not inflict on the reader my unedited notes or a stream-of-consciousness account of my research activities. Such strategies would so violate the conventions of social scientific authorship that readers would miss my central points, negating the very reason for my research and this study. Hence the remainder of this chapter adopts the general form of an introduction built on reconstructed logic. It sets forth my starting point without detailing precisely where my theory ends.

This introduction acknowledges and explicates my considerable debts to the dramatic social theories of Erving Goffman and Victor Turner. My initial, partially reconstructed, effort to outline a critical theory of dramaturgy is presented at the end of this discussion of Turner and Goffman, along with the work of T. R. Young. The introduction also contains the usual general notes on methodology (the specifics, however, are reported in each empirical chapter) and introduces my one significant acquiescence to organizational convention, a discussion of two major types of ritual: participatory rituals (chapters 2 to 4) and media-constructed rituals (chapters 5 to 7).

Participatory and Media-Constructed Rituals

Two major categories of ritual in American life are examined here. First, I focus on what I call "participatory rituals" and explore three exemplars in detail: singles bars, household estate auctions, and college football. These participatory rituals exhibit common characteristics: (1) they involve face-to-face, participatory interaction; (2) they are socially situated in a matrix of roles, social statuses, and culture; and (3) they are organized by a set of rules for ritual action (Goffman, 1967). Ritual events of this type are deeply embedded in the lore and traditions of local American communities.

Second, I turn to a different and very modern event that I call a "media-constructed ritual." The following characteristics highlight these events: (1) the rituals are constructed by professionals who work in the mass-media industry; (2) the professionally constructed products are presented to an audience; and (3) the products and presentations are organized by a set of rules for portraying ritual action. Three examples of media-constructed rituals are analyzed: the visual presentation of the city on fat-letter postcards, the television and film series *Star Trek*, and the written adventures in the magical land of Oz. Ritual events of this type create shared symbols and meaning over widely dispersed regions and communities.

Although the six rituals analyzed here use similar rules for action, they combine these rules in different ways to generate distinct patterns. Indeed, American life is filled with extraordinarily varied ritual fare. The many possible patterns of American ritual are far from exhausted by this study. It would be a herculean job merely to catalog the permutations. What is accomplished here, however, is an examination of underlying patterns that combine to generate American rituals. My empirical investigations clarify two aspects of ritual life in America: the long-term ritual patterns unique to our world view and material life, and the rapid innovation of new rituals that generate ongoing life.

Empirical Methodologies

I empirically studied six American rituals using a variety of methodological procedures, employing a range of different data bases for each ritual. This provides a dense and multidimensional perspective on American culture. Multiple data collection techniques are increasingly accepted (and, in some quarters, strongly advocated) in the methodological literature (although many sociologists continue to use only unidimensional, questionnaire-based approaches). Norman K. Denzin (1970) calls this multiple methodological approach "triangulation." Barney G. Glazer and Anselm Strauss defend using a variety of different techniques to generate theory and practice (1967). Eugene Webb et al. (1981) argue that no social science research method should be used in isolation. Finally, Reinharz (1984) transcends the hurdle of abstracted empiricism to discuss ways to bring the "experiencing self" into research processes from which it has traditionally been excluded and alienated. The arguments against methodological rigidity are clear.

It is not my aim to justify the use of multiple approaches; others have already offered convincing arguments. Instead, I simply announce that I employed a variety of traditional research techniques to uncover and discover ritual life in America. These techniques include: ethnomethodological breaching demonstrations participant observation, and content analysis. This rich information supports a critical study of ritual elements in our culture.

Dramaturgy

My analysis employs a dramaturgical perspective and it may be useful to set this perspective in context and give a few indicators as to why I chose it as a framework for my investigations. Dramaturgical theory explains human action as a product of rules and "scripts" for action. Several theorists, particularly Erving Goffman, Victor Turner, and T. R. Young, developed this area of study by applying the dramatic metaphor to their analyses of social life. Considered alone, each of these theorists makes potent and significant insights. Considered together, however, their combined works are a powerful and brilliant analytical force with few equals in the world of social science. Their ideas are combined here for the first time to generate a critical theory for analyzing the social structure of everyday life and its relation to times of celebration. The remainder of this chapter outlines the dramaturgical sources and elements of my critical theoretical analysis of American rituals.

The theory I propose in the remaining pages of this introductory chapter forms the conceptual framework for the book as a whole. I begin and end with dramaturgy, but the final version is informed by empirical study and attendant theoretical evolution. Although I draw heavily at first on Goffman, Turner, and Young, I bear responsibility for the subsequent elaboration of their themes. Each subsequent chapter extends or informs this design, provides new perspectives from which to view it, and weaves my emerging theoretical ideas into an integrated and emancipatory argument.

THE DRAMATURGICAL THEORIES OF ERVING GOFFMAN AND VICTOR TURNER

Dramaturgy is a powerful tool for analyzing social life. Invoking the dramatic world of the theater, it allows us to analyze the profane world of everyday life and the sacred world of "extraordinary" life (Goffman, 1967). In the common usage of the dramatic metaphor, the theater is a depiction and enaction of the mundane and extraordinary events that occur over the course of human lives. In dramaturgy, the relationship between action and its reenactment on stage is reversed. Dramaturgy views human life as an enactment of learned roles, settings, language, and patterns of interaction. Everyday life, therefore, is like the theater, because both rely on the structure of social meanings, rules, and expectations. With a dramaturgical perspective, everyday people are viewed as performers. Like actors on a theatrical stage, we fit into the dramatic expectations of others and thereby construct our lives and actions.

Erving Goffman, the most innovative writer and leading proponent of dramaturgy in sociology, elaborated a theory of self-presentation and human interaction. The social principles guiding and structuring action and presentation are skillfully revealed by Goffman in his interpretation of everyday life as theater (1976, 1974, 1969, 1967, 1963a and b, 1961a and b, 1959). He defines human experience as a product of the rules used to organize that experience. These rules are called "frames" (1974: 7), and they enable the individual to guide and interpret experience in a fluid and socially created reality. The capacity to internalize and use social rules and expectations allows for human creation and control, and this underlying power of the person can be explained by the dramaturgical perspective. Despite this built-in potential for human creativity and liberation, however, Goffman generally depicts life and its dilemmas as generating alienated and manipulated individuals (Psathas, 1977; Deegan, 1978). His early doctoral dissertation on Ireland to the contrary, Goffman primarily studied the everyday life of modern, industrial America. This influenced the character of his findings, for reasons that become clearer as the studies in this book unfold. His cynical, gloomy outlook pervades his writings.

Goffman, long a contentious and abrasive critic of mainstream sociology, was eventually recognized by his colleagues when they elected him president of the American Sociological Association. His brilliant contributions (see bibliography) to social science are legendary and inspire profound sociological and philosophical inquiries (see, for example, Combs and Mansfield, 1976; Harre and Secord, 1972; Hare and Blumberg, 1988; Lyman and Scott, 1973; Deegan and Hill, 1987). Anthony Giddens (1987) remarks:

No one would question the claim that Erving Goffman was one of the leading sociological writers of the post-war period. His writings have been more or less universally acclaimed for their luminosity, their charm and their insight. Probably no sociologist over this period has been as widely read both by those in neighboring social science disciplines and by the lay public. (p. 109)

Popularity, of course, does not (and did not, in Goffman's case) automatically elevate writers to positions among the major theorists in sociology. Giddens observes, however, that Goffman should "be ranked as a major social theorist, as a writer who developed a systematic approach to the study of human social life and one whose contributions are in fact as important" as those of Parsons, Merton, Foucault, or Habermas (pp. 109–10).

Goffman's conception of people chained to norms of tact and mundane social expectations differs starkly from the views held by Victor Turner. Turner, the most innovative and leading proponent of dramaturgy in anthropology, elaborated a theory of life based on data gathered largely in nonmodern societies (1974, 1969, 1968, 1967). In Turner's studies, communities are found to have formal rituals that transcend and order everyday life. These "extraordinary" events portray the individual as part of a society that generates dignity and meaning. These rituals employ rules that separate the people and the events incorporated in the ritual from everyday life. The rules governing everyday life are distinct from those governing ritual events, but the common thread in both realms of life is the shared experience of community. In fact, for Turner, the experiences generated by formal rituals bind the individual to the group in everyday life. The symbolic structure of rituals is the means for connecting experience and meaning between the individual and the group. The social appears in the individual through the union of group experience and meaning.

Turner was a major theorist in anthropology who inspired and edited the prestigious monograph series on symbol, myth, and ritual published by Cornell University Press. His own theoretical and empirical accomplishments are stellar (see bibliography). Not every theorist of Turner's stature is simultaneously humane or collegial. As a student in Turner's seminar at the University of Chicago, I gratefully remember his wise insights, encouragement, and generous spirit.

Goffman and Turner provide different views of rituals, symbols, rules, and human experience. This seeming contradiction is not rooted in a bifurcated definition of dramaturgy: both use a similar approach to study different aspects of life and experience. In contrast to the despair, fragility, and vulnerability of the person that Goffman depicts so poignantly, Turner depicts hope, strength, and survival.

Goffman minutely details the everyday, routine, continual process of defending the "self" against manipulations by the "other." Turner, on the other hand, explicates the ritual process in which a sense of "self" and "community" is found *with* the "other." Goffman's modern world is governed by unending social structure and rules that generate alienation and isolation, whereas Turner's traditional ritual world is governed by distinct forms of social structure that reincorporate the individual with the group. Most importantly, Goffman emphasizes the commonplace rituals found in American everyday life and Turner emphasizes the formal and sacred rituals found in nonmodern societies. In order to understand their commonalities and differences, Turner's ritual world and Goffman's moving description of the modern person must be examined.

Turner's Ritual World as Betwixt and Between

Turner's imagery of nonmodern ritual is filled with human vivacity, drama, and renewal. Drawing heavily on Arnold van Genepp's work on *rite de passage* (1960), Turner stresses the uniqueness of ritual life. The power of the ritual is based on this distinctiveness, the world of mystery, and new definitions of action. Traditional roles of power and stratification are often inoperative, if not reversed, during ritual events and the community experiences a shared life built on this new context. The everyday world is specifically set aside. The rules of everyday life form a "social structure" while the ritual rules form what Turner specifically calls an "anti-structure," or new structure of meaning.

The mundane world is left behind during the ritual, and the people who enter the new passage or stage of life are "betwixt and between" the sacred and the mundane. They are seen as different, perhaps dangerous, perhaps frightened (or frightening), and this passage is marked by heightened awareness and meaning. Turner calls this "betwixt and between" process "liminal": it is an extraordinary world created and entered through the ritual process. The persons who share this liminal world are special. The experience they share is unique to the ritual and reveals both the individual and group in a personally and emotionally complex way. This experience of the self and the other as one in community is called "communitas."

Turner's concept "communitas" expresses much more than the now rather limp expression "the brotherhood of man." Communitas refers specifically to the emotional surety that one's world is just and shared; that being with others can be a unifying experience; that the actor is not always "acting" and pushing the self forward to the detriment of others. It forms the basis for human commitment to the group, to the other, and to oneself. Rituals perform the function of uniting meaning, action, the abstract, and the real. They are crucial to being human and part of society.

The ritual world, according to Turner, binds people through ties of commitment and love.

Here the notion of love as the basic societal bond is related to the notion of both real and symbolic death—to be in a true social relation to another human being one must die to one's "selfhood," a term which . . . is *inter alia* a shorthand for the ambitious, competitive world of social status and role playing. (1974: 68)

Turner's ritual world based on love differs sharply from Goffman's perspective where, often as not, the social glue is coercion, fear, or tact.

Rituals also become sources for social and cultural creativity. They provide a rich resource for "the production of root metaphors, conceptual archetypes, paradigms, models for [action] and the rest" (Turner, 1974: 50). This is significant because root paradigms are the mechanisms for intergenerational transfer of cultural meaning and tradition.

Steeped in cultural tradition and a mechanism for human renewal, ritual is also a model for liberation. Through their ability to transcend the categories and existence of everyday life, rituals are the antithesis of alienation. The dramatic metaphors and symbols of rituals create the human space for the generation of meaning and a lived experience of the sacred as communal. Turner holds that liberation is not found in escape from rules and group experiences. Rather, liberation through the "extraordinary" realities of liminality and ritual process are grounded fundamentally in the rules and the group.

The rich and powerful ritual world of premodern societies studied by Turner contrasts starkly with the ritual world of modern societies studied by Goffman. It is striking to find that Turner started to struggle with the modern ritual and its relation to human experience. His untimely death left these analyses in a more rudimentary stage than his earlier work.

From the mid-1970s to the early 1980s, Turner tried to expand his theory to include modern rituals. By and large, his efforts were unsatisfactory, for the complexity and problems of modern life are ill-adapted to the optimistic, apolitical model of a cohesive nonmodern society. A few distinctions between modern and nonmodern societies that he developed are introduced here to show both some areas of innovation and some of the problems with this expanded approach.

Turner contrasts modern and nonmodern societies on several dimensions. In the nonmodern world, everyday structure and anti-structure are two forms of *work*. The profane work of normal reality is less playful, however, than the sacred work of rituals. "Thus, the play is in earnest and has to be within bounds" (Turner, 1982a: 32). In postindustrial societies, work and play (or work and leisure) are divided by Turner into two separate spheres. But such a distinction between work and leisure rarely exists, and this blurring of the two worlds appears repeatedly in my analyses.

Turner idealizes leisure and uses this ideal as if it actually typified modern society. For example, he writes: "Leisure can be conceived as a betwixt-and-between, a neither-this-nor-that domain between two spells of work or between occupational and familial and civic activity" (Turner, 1982a: 40). The case studies presented in this book show, however, that most modern rituals are intertwined with bureaucracies, family "fun," and loyalty to the government.

The edges between mundane structure and ritual anti-structure overlap. Turner did acknowledge this blurring when he noted that when artistic genres "also buttress, reinforce, justify, or otherwise seek to legitimate the prevailing social and cultural mores and political orders . . . they are 'liminal' or 'pseudo-' or 'post-' liminal rather than 'liminoid' " (Turner, 1982a: 40).

Turner's new term, "liminoid," will be considered shortly but first it is important to emphasize that Turner here significantly revised his concept of liminality. His interpretation of liminality now differs considerably from his multilayered use of the term in earlier texts. In the passage quoted, Turner interprets liminality as politically conservative, and he subsequently characterizes it as a potential "scene of disease, despair, death, suicide, the breakdown without compensatory replacement of normative, well-defined social ties and bonds. It may be *anomie*, alienation, *angst*, the three fatal *alpha* sisters of modern myths" (Turner, 1982a: 46, italics in original).

Although the potential for the "darkside" of liminal experience was always present in Turner's earlier interpretations, it was embedded in analyses emphasizing community strength, union, and transcendence. In my view, Turner turned his concepts of liminality upside down to make room for a concept to refer to a more pure form of play ideally possible only in modern life. Turner's new term is the "liminoid."

The liminoid realm is restricted to cultural productions and carries an elite or avant-garde connotation. Compared to the weight of tradition embedded in liminality, the liminoid is completely voluntary. "Optation," states Turner, "pervades the liminoid phenomenon, obligation the liminal" (1982a: 43). He continues: "In the liminoid genres of industrial art, literature, and even science (more truly homologous with tribal liminal thinking than modern art), great public stress is laid on the individual innovator, the unique person who dares and opts to create'' (1982a: 43). Turner's liminoid, instead of emerging from the group and renewing it, emerges from the individual leader who dares to break all bounds and obligations. In short, Turner defines the ideal bourgeois artist.

Turner idealizes modern leisure as composed of manifold options and sources of renewal. In contrast to nonmodern societies, ''liminoid phenomena develop apart from the central economic and political process, along the margins, in the interfaces and interstices of central and servicing institutions—they are plural, fragmentary, and experimental in character'' (1982a: 54). Turner ignores the mass culture, its attendant industry, and the central functions of such institutions. His investigations pursue a line of thought outside the orbit of social scientists who articulate an integrated, specifically institutional conception of artistic production and creative cultural work (Wolff, 1981; Becker, 1982; Hill, 1984). Janet Wolff (1983) shows clearly that idealizing artists as independent and detached from larger institutional structures is unjustified. Creative independence is a significant cultural myth, a myth that Turner, in this case at least, helps perpetuate.

Turner notes that the liminoid is more like a commodity—indeed, often *is* a commodity, which one selects and buys—than the liminal is. He does not see this commodification of innovation and play as problematic. No doubt Marx would have disagreed that things are so simple, given his opening position on the fetishism of commodities: ''A commodity appears, at first sight, a very trivial thing, and easily understood. Its analysis shows that it is, in reality, a very queer thing, abounding in metaphysical subtleties and theological niceties'' (Marx, 1936, p. 81). Turner, however, focuses on play and its meaning in modern life, not on classical economics. He poses the dichotomy that ''one *works* at the liminal, one *plays* with the liminoid'' (1982a: 55) and sees no difficulty if playfulness is purchased. Further, Turner's new conceptualization of the liminal as ''work'' ignores the former majesty and joy that were consistently part of his liminal analyses of nonmodern ritual.

A final terminological distinction must be discussed here, namely, Turner's technical use of the concept ''anti-structure.'' In my view, Turner disastrously redefined this central concept in his later work on modern societies. He moved to equate his formerly very precise term ''anti-structure,'' meaning ''different from everyday structure,'' with the more popular meaning, ''opposed to everyday structure.'' Not only in his many earlier books but also in his seminars in 1972–73, Turner emphasized the earlier meaning of anti-structure. It did not refer to spontaneity, to anarchy, to the everchanging and the evernew. Rather, anti-structure referred to something stable, known, and organized to reincorporate the individual into the group.

I am confident, however, that Turner's struggle to apply his theory to modern rituals would have developed in a variety of exciting and insightful ways if he had lived longer (he died in December 1983). His writings in the last decade of his life reveal his attempt to move into new theoretical analyses. Politics, bureaucracies, alienation, and oppression are all areas that are underexamined in his work but intrinsic to modern ritual life.

I do not introduce more of Turner's new directions here since my work builds on his earlier and more complexly developed insights. Suffice it to note that modern society is not easily incorporated within the social drama metaphors used by Turner in his studies of nonmodern societies. The beauty and vision of community life as one lived with meaning and transcendence organized through shared rituals was lost when Turner began to study modern society. He tried to analyze play through the experimental play-theater. An avant-garde group of actors became the source of data for a new, emerging theory. Turner died shortly after this study was completed and did not work through the problems attendant to studying modern life at the margins.

Goffman also studied this same theater group (Turner, 1982a: 90) and he too died shortly thereafter, but no interaction between Turner and Goffman is noted in Turner's accounts. Goffman's view of this same theatrical situation, had he lived to write it, would have provided us with a working contrast between the two men's visions. My analysis of modern rituals attempts to reconnect the lost threads of Turner's ritual theory, threads that apparently become tangled when Turner confronted the bumps and confusions of modern life. It was Goffman who knew and best understood the modern muddy world, albeit on a small stage with face-to-face scenes, and it is to his dramaturgical theory of everyday life that I next turn.

Goffman's Everyday World as Interaction Rituals

Much of Goffman's work centers on the presentation of self in everyday life. For Goffman, the "self" is a performed character, it

is not an organic thing that has a specific location, whose fundamental fate is to be born, to mature, and to die; it is a dramatic effect arising diffusely from a scene that is presented, and the characteristic issue, the crucial concern, is whether it will be credited or discredited. (Goffman, 1959: 252–53)

This staging of the individual involves a "front" (1959: 22), a "manner" (1959: 24), and a "performance." Each actor needs an "audience" and is a member of a "team"; the play unfolds on both a "backstage" and a "frontstage" (1959, chapter 2). People often follow rules of tact in interaction so the drama may continue with minimal flaws. Such tact does not have to be extended to the "other," however, especially when the actor feels safe and secure as cast. These are the major elements underlying the "structure of presentation" in everyday life.

People who are unable to maintain their desired social roles are often "stigmatized" as having a discrediting attribute (Goffman, 1963b). Mental patients are one major group of discredited actors, and it is this discreditation that generates the "self" of the mentally ill and not their state of mind (Goffman, 1961a). The mentally ill, as discredited "normals," thus reveal the fragility and vulnerability of the self. Unlike others, the mentally ill "learn that a defensible picture of self can be seen as something outside oneself that can be constructed, lost, and rebuilt, all with great speed and some equanimity" (1961a: 165).

Flawed performance is a crucial fulcrum for ordering and explaining everyday life. As a result, Goffman studied a wide array of failures in performance: "embarrassment" (1961a, 1963b, 1967), "degradation" (1961a), "alienation" and "role distance" (1961b: 85–152; 1967: 113–36), "abandonment," "disloyalty," "embitterment" (1969: 133), and "discreditation" (1961a, 1959, and 1963b). Emphasis on these negative experiences of the world permeates the everyday life of modern people. Even when working with others through "teamwork," the emphasis on "showing-up" the audience is central:

Secret derogation seems to be much more common than secret praise, perhaps because such derogation serves to maintain the solidarity of the team, demonstrating mutual regard at the expense of those absent and compensating, perhaps, for the loss of self-respect that may occur when the audience must be accorded accommodative face-to-face treatment. (1959: 171)

According to Goffman, "individuals are treated relatively well to their faces and relatively badly behind their backs" (1959: 175). Thus, although tact governs face-to-face relationships, it is a facade that is easily cast aside. The world behind our backs is filled with the possibility of betrayal and secrecy.

In Goffman's interpersonal world, performances are the substance of interaction. Interactions are based on a series of codified principles of organization, called "frames" (1974: 10). Experience itself is organized by frames. They provide the actor with cues for subjective involvement in a slice of ongoing activity, the "strip." Frames can be physical processes ("natural," p. 22), or initiated by human agency ("social," p. 22), characterized by pretense (i.e., a "fabrication" wherein frames contain a manipulated dupe so that the true state of affairs is misunderstood, p. 83), or altered systematically ("keyed" or "re-keyed," pp. 43–44). All interactions are in one way or another framed or "made sense of" by the interacting participants.

Goffman concludes that everyday experience is characterized by the ever-present possibility that interactions are deceptive, that is, organized by making reference to fabricated frames. This chronic condition generates alienated experience because actors are never sure if they are being duped. Acute instances of being deceived serve mainly to punctuate and underscore the chronic condition of vulnerability.

Goffman's use of "frame" to mean an organizing principle for social action is a powerful concept, and I utilize it here to interpret Turner's original notion of anti-structure. Specifically, I define ''anti-structure'' as the rules for organizing extraordinary reality; it is a particular type of frame. This special frame has several characteristics. It is not a fabricated frame; at least there are not separate categories of dupes and manipulators. Its rules are distinctly different from the frames for everyday life. Anti-structural frames generate communitas rather than alienate the individual from the group. Finally, such frames are controlled by the community as a whole.

Few anti-structural frames exist in the participatory or media-constructed rituals that characterize American life. This is a central reason for the failure of most American rituals to generate communitas. In particular, the participatory rituals presented in this book (chapters 2 through 4) create divisiveness and alienation. At the same time, they incorporate some anti-structural elements, enough to generate ''fun'' despite their deeper, alienating flaws. Anti-structural frames also characterize two of the media-constructed rituals examined here (chapters 5 through 7). Although professionally constructed rituals can incorporate significant anti-structural elements (Baum's *Wizard of Oz* books, for example), most of them are tied to structural constraints. By careful study and analysis, however, we can learn the rules of anti-structural frames and apply them to both participatory and media-constructed rituals. The theoretical basis for this emancipatory project is more fully explored in chapter 8.

It would be unfair to end this discussion of Goffman's work with the impression that his theoretical world leads only to manipulation, alienation, or an amoral universe of schemers and dupes. Despite Goffman's emphasis on the manipulated and manipulating facade of the actor, a moral element does exist in his work. ''Moral'' in this context refers to a judgment of performance, its appropriateness, and the consequences of such judgments (Goffman, 1959: 128). Morality is thus determined relative to the frame of a specific interactional performance. This is situational, frame-bound morality, but morality nonetheless.

Finally, for Goffman, rituals are daily events that occur with some regularity. They are the minutiae of life that create the context of morality and meaning. In direct contrast to Turner, Goffman spends the majority of his time on the mundane, and rituals are a piece of this world. They are part of the system of rules and frames that organize experience, generate tact, and characterize the modern, often alienated, life. In this way, Goffman and Turner complement each other, filling in some of the gaps in our understanding of face-to-face ritual life. Even taken together, however, they still fail to adequately confront or account for the flawed anti-structural patterns that define ritual life in modern America. The variability and experience of these ritual patterns is my next point of departure.

THE VARIABLE STRUCTURE AND EXPERIENCES OF AMERICAN DRAMAS AND RITUALS

In contrast to rituals in nonmodern societies, rituals in the United States vary widely for different groups of people in various regions, for different classes, races, sexes, religions, occupations, ethnic backgrounds, and generations. American rituals can also be temporally fluid, and the rules for interpreting them may change rapidly. Formal rituals, and the publicly acknowledged institutional power that defines and legitimates them, are in the minority. The more common rituals are informal and organized by very different sets of social rules. Not infrequently, they are supported by powerful but effectively anonymous institutions.

The formal, participatory ritual of traditional religious marriage is a case in point. It is increasingly rare for a couple to participate in a religious marriage ceremony conducted in a church by a cleric who follows an official order of service that is not subject to revision. Instead, marriage rituals, if seen as desirable by a couple (who may be heterosexual or homosexual), are generated in a context of civil or religious ceremonies exhibiting an increasingly wide range of participants, language, religious meanings, settings, and definitions.

The rules separating these rituals from daily life are, therefore, more ambiguous than in nonmodern society. This amorphous quality is compounded by complex mixes of participatory and media-constructed ritual events within everyday life. Thus families may gather weekly to watch televised dramatizations of fictitious, media-constructed families in "Father Knows Best," "The Waltons," or "The Bill Cosby Show." College dormitory residents may meet daily while eating lunch to jeer and cheer collectively at contestants on "participatory" media-constructed television game shows like "The Price Is Right" or "Hollywood Squares." This variegated dynamic, and frequently blurred intermingling of anti-structure with structure characterizes American ritual.

The old-fashioned, formal ritual supported by an identifiable institution can still be found in American life, but it is embedded in a context of competing rituals, rules, symbols, experiences, and participants who advocate them. The power of any one symbol, ritual, or institution is thereby challenged. As a result, the power of traditional institutions to control any ritual is lessened in the general society. The competition for institutional control is augmented by the appearance of new types of authorities and sources of legitimation. A powerful example of a new institution is television, which can incorporate a wide range of new forms of mass media, technologies, and ways of defining human action. Traditional institutions, such as religion, can enter the televised world of rituals, but they are part of a competing set of authorities, entertainments, and views of human meaning and action.

Contemporary institutions operate in a world where rituals may be significant today but not tomorrow. Rapid alterations of rules and symbols are possible, if not defined as desirable progress. And when continuity does exist, it may be disguised due to the rhetoric of change and newness that is part of American values and ideology.

Ritual cohorts, or members of the group sharing the same experience, may be difficult to determine. Turner's liminal group shares the same lifelong experiences, thereby generating a deep understanding of each other that is absent in modern life. Identifying cohorts in the modern world is difficult. Each person may be "doing his or her own thing" or acting for a short period of time within a small group that shares a reality different from others in the larger group. A pattern of separation is maintained even during ritual times. For example, each person or small group at a football game pays separately for entry fees, food, drink, and souvenirs. They do not buy and share with all others. They act in relation to food, drink, and goods as private property controlled by private capital. Community is not generated when those who engage in similar activities within the same spatial and temporal coordinates still remain distinct "others." These others, if they come to one's attention, often appear to be different from the observing self. This is particularly true if the others are of a different race, age, sex, or class status than that of the self or "our group" (Deegan, 1987a, 1985).

Modern ritual rules may also be ambiguous. They may contrast starkly with everyday life, but they may also be continuous with it, or blend structural and anti-structural rules and characteristics. The rules that organize rituals may stand for or symbolize any number of things (a defining property of ritual), but if their symbolic referents become unclear (or lack common understanding), the ritual's power is greatly reduced. Simultaneously, ritual rules may possess a great deal of unintended power. Unintended power and the dissolution of power occur commonly where the participants' experiences have been excluded from the process of generating the rules and the rituals. Without community or democratic feedback into the construction of rituals, dysfunctional aspects are unchecked by the community. Without ongoing democratic input, rituals come to be meaningless for some, very important to others, and only partially meaningful for most.

Without the unity characteristic of nonmodern societies, there may be disagreement about the type of experience that it is desirable to generate ritually. There may be confusion about the purposes a ritual is intended to fulfill. Different goals for a ritual may employ the same symbols but convey vastly different experiences. Individuals who are part of a ritual, moreover, may bring different interpretations to the rules and symbols due to their different experiences with previous rituals.

Myriad factors, therefore, have generated ritual experiences for Americans that differ sharply from those found in nonmodern societies. Some of these differences have generated, in turn, an alienated and relatively powerless populace. Turner's nonmodern world of ritual renewal contrasts clearly with a more complex modern world where both rebirth and alienation are possible ingredients and outcomes of ritual. The nonmodern world is now part of our past, but Turner nonetheless provides us with a few keys for unlocking the modern labyrinth of ambiguity and alienation. These keys may open a new world of community incorporation and a shared "forest of symbols" (Turner, 1967). His concepts of anti-structure, liminality, rich community imagery, communitas, and the social creation of community through shared experiences based on equity are creative and liberating alternatives to an alienating and oppressive modern life.

My analysis of American rituals elaborates the continuum of ritual that extends from small, everyday rituals to the more common, shared rituals, and finally to an example of an American ritual world that transformationally and creatively incorporates the liberating, nonmodern "rules" explicated by Turner. Each ritual "type," or point on this continuum, concerns the generation of experience and relates in various ways to mundane life. The most minute rituals of daily life are intimately connected to the construction of mundane life, and the more complex rituals exhibit characteristics of both extraordinary rules and ordinary ones. Few American rituals display the openness and anti-structure of nonmodern rituals, but those that do reveal a forest of symbols that are recognizable but largely unexplored in American life.

The reasons our ritual life is stunted and so often fails to exhibit any deep anti-structural capacity for renewal and liberation are rooted in our larger social structure. Goffman's and Turner's analyses provide essential clues in the investigation of links between ritual life and social structure, but their analyses alone are insufficient. Goffman, insightfully engaged in the modern world, is too focused on face-to-face interactions to fully explore abstracted institutional forces at play in the society as a whole. Turner, also focusing on small group interactions, did not successfully transform his perceptive understanding of nonmodern ritual into a workable theory of modern ritual life. Useful critique and exploration of rituals in the modern world requires a more reflexive and comprehensive dramaturgy. Fulfilling this requirement, however, builds upon and extends Goffman's and Turner's pioneering analyses of small group interactions. The next section presents such a synthesis and extension.

CRITICAL DRAMATURGY: DRAMATURGY, THE SOCIAL STRUCTURE, AND ISSUES OF FREEDOM

The social structure of modern society was not explicated by either Goffman or Turner. For Goffman, everyday life was composed largely of face-to-face, often anonymous, interactions. The largest social unit that he analyzed was the "total institution." Examples include asylums, prisons, and military boot camps. Power in total institutions is organized bureaucratically, spatially, temporally, and hierarchically to control every aspect of self-definition and daily rituals (Goffman, 1961a; Giddens, 1984). Insightful as his analysis is, the larger social institutions—law, religion, family, economy, and so forth—do not fall within his purview. *Frame Analysis* (1974) is Goffman's closest brush with structural patterns of societal scope and here he pointedly puts aside questions of structural control and ideological hegemony to concentrate on the experience and organization of meaning in everyday life and face-to-face encounters.

For Turner, the nonmodern society structured everyday life through a rich array of relationships, symbols, and rules. There are some similarities between Turner's nonmodern society and Goffman's "total institution." Power in nonmodern societies, however, emanates from the people, it is neither anonymous nor bureaucratic. The community creates rather than manipulates the self.

In this section I delineate the structure of modern society and explain how it affects the elaboration and enactment of ritual life. In this way the lacuna between the work of Goffman and Turner is partially explained. By making closer connections between modern society and dramaturgical theory Goffman, the existential and pessimistic observer, is by and large focusing on the mundane, noncelebratory world around him. Similarly, the creative and rich social milieu uncovered by Turner owes much to the social structure enacted by members of nonmodern communities.

While Turner's later work did, in fact, focus on modern events, he narrowed his scope as did Goffman, abandoning any attempt to look comprehensively at modern social structure. Turner's early work describes a living forest of symbols and reflects a reality generated in a community not alienated by capitalist, technological, and anonymous power. In his later attempt to study modern ritual, Turner sought out a highly creative ritual, relatively untainted by the destructive patterns so common in American life. In other words, when Turner did focus on modern life, he purposefully tried to find the most creative community he could locate, in his case an experimental theatrical troupe. He completely ignored the most mundane and important rituals for the common person.

In contrast, I emphasize popular rituals and their embeddedness in inequality and modernity, in society as a structured whole. Turner's interest in the liminoid playfulness of an elite intellectual enterprise is just as foreign to my purpose here as is Goffman's emphasis on the mundane, noncelebratory interactions of ordinary people. Nonetheless, there is great value in Goffman's and Turner's work; they provide key concepts and important insights. Before I explicate a theory of modern social structure and inequality that overcomes the deficiencies in Goffman and Turner, however, there is more to learn from Turner's analysis of conflict resolution and inequality in nonmodern societies.

The Structure and Process of Conflict in Nonmodern Societies

Conflict resolution and its relation to ritual healing were major issues for Turner, particularly in his earliest writings. His first book (1957) was the in-depth analysis *Schism and Continuity in an African Society*. In this text he elaborated on the origin of conflicts as a result of ambiguous structural situations and the appearance of everyday "evils" in people's lives, such as illness, death, and unhappiness. Often these two events, ambiguity and suffering, coincided. People who occupied ambiguous situations of power, for example, were subsequently accused of causing harm to the people or families who opposed them. These situations of conflict occurred within small groups and involved face-to-face conflicts. Power was not located in anonymous corporate structures or a distant capitalist elite. Power emerged from traditional lines of inheritance, and conflicts were sometimes resolved by an entire group leaving the village. The "dissidents" then established another village in a new spot in an unclaimed jungle area.

Turner analyzed conflicts as social dramas in which the following phases unfold sequentially: (1) breach, (2) crisis, (3) redressive action, and (4) reintegration or recognition of schism (Turner, 1957: 92). Turner emphasized first the role of consensus in achieving compliance, and second the links between values and acceptance of authority (Swartz, Turner, and Tuden, 1966: 14–15). In the conflicts he studied in Africa, kinship plays a major role in both the origin and the resolution of problems (Turner, 1957: 93).

In nonmodern, close-knit, and largely homogeneous societies, Turner depicted ritual as an event that can ameliorate conflicts (Turner, 1966: 239–46). This consensus is developed, however, at the cost of making members obey authority rather than question it. "Clearly, an important emphasis of religious action is upon creating and restoring in members of a political community the capacity to obey officials, commands, and judgments that it simultaneously declares to be legitimate" (Swartz, Turner, and Tuden, 1966: 188). Turner thought modern liminoid (as differentiated from nonmodern liminal) phenomena could institute change, but he did not explain how, where, and when this occurred.

Turner's analysis of politics ceased to be a central focus in his work after 1966. The nonmodern situations he analyzed, in any case, were not comparable to modern life and politics. His dramatic, sequential four-phase model does appear to fit his data well. He noted also that "secularizing" and "modernizing" trends began generating conflict in these villages in the 1950s. Nonetheless, he did not analyze in any depth the role of colonialism, African independence movements, or national politics in any of his books or articles. Such work would have provided a bridge between these modernizing forces in nonmodern societies and their counterparts in modern society. The hallmarks of modern society— patriarchy, capitalism, bureaucracy, and the commodification of time—were not systematically linked in these nonmodern worlds.[1] The structural differences between these worlds provide a key to the potential differences in their ritual domains.

The Dramaturgical Society

Critical analysis reveals that modern life, in direct contrast to nonmodern societies, is increasingly organized on the basis of theatrical metaphors that are controlled by anonymous and powerful elites. Young and Garth Massey analyze this increasing control as a fundamental characteristic of a dramaturgical society. Such a society is "one in which the technologies of social science, mass communication, theatre and the arts are used to manage attitudes, behaviors, and feelings of the population in modern mass society" (Young and Massey, 1978: 78). These technologies provide images of equality, democracy, and service that shape the needs of people while advancing the vested interests of the elite. These elites, moreover, are maintained through interlocking systems of discrimination against women, blacks, Hispanics, native Americans, the physically and mentally disabled, the poor, homosexuals, and the aged (Deegan, 1985). The cultural hegemony (Marx and Engels, 1939) of technologies, organizations, and elites is understood by Young in terms of a critical analysis of the drama of everyday life. This social critique reveals the construction of theatrical control and the mechanism to alter this control. Critical dramaturgy illuminates the problem of controlled and alienating images and the solution to such inauthenticity.

When individuals do not control their community rituals, they enact patterns of alienation, role distance, and inauthenticity. In modern societies, individuals are socialized into patterns that link community experience with inequality. Rituals maintain their power to incorporate individuals into social life in this context, but the process of incorporation simultaneously requires the reinforcement of discrimination, alienation, and inauthenticity.

The increasing significance of bureaucratic organization of work and interaction reinforces the hegemonic ideology of the dramaturgical society:

Such a society is devoid of permanent, inclusive social relationships because anonymity norms, bureaucratic order, and power inequality all reduce sustained reciprocal interaction and accountability. The social-life-world produced in the polity, in the marketplace, and in the university has little more authenticity than the dramas produced on television or in the cinema. (Young and Massey, 1978: 88)

The life-world characteristic of modern, bureaucratic societies maintains structured sex and class differences and a unique orientation toward time.

The modern world is typified by the commodification of time. The cliche "time is money" aptly summarizes the equation of time with a valued commodity. Thus, time is measured, routinized, controlled, and coordinated in a systematic alienation of self that reinforces the patterns of inequality and bureaucratization characteristic of the dramaturgical society.

The Core Codes of the Dramaturgical Society

Bureaucratization and the commodification of time are major components of repression in America. Their repressive effects are reinforced and intensified by the two major forms of inequality in this society: sexism and capitalism. These four factors (bureaucracy, commodified time, sexism, and capitalism) are here called "core codes." These four factors interact, forming a united system of rules for alienating the self from the other. I call each of these four factors a core code because (1) each embraces a set of rules covering behaviors in a variety of social situations, (2) each is a major category for action covering a diverse range of activities, and (3) each organizes experiences in everyday life and in most ritual settings as well. A core code is a basic component of everyday structures that *oppress* and *repress* people in America.

The editors of the *Oxford English Dictionary* define "oppress" as both "to lie heavy on, weigh down, crush (the feelings, mind, spirits, etc.)'' and ''to keep under by tyrannical exercise of power; to load or burden with cruel or unjust impositions or restraints.'' Thus by ''oppression'' I refer to both the crushing of experience and feelings, and the exercise of power leading to unjust impositions or restraints. Oppression is typically experienced as an external imposition that crushes or blocks human action.

In the *Oxford English Dictionary*, ''repress'' is defined as both ''to check or withstand (some passion, feeling, etc.) in another by opposition or control'' and ''to reduce (troublesome persons) to subjection or quietness; to put down by force, suppress.'' By ''repression'' I refer to both the containment of passion and the forceful check on action resulting in passivity and apathy. In many cases repression involves self-checking and self-restraint and often appears as an internal imposition although its sources are frequently external to the repressed individual.

The core codes structure activity such that they oppress certain groups and repress large segments of the community. Those who oppress others may be repressed themselves, and only a very small elite is exempt from both oppression and repression. The core codes are a system of rules for action that structures both everyday repression and oppression.

This structure orders many of the mundane interaction rituals in everyday life as well as the course of action in more special ritual settings. These core codes form a grid for the analyses in this book. They are composed of two major interrelated parts: (1) a series of group inequalities that are (2) ordered through the manipulation of bureaucratic rules and the commodification of time. Each axis of this grid is analyzed more carefully below.

The Structure and Social Construction of Inequality: Sex and Class Codes

Goffman, like Turner, was increasingly concerned with larger social patterns in the years immediately prior to his death. The first (and only) major structure of oppression that Goffman analyzed was sexism. He noted that:

The most fundamental inequality in society is sexism. In modern industrial society, as apparently in all others, sex is at the base of a fundamental code in accordance with which social interactions and social structures are built up, a code which also establishes the conceptions individuals have concerning their fundamental human nature. (Goffman, 1977: 301)

Hereafter, I refer to the rules that produce this fundamental inequality as the ''sex code.''

This sex code is a fundamental component of the rules that govern rituals as well as everyday interactions and organizations. Rituals that reinforce everyday structure empower that structure and associate it with individual experience—

often pleasant communal experiences. Sexist rituals simultaneously generate ideas and emotions of belonging and not belonging.

Sex codes in rituals are an instance of Goffman's notion of "institutional reflexivity." This concept refers to social patterns or conventions "which have the effect of confirming our gender stereotypes and the prevailing arrangement between the sexes" (1977: 319). An example from everyday life: gender-specific clothing rules exemplify institutional reflexivity because they enable gender identification at a distance, permitting social interactants to correctly initiate gendered greetings or comments, such as "wolf whistles." An example from an American ritual: gender-specific clothing in the Miss America beauty pageant, particularly bathing suits, high heels, and evening gowns, are specific to that particular pageant but serve to reinforce stereotypic, socially constructed gender ideals.

I will explicate "institutional reflexivity" in reference to both sex and class in a series of rituals in the following chapters. This analysis can be extended to the status and experiential inequalities of other groups (for example, racial and ethnic minorities, the physically disabled), but the sex and class codes are the most fundamental rules in modern capitalistic societies. The general process of inequality is, moreover, modeled after these two basic codes. There is a repetitive process of disenfranchising others that is common to the various forms of structured discrimination (Deegan, 1985). This process per se can be revealed by an analysis of only two types of inequalities, those based on sex and class. This does not mean that either group is identical in its form, historical origin, variation, significance, or resolution of key problems. It does mean, however, that different, discriminated groups are generated by a series of similar steps and legitimations in any given society. This pattern arises from the elaboration of a cultural set of symbols and rituals that maintain and legitimate everyday reality.

Class codes comprise the other set of fundamentally important codes of oppression. Class is the key factor organizing the economy and the ownership of private property. Selling of one's labor to capitalists to obtain wages necessary for survival is intrinsically a commodification of the self and a source of alienation. Marxist interpretation holds that the profit gained from this alienated labor is used by the elite to increase their power and control over the working class (Marx, 1936; Marx and Engels, 1939).

The basically Marxist explanation of society outlined above has been greatly altered by contemporary Marxists. A major change is an understanding of the increasingly complex nature of class divisions that are now based not only on differential control over capital but also the various patterns of access to education, knowledge, status, consumer goods, and lifestyles (Giddens, 1975). Communist and socialist societies have made extensive efforts to reorganize private property, the state, education, and the economy for the purpose of eliminating or reducing the sources of economic exploitation by one class against another, but they have had less success in eliminating new forms of class distinction. Many of these new forms of inequality are directly linked to changes in the nature of work that accompany bureaucratization (Lane, 1981).

The Structure and Social Construction of Everyday Repression: Bureaucratic and Time Codes

Max Weber's early work on bureaucracies remains the most powerful analysis of their extensive power to control both objective and subjective life. While decrying the anonymous and dehumanizing power of bureaucracies, Weber was also the first to note their impending supremacy and their independence from economic forms of organization (Weber, 1948: 337–39). Bureaucracies (1) become a form of controlling knowledge, (2) orchestrate and coordinate work processes, and (3) structure social interaction. Efficiency becomes a major criterion for judgment—and profit is a concomitant concern—in capitalist bureaucracies.

Modern societies are characterized by bureaucratic methods for doing things that are highly patterned or structured. Bureaucratic structures are based on legal authority, offices, hierarchical divisions of labor, procedural rules, record keeping, and anonymous control (Weber, 1948: 339–40). These structures, in turn, generate ways of thinking about the self and the other that lead to alienation. Peter L. Berger, Bridgette Berger, and Hans Kellner (1973) defined this type of modern consciousness as a "homeless mind." These authors also link the process of modernity to technological and bureaucratic organizations that make the person increasingly dependent on a "private" world that is fragmented and underinstitutionalized (p. 186). As a result, the modern person is "inflicted with a permanent identity crisis" (Berger, Berger, and Kellner, 1973: 78).

It is difficult to overemphasize the centrality of bureaucracy in any study of modern life. Sociological studies of bureaucracy are legion. Giddens (1985), for example, recently underscored the crucial importance of data collection and surveillance by bureaucracies as a fundamental aspect of power in nation-states and, ultimately, the control and use of the means of mass violence in the modern world. Rosabeth Moss Kanter (1977), Susan Martin (1980), and Kathy E. Ferguson (1984) note the intersections between class, gender, and bureaucracy in everyday life. Bureaucratic structures and the codes for their organization and maintenance are fundamental components of modernity in the twentieth century.

The control and use of time is deeply influenced by modernization and bureaucratization. A major problem for modernization efforts in nonmodern societies is the resistance by nonmodern people to repressive control over their temporal pace and daily rhythms. Modern values associated with time give priority to the workplace schedule. When a person wakes up and goes to sleep is directly related to the workplace.

Adopting "modern" time involves objective and subjective dimensions of change. Large groups of people who are similarly controlled and coordinated by clocks and interrelated schedules provide the objective indicators of change. Individual compliance with and adoption of modern temporal values in everyday life are signs of subjective change. Individuals now "budget" and "invest" their time not only during work, but also during their leisure and rest hours.

Corporate groups and private individuals actively determine the duration of their activities, how long to talk to friends, play, eat, sleep, work on a task, or spend visiting various kin and participating in community projects.

When individuals and groups prepare time budgets they make trade-offs, choosing some activities rather than others. Time becomes a commodity in human relationships when shared activities become objects associated with various time values. Thus an activity is seen as "worth so much time." Viewing time as limited, quantifiable, and equivalent to capital is modern. Time allocations wherein time is exchanged for some other type of commodity are here called "time exchanges." People are limited in how they can "spend" their time, and a number of time exchanges are negotiated daily.

A powerful example of the pervasive nature of modern time is the fast-food restaurant. Customers engaged in the "fast-food time exchange" know and quickly report what food commodities they want, and their orders are served quickly. In a local fast-food restaurant, for example, one employee takes orders sequentially from customers organized in a queue; another employee, the cashier, takes one customer's order with one hand, while making a cash exchange for the previous customer with the other hand. To maintain the speed of the trans-action, the cashier impatiently says "Next!" to each customer at the head of the queue before the cashier finishes the time/money exchange to the customer in the process of leaving. Failure by a customer to immediately respond to the cashier results in the cashier's voice being raised, repeating his "command," and grimacing at the customer.

The pace of modern life is a recurrent theme heard in everyday phrases: for example, "Time is money," "I can't talk to you now but we should get together soon," "I'd love to see you but I don't have the time," "Do we have time to stop for some ice cream?" and "Do you have time to talk?" The internalization of time scheduling is a basic code for ordering everyday life. This ordering distances us from the self and from the other. We have to "make time" to be in a nonbureaucratic, nonsexist, noncapitalist relationship. These pervasive bu-reaucratic and temporal codes commodify social relationships, subjecting them to judgments outside community control.

Alienation Versus Communitas

The core codes generate alienation rather than communitas. A central reason that repressive codes are maintained is the conjunction of "good times" with community celebrations and ritual behavior. A symbolic universe is created through ritual occasions that allows our disparate elements of behavior to be joined into a meaningful whole that is emotionally internalized and learned (Berger and Luckmann, 1966: 92–128). These are fractured wholes, however, with internal divisions that cannot be completely welded together. Our symbolic universes do not transcend oppression and repression; they incorporate them.

Our forest of symbols is fed the acid rain of inequality within the bounds of rigid social control, generating alienation.

Alienation is not only a key concept in Goffman's corpus, it is also central to Young's critical dramaturgy. In the latter approach, however, "alienation" is rooted in Marx. The distinctions between Goffman's and Marx's definitions of the concept must be delineated to make a useful, coherent concept here.

For Goffman, alienation refers to an individual's degree of involvement or engrossment with a frame or situated encounter. The smaller the involvement, the greater the alienation (Goffman, 1974). In many ways, then, this use of the term is similar to Goffman's other concept of "role distance" although in this latter concept, the definition of involvement applies only to the behavior in a delimited role. Alienation embraces the more comprehensive situation covering a set of rules defining experience, perhaps for a number of people.

Alienation for Goffman does not specifically consider the macrolevel context that generates the experience of involvement. This is in direct contrast to Marx, who considers alienation as a separation of wage laborers from their experience arising from their lack of control over capital and the inability of the working class to control their labor, use of time, ideas, and experience. This primary division in action and thought yields a painful separation within the person. The person feels a distance from both the interior experience and the exterior, communal bonds with the group (or "generalized other," Mead, 1972). The pain resulting from the separation of the self remains unarticulated, beyond the grasp of awareness for many people.

Critical dramaturgy employs the concepts of "alienation" developed by Goffman and Marx and extends them to a macrolevel analysis of modern society. In this use, adopted here as well, "alienation" is a separation of the individual from the self and the other arising from lack of control over capital, technology, and rituals. Communitas, however, Turner's concept of the meaningful experience of identifying the self with the community, is the antithesis of alienation.

I use "communitas" in this book to designate the desired goal of ritual experiences. Communitas is generated by the manipulation of structural elements of everyday life and provides opportunities to transcend everyday structural divisions and social inequalities. Communitas is a mechanism for changing everyday structures through the experience of alternate ways of being and relating to others. I do not assume that communitas automatically yields less alienating structures, only that it creates a potential for generating such structures. Communitas emerges from anti-structure, and it is now appropriate to examine anti-structure and American experience more fully.

Anti-Structure: Fun Versus Play

Anti-structure, as I use it here, involves playfulness.[2] Operational and comprehensive definitions of playfulness violate the concept itself. It is easier and more accurate to define what it is not. Playfulness cannot be contained and specifically defined. There are many ways to be playful and an element of surprise is often present. In other words, playfulness is not the ordinary way of looking at things. It is not serious in the usual meaning of the word, but it is intrinsic to being human. Playfulness is different from everyday life in the modern and grimly serious world. It is this difference that makes it anti-structure. It may or may not signal ''opposition to'' everyday structure, but it does mean ''different from.''

A common word for describing a pleasant experience is ''fun.'' ''Fun'' in this book refers to neither communitas nor playfulness but a particular American experience that emerges from American rituals. Because of the structured nature of ''good times'' in America, many enjoyable experiences are generated in contexts of discrimination and technological control. Therefore, emotional investments in the rituals occur, often with some partial identification with others involved in the ritual, but the individual remains distanced from the other and the community and therefore the self in fundamental ways.

Fun is, by definition, a flawed playfulness or communitas experience. It allows the individual to be partially incorporated in the group and because of the presence of considerable alienation, this partial tie is strongly held and defended. ''Good times,'' the events associated with fun, maintain inequality and alienation because they create the appearance of an escape from these very problems. Note too that fun experiences in capitalist societies frequently generate alienating work for others. The ''boys' night out on the town'' may be touted by the celebrants as ''great fun,'' but consider the work performed by bartenders, drink and food servers, dishwashers, cooks, waitresses, exotic dancers, and others who suffer rather than enjoy this evening of ''fun.''

Fun may be a form of ''false consciousness'' (a Marxist concept), but fun may also be distinct from it. Fun may help the individual feel at one with a select group of others: for example, family, friends, sorority sisters, the in-group, or the team. The wider community, that is, those different from the self and the self's emotionally attached others, is *not* incorporated, however. Fun often creates a ''flow'' experience (Csikzentmihalyi, 1975a and b) wherein a person loses contact with ordinary reality and experiences heightened sensory appreciation and flow of time and space. This is not liminality, however, because flow is not comprehensively anti-structural. During flow, a person is taken out of the ''natural attitude'' and experiences another reality, an ''extraordinary reality'' (Schutz, 1971a). Flow may additionally help individuals to create beautiful worlds of fantasy, equality, and communal meaning.

Flow may enable the oppressed, in other words, to continue to survive against their oppression. ''Survival'' is used pointedly, however, for survival is not necessarily liberating. ''Survival'' and ''struggle'' are two distinct concepts. Struggle involves a battle against alienation and its structured generation. Struggle helps eliminate alienation and becomes part of the change process. Survival involves the continuity of the self despite alienation. Survival is a more limited strength than struggle because energy is directed toward maintenance of the self instead of its expansion. Fun is enmeshed in the forces that continue alienation and allow for survival. Fun, therefore, perpetuates alienation under the guise (if not the limited apolitical reality) of communication and identification with others.

My conceptual strands can now be woven together to reveal the tapestry of American rituals. The variety and range of American rituals is narrowed here to the two types examined in this book: participatory and media-constructed rituals. The structures, anti-structures, and experiences generated by these rituals, and their relation to the four core codes, are anchored in this study in concrete examples and patterns.

PARTICIPATORY AND MEDIA-CONSTRUCTED RITUALS

The empirical studies in this book provide insight into the nature of flawed playfulness (and its potential remedy) in American ritual. Rituals always involve rules, and the performance of rituals is guided by principles designed to show and create particular experiences. Here, I examine examples of rituals intended to be fun and entertaining. The behaviors, settings, and rules guiding these events are special but rarely sacred. They involve leisure instead of work. Finally, they can be loosely scripted and performed frequently (characteristics typical of participatory rituals), or closely scripted, carefully produced, and perhaps performed by special actors witnessed by others (characteristics typical of media-constructed rituals).

Rituals involving rules performed by the common person as actor are called here "participatory rituals." Although they sometimes involve special, more formal roles, the focus here is on the everyday actor. Participatory rituals are a part of the social construction of ordinary and extraordinary life for each member of the society. Participatory rituals studied here include the settings for singles' bars, auctions, and football games.

Rituals involving rules to be performed by the professional actor, or observed in the production of a popular drama or artifact, or used to generate an imaginary world of fiction, are called here "media-constructed rituals." These forms of popular culture are created by specialists whose work is to generate fun or play for others. The rules for generating the particular "story" or "plot" of media-constructed rituals are highly patterned, repetitive, and rigidly controlled. The particular set of rules for a media-constructed ritual is called a "formula frame."

These formulas have some similarity to the highly patterned and formal rules for sacred rituals in nonmodern societies, but media-constructed rituals are not intended to be sacred but entertaining. These latter rituals, moreover, are dominated by the rule to make money: they intend to sell something. Media-constructed rituals examined here are the television and film series *Star Trek*, fat-letter postcards, and the fantasy series chronicling the adventures of Dorothy and Ozma in the land of Oz.

Neither participatory nor media-constructed rituals were studied by Goffman or Turner. They are betwixt and between the categories developed by each. The rituals studied here combine both anti-structural and structural rules; both mundane and special characteristics, and they tie the modern person to an everyday world that is fundamentally distanced from the self. Rituals are the only public home in a heartless community.

CONCLUSION

In this chapter, I explored the foundations of critical dramaturgy and its relation to structure, anti-structure, and alienation. The structure of everyday life in a dramaturgic society is manipulated by elites who control symbols and images of the self and community that are incorporated into ritual events and products. Alienation, therefore, is a characteristic experience of rituals that manipulate the self and the other in a context of good times. These limited feelings of enjoyment are directly tied to systematic oppression and exploitation. Because the community and individuals who comprise it are not allowed control over their rituals, the potential for structural critique and change is sharply circumscribed. The renewing power of communitas is frequently limited if not absent in American experience, while the less creative and generative experiences of fun and good times are used as substitutes. Because of the painful nature of everyday alienation, the *appearance* of playfulness, that is, fun, is strongly defended and emotionally significant to many oppressed and repressed people. Critiques of the fundamental injustices of American life are seen as not only attacks on those in power, but as threats to that narrow realm of enjoyment that is central to the survival of people in an alienated world.

NOTES

1. Turner helped prepare a display of celebratory objects from around the world at the Smithsonian Institution (1982b). A collection of articles on their ritual use was published, and a portion of these rituals were from the United States. These American rituals tended to emerge from very small, homogeneous groups marginal to mainstream society, for example, small religious sects or communes in the nineteenth century. Turner's model fits such groups more closely than the modern people and world of interest here.

2. Turner stated that "play" was not intrinsic to anti-structure. He restricted play to modern societies because of his dichotomy between nonmodern society with its sacred and profane *work* and modern society with its *work* and *play*. Turner's interpretation is modified here, where anti-structure is seen as the rules that allow playfulness to occur in modern society. Many modern rituals, moreover, generate fun for some people, and work for others. Play is rarely realized.

PART II

PARTICIPATORY RITUALS

2

The Meet/Meat Market Ritual

My first analysis of American drama and ritual began in a singles bar. Here, I experientially discovered the sex codes structuring interaction rituals between women and men. Ostensibly, singles bars are a place to meet people; however, participants in the singles bar scene often deny their wish to meet people at a bar. Instead, they emphasize that singles bars are "fun."

These bars exemplify the frequent combination of structural and anti-structural rules in American rituals. The bars are often dimly lit, perhaps having corners with colored lights, lasers, or disco light shows. Rhythmic music, alcohol consumption, and dancing are powerful anti-structural elements. Nighttime patrons frequently dress in party clothes, buy drinks for themselves and their friends, and escape from the nine-to-five workaday world. The singles bar holds forth the promise of possible sexual liaisons and romantic adventures. These anti-structural dimensions of singles bars make them potentially liminal, but the introduction of the core codes of oppression and repression makes them merely "fun."

The four core structural codes—class, sex, bureaucracy, and commodified time—are fundamental patterns for action undermining the anti-structural aspects of the singles bar. Thus bars in the United States are licensed establishments with bureaucratic requirements for entry. Age is frequently a way to determine eligibility for access, but dress and manner may also be judged. The patron's age is determined frequently at the door by comparing his or her likeness to information on a bureaucratically issued identification card (typically a driver's license).

The bar's operation is regulated further by legislatively generated rules. The hours for opening and closing are more or less strictly enforced by uniformed police officers.

"Fun" at a singles bar is built on a commercial enterprise in which patrons pay for drinks, cover charges, cigarettes, and so on. The bar is operated by paid workers including bartenders, waiters and waitresses, bouncers, disk jockeys, and other staff. The fundamental split between paying patrons and paid staff creates a rift that cannot culminate in communitas. Neither side is fully liminal. An evening at the singles bar is work for the staff and, at best, fun for patrons.

Singles bars provide a particularly good opportunity to observe sex codes in action. Although all four codes are operative to some degree in singles bars, the sex code predominates and most fundamentally structures ritual interactions between male and female patrons. This chapter focuses on my study and explication of sex codes in singles bars.

A sex code is "a fundamental code in accordance with which social interactions and structures are built up" (Goffman, 1977: 301). In this chapter I explore interaction rituals (Goffman, 1967) for men and women (what I call "gendered interaction rituals") and relate them to the construction of the self and the other as commodities, within the singles bars setting. I call the particular ritual I study here the "meet/meat market" ritual. Specifically, it is a heterosexual interaction in gendered space whereby one sex appraises the "sexual value" of the opposite sex by the use of commodified ratings based on an anonymous presentation of self. Both sexes engage in this ritual but with differential criteria for judgment and differential power to act on this appraisal.

Singles bars are public settings frequented by customers who want to meet others to arrange dates and sexual encounters. These meetings and negotiations are facilitated through anti-structural elements, for example alcohol, or other drugs, music, perhaps dancing, and the intended use of leisure time to have fun, usually after work. Clearly, this setting is part of one's leisure only for customers, not for the laborers who serve them. The bar's staff go to other "fun" settings for their leisure. For the customer, however, everyday structures appear distanced by the customers' self-selected use of generally informal norms concerning desirable age, race, sexual preference, and class. Marital status for heterosexuals, the population studied here, is often assumed to be single or divorced, as suggested by the name "singles bars," but participants may be married in fact.

Face-to-face but anonymous encounters, or meetings, between strangers are typical. The rules for these "meeting rituals" are primarily based on the presentation of self. Goffman's (1967) description of interaction rituals as rules for face-to-face encounters where people exhibit tact to save face in everyday life applies precisely to meetings in singles bars. The processes of maintaining, protecting, and generating fronts, facades, audiences, and performances are the ritual components that organize interaction and the presentation of self.

Life in singles bars is predicated on the manipulation of performance rules where the power to openly initiate action is retained by males. Females are therefore subject to detailed "ratings" before being approached by males. Such ratings are part of the ritual rules of meeting and judging "meat."[1] This term, "the meat market" ritual, captures the context of a standard of performance and appearance that is applied to the presentation of self as a commodity to be judged on a sexual scale. A popularized version of such a scale was the "10" rating of Bo Derek in the movie of that name. In this movie, ten was the perfect rating and the mere seeing of such a beauty disrupted all other rules for action in everyday life. The set of *meeting* rules is coded by sex and the basic assumption is that the male is in control of initiating encounters. An important part of the process involves male judgment of females' performances and presentation as commodities. The meet/meat market ritual is more than a clever turn of words.[2] It incorporates the concepts of encountering the other (meeting ritual) through an alienating process of objectification (meat market ritual). It is a style of meeting that is displayed particularly clearly in singles bars but is not confined to them. This set of alienating, patriarchal rules was discovered through a series of breaching experiments I conducted over a period of years. Some of the problems of commodizing the self and the other, particularly women, are explored in this chapter.

METHODOLOGY

Breaching demonstrations involve the breaking of everyday rules as a technique to discover social order through its disruption. The format was introduced in the early 1960s by Harold Garfinkel (1963) under the title "breaching demonstrations" as a way to make tacit understandings clearer and to show the power of the taken-for-granted world. The concept and procedure immediately became a popular way to conduct research into everyday life and, in particular, to train students to see and experience the complex web of rules in which we live. Its popularity and ultimate failure as a methodology are directly correlated with its power to reveal the social construction of mundane life in a dramatic and often anxiety-producing way. With this methodology, the usually unreflected natural attitudes and habits that underlie everyday life become revealed as fundamental ways of being in the world. Basic threats to such important underpinnings can result in anxiety for the actor engaging in the experiment and for the other who observes and shares it. By 1975 H. Mehan and H. Wood warned researchers that breaching procedures were too "real" and advised against their widespread and unreflective use (p. 113). They suggested that such demonstrations could be used in limited contexts, especially where the researcher used them as ways of thinking about the world and social interaction (pp. 225–38).

This introduction to breaching demonstrations is necessary to understand the research conducted here, its context, and reflection on the technique. From 1969 to 1972 I engaged periodically in participant observation of singles bars. My presence was similar to Sherri Cavan in her study of bars. She stated:

I visited all establishments in the guise of a "typical patron," attempting to be indistinguishable from other patrons present. The fact that the public drinking place is a setting open to all members of the community who have reached their majority made it unnecessary to justify my presence as a patron to those present and in this sense actually facilitated the use of participant observation. (1966: 16)

Like Cavan, I limited my research to the bar and did not continue outside its setting. Unlike Cavan, however, I breached the typical female rules of seating, evaluation, and initiating interaction.

The bars were located in cities of various sizes ranging from thirty thousand to several million people in three states in the Midwest. About thirty different bars were included at various times. The patrons frequenting the bars were generally about thirty years of age, white, middle class, and heterosexual. Although the clientele were usually white, when blacks were present they were usually males. Many of the clientele were students or recent college graduates just beginning their work careers. Both small-town and urban settings were included in the study. Thus, in general, the bars catered to white, middle-class college students or graduates and provided a rather homogeneous subculture in a variety of settings.

The tendency of singles bars to be segregated by class, race, sexual preference, and age creates a setting where it is easier for "egalitarian" norms to appear to operate in a racist, homophobic, and capitalist society. In other words, discrimination against outsiders in bars is so strong that few people violate them. For example, if a male asked another male to dance in a heterosexual singles bar a very dramatic rejection, possibly involving physical violence, would undoubtedly ensue. Because these "others" are not present, there is the illusion of open conviviality. Unlike Cavan, I see the apparent openness of public bars as deeply entrenched in codes of oppression.

For one month the observations were gamelike, with myself as a budding sociological student who enjoyed going to such bars with her friends. I was originally motivated by my women friends who talked about the degradation and humiliation they experienced at these bars. From my new perspective as a sociologist, I could explain to them that they were being evaluated by inegalitarian gender rules designed to make them feel powerless. It became clear to me that my friends' emotions and self-evaluations were tied in these situations to institutionalized social arrangements where they were structurally disadvantaged. For myself, at least, here was an opportunity to demonstrate the liberating potential of reflexive sociology.

Subsequent interactions and discussions with my friends led me to elaborate a then-rudimentary theory of male ritual interaction. This perspective emerged from my observation that males were given the power of initiating social interaction while "nice girls" (Fox, 1977) were expected to be passive "victims" of superficial ratings. My skeptical friends did not believe that such rules existed. After all, as they saw it, several women who appeared to be "just like them" were selected by men all around them while my friends were not. My friends interpreted their lack of selection as some kind of failure in their sexual desirability, an inner lack rather than differential power in an external social exchange.

During this same period, I read about breaching demonstrations in my coursework. The criticisms later mentioned by Mehan and Wood, among others, had not yet surfaced. I decided to test my theory and show the existence of such rules, discover their form and location, and their association with gender roles. The sequential development of my ideas and research is discussed later in this chapter, when I focus on the ritual itself.

A major ethical concern argues against the use of breaching demonstrations due to the generation of anxiety in both the unwitting actor—most of the early norm breakers were students doing a class assignment—and in the unknowing or "victimized" other. This criticism did not apply in my situation. As an independent researcher, I actively decided to conduct the experiment. Although I was initially anxious, once the dramatic role had been learned, this disappeared. I belonged to the typical population of white, heterosexual college students, and I was already being victimized by males who used these rules. This set of criticisms of the technique did not, therefore, apply directly to this study. In other words, I found that the legitimate use of this methodology varies according to the relationship of the researcher to the population and the amount of power that the researcher has over this population. The use of power by those who have been disenfranchised is different than the use of power by the powerful. This differential power makes the assessment of this technique more than a "right or wrong" issue. In this sense, the breaching experiment can be a way for the victimized to learn about the process of victimization, an empowering and potentially liberating process.

Carol Smart also analyzed the interconnected problems of ethics, feminism, and the study of men who have greater power than women. In her study of judicial magistrates, she found that:

The current writings on the ethics of feminist research have fallen into the presumption that feminists will only study women. . . . The methods and practices we employ when interviewing the powerful must be different to those employed with women, or feminist research will become trapped into a perpetual study of women's powerlessness and will fail to adequately address the mechanisms of power most frequently (although not exclusively) exercised by men. (Smart, 1988)

Although I focused on women's powerlessness and the exercise of power by men, I learned what was for me an important lesson about the alienating dimensions of male power. Males who assess females by using a commodity rating in singles bars are aggressors, actively turning women into objects. As I knew from the start, the male-controlled meeting and evaluation process generated extreme feelings of powerlessness—as well as humiliation and alienation—in women. However, males who participate in this process also experience alienation because conceptualizing women as "the other object" is an act of violation against human subjectivity. By turning the tables on males through breaching demonstrations, I experienced this violation and alienation. This aspect of my project became increasingly clear to me as my research progressed. Ultimately, I decided against further use of the breaching demonstration technique. My eventual rejection of the technique—and the effect of the passage of time on this project—are discussed following the analysis of the ritual below.

SEX CODES AND THE MEET/MEAT MARKET RITUAL

The meet/meat market ritual is a heterosexual interaction whereby one sex appraises the sexual value of the opposite sex by the use of an objectified rating based on an anonymous presentation of self. In American society the male sex is assumed to be the correct sex to openly appraise females, both individually and as a group. In this way women become commodities to men and men become distanced from the self and the other. Obviously, this ritual appraisal generates two radically different points of view and experiences: the male's and the female's. Both sexes experience alienation, but these emerge as sex-linked experiences. The male learns to "commoditize" women/"the other" (Beauvoir, 1953), and women learn how to "package" themselves and think of the self as other. The male is corrupted by power while the female is victimized by it. Once approached by a male, the female can then appraise the male's presentation of self. But the power to say "no" is much more limited than the power to choose. Such settings facilitate the traditional roles of males and females. They are, in other words, institutionally reflexive (Goffman, 1977).

The words used to assess the other as a sexual commodity carry this "meat market" analogy. For heterosexuals, these include the males' evaluation of females as a fresh "piece of meat." For example, the vagina is referred to as "meat" (see Wentworth and Flexner, *Dictionary of American Slang*, cited by Penelope, 1970: 58). Other linguistic analogies include: wanting "to be eaten," and, for a man, being "well-hung." For homosexuals, the "meat market" or "meat rack" refers to a "street on which homosexuals gather, cruise, and pick up tricks" (Penelope, 1970). This homosexual usage was apparently popular in the early 1960s and predates the heterosexual use of the term. The popularization of meat imagery is also seen in feminists' use of the meat market analogy in connection with beauty pageants. It is instructive to note that the British television system banned the showing of beauty pageants because of the offensive practice of rating women, while such shows are considered fun entertainment in the United States. Grading and labeling a side of beef is closely analogous to the sex-coded meeting and evaluation ritual in singles bars and vividly symbolizes the experience of being considered as nonhuman and subhuman.

Actual encounters between the sexes take place following the opening meet/meat market evaluation ritual. This study focuses only on the opening gambits of this ritual and the insights learned by breaching the rules guiding this ritual.

Encounters between the sexes subsequent to the completion of this ritual are not considered in this paper. Here, the male and female components of the meet/meat market ritual are separately detailed.

The Male Meet/Meat Market Ritual

The male meet/meat market ritual involves the male's appraisal of females on various physical attractiveness ratings. The primary evaluation focuses on women's bodies. High marks go to women who possess medium to large breasts, small waist, medium to full hips, and nicely shaped legs. Additional attributes are evaluated in turn: clothing, carriage of the body, way of dancing (if dancing is an option), face, hair (preferably fashionable), and, of course, estimated approachability for later sexual encounters. This ritual evaluation is dramatically akin to buying a good piece of meat at the market. Erving Goffman (1976) minutely depicted the "right" gender displays for women who appear in advertisements. These displays include facial expressions, body language, and so on. Strikingly, these media patterns are seen over and over in presentations of self by women patrons of singles bars (a point of contact to be remembered when I turn my attention to media-constructed rituals in chapters 6 through 8).

Blatant assessment of the female's bodily assets is a central part of the male method of encounter (Goffman, 1961b). This strategy is enhanced by the male's dominance of space. In singles bars, men usually stand by or sit at the bar, a spatial location that provides good visual surveillance of the movement and placement of women throughout the premises. Men often leave the bar to walk around or lean against walls, thereby showing their control over the "unclaimed" spaces in singles bars. Obvious positioning and evaluating by males are core elements in the meat/meat market ritual.

The Female Meet/Meat Market Ritual

Women also make evaluations, but the female counterpart of this ritual is more subtle and complex. Male attributes considered attractive include body build: broad shoulders, small waist, narrow hips, height (preferably three to six inches taller than the woman), and facial characteristics. Dancing is evaluated, but less severely than the woman's since the white female often still waits to be asked to dance and is often a better dancer than the white male.

Other desirable characteristics of the male include his class status, education, and access to capital and his potential ability to finance "good" (i.e., expensive) dates. These factors are less visibly displayed than the female's largely physical evaluation. Evaluation depends more on interactional and conversational clues (e.g., etiquette, willingness to buy expensive drinks, information about education and occupation, etc.). Although clothing is often an indicator of social class, in singles bars the clothing worn is often standardized and relatively inexpensive. This means that even "scrounges" may be potentially interesting if they might have a "good car," "nice apartment," or "taste." The range of factors evaluated by women extends well beyond simple physical attractiveness.

Conversely, males are not limited to a one-dimensional physical presentation of self. Physically unattractive men with money and relatively good social position can overcome low marks on the physical attractiveness scale. This gives males generally a major structural advantage. Since men have structurally greater access to capital resources than women, they have more potential power as a person than women. This is also another form of commoditization, but one that is differently structured for each sex. Men become for women the mediating commodity needed to obtain material goods and good times. This type of male commodity ranking, moreover, is more capable of being achieved than the female commodity rating on ascriptive physical traits. Plastic and cosmetic surgery, open to women with access to surplus capital, has somewhat changed the givenness of physical presentations. The male capital commoditization enters not only into heterosexual ratings but also into male ratings of each other's performances in a variety of settings (e.g., housing, cars owned, business *savoir faire*, education, vacations, etc.).

Females' more complex appraisals of males are reinforced by "feminine" traits that favor demureness in eye contact. Operationally, this means that women do not openly stare at a man and appraise him without openly inviting a male approach or rejection. Women are schooled from childhood in the manner of "being nice" (Fox, 1977), and not being so "immature" as to measure people in strict physical concepts. Women are taught to grow out of this "adolescent" assessment stage. Men, to the contrary, are taught to sharpen their skills and to look on an ever-increasing number of women as part of their available field of conquest. This means that the older a man gets, the more experience in appraisal he gets, the more success in this approach he receives (even allowing for rejections), and the more eligible women he can assess. It is into this male network of sophistication and support that the younger woman enters without social norms of open aggressiveness or equal appraisal systems available to her.

Actual encounters between the sexes take place after this assessment process and are not considered in this paper. The next topic of interest is, instead, the effect of violations of this ritual act and the norms governing it.

VIOLATING THE MEET/MEAT MARKET SEX CODES

Once the meet/meat market ritual is understood, its gendered nature and the way it governs interaction between the sexes can be examined through breaching experiments. In this study I purposefully violated some of the female rules for the meet/meat market ritual and adopted some of the rules governing male comportment.

Upon reaching the age of twenty-one, I immediately joined my friends in the mad and popular scramble to go to singles bars. Thinking of the setting as a game (and not a research setting!), I went to a large urban area and tried out various personalities and stories on unsuspecting males. I participated initially on the basis of having fun and being anonymously involved in ritual "bar-hopping." My behavior was already in direct contrast with many of my friends who approached these situations with ambivalent feelings of dread and enjoyment—as well as questions concerning their attractiveness and desirability. Originally I treated the bar system as a game to be conquered. I demonstrated (to my friends as well as myself) that anyone could be selected by playing the game correctly. This included acting provocatively but within a limit of not being openly available. Barbara Risman (1982) calls this "coy sexuality" and perceptively describes how it is learned in sororities where "there is a conscious desire to portray coy sexuality—attractiveness—without suggesting 'cheapness.' Sexy mannerisms are used as bait, assuring the green first-year student that she too, will become cool, hip, and sexually attractive if she pledges their sorority" (p. 130). None of my friends was in a sorority so they lacked this structured learning. In fact, we lived together in a dormitory, suggesting that there may be more parallels between "Greeks" and "dormies" than many students think.

Rules for avoiding "cheapness" vary from generation to generation. At the time of this study, sprayed and "ratted" hair was strongly avoided since these practices were associated with "easy girls" and prostitutes. Low-cut outfits were in the same category, as was overly tight clothing. (The rock singer Madonna has recently helped to change these definitions, albeit temporarily.)

After trying out rules with my friends for a month, I saw the process as an important sociological question and began doing participant observation, taking notes, and making systematic analyses. After adopting the more professional role, I did not continue any interactions begun in the bar outside of this setting. I mention the more informal process, however, because my friends motivated me, poignantly revealed the problems of not understanding the rules, and helped shape the research. It is professionally expected that researchers acknowledge the innovating thought of "correct" influences—professors, published writers, and mentors. The role of our personal friends is often defined as unprofessional or minimal. In this research, however, my work was tied to the lives of my friends and my own initial experiences in the everyday life of the meet/meat market ritual in America.

Breaking the Sex Codes of Space and Evaluative Process

When the hypotheses that generate breaching demonstrations are not only correct but also touch on deep, culturally unreflexive patterns, the results can be striking. Strong responses to breaching demonstrations are a good indication that culturally significant codes have been violated. In my research I purposefully violated (or breached) the sex codes that guide the use of space and the evaluation processes in singles bars.

Gendered Space

Cavan (1966) provided a detailed understanding of hierarchical space and social interaction in bars. Her observations did not focus on the gendered characteristics of bar space, but her descriptions are nonetheless insightful and compatible with my own observations. She explained that "the physical bar is typically the focal point of the public drinking place" (p. 95). While sitting at the bar is the literal seat of power in singles bars, standing next to this location is the second most powerful location for interaction and control. Cavan reported that, "In many public drinking places, in addition to the standing area behind the physical bar there is what might be called the 'milling area' "(p. 101). The least powerful space, and that most frequented by women alone or in same-sex groups, is found in chairs, booths, and tables. Cavan did not examine how these spaces are gendered, although she noted that "B-girls (who receive money from the bartender for the drinks they encourage male customers to buy) and prostitutes customarily sit at the far end of the bar" (p. 182). The changed moral evaluation ("B-girls" and "prostitutes") of women who dare move from the table area to sit at one end of the bar reflects the gender geography of singles bars. Cavan's observations show how Fox's (1977) "good girl/bad girl" dichotomy is often realized in practice through spatial signals. Focusing initially on the array of gendered space rules, I began my investigation by specifically examining the spatial patterns of women in singles bars.

Women generally travel to singles bars in groups and also sit in groups once they arrive. This apparently paradoxical grouping is problematic for males who want to approach a particular woman without interacting with the other women in her group. In short, group travel and group sitting partially frustrate the purpose of the outing—to meet men.

Women's group behavior in singles bars, however, is not generated by any lack of sociability on their part, but by male practices that make group patterns necessary for women. Two factors are especially important in generating women's shared travel and clustered sitting rules. First, group travel is necessary for safety in getting home when the evening outing comes to a close. This is especially true for women whose purpose is only to have fun and meet men rather than go home with them. Because many men are willing to interpret accepting a ride as obligating women to perform sexual favors, it is dangerous to depend on recently introduced men for transportation. Women's travel groups provide practical and safe alternatives to accepting rides from men.

Second, women sit together in groups because a woman sitting alone is automatically suspected of being at the bar in order to go to bed with a man she will "pick up" there. There are few places, if any, where an unknown young woman can enter a bar alone and not receive a proposition from a male. If the female ignores or rejects his "friendly" advances, he usually reacts indignantly since the woman—as far as he was concerned—obviously "signaled" her desire to be picked up. This is a general problem faced not only by women in singles bars but by all women who travel alone (Hill and Deegan, 1982). Sitting in groups, however, signals a very different moral message and greatly reduces the frequency of male harassment. Simultaneously, this pattern increases the complexity of (and often frustrates) what might otherwise be simple, unencumbered meetings between men and women.

In contrast to women, many males arrive and leave alone. Single men can observe, drink, and talk to male and female strangers in these settings without being labeled "easy" or "cheap." Males are thus free to "work the room" and to freely schedule their arrival and departure times independent of group decision-making processes. Males can also go to bars in groups, although pairs are more common than groups, but this is a matter of choice rather than necessity. Further, males arriving in groups or pairs can split up or "disappear" at will. These options are generally unavailable to women without jeopardizing their safety or moral standing.

Even if males do not successfully meet women at a singles bar, they may well meet other men and establish friendships or business contacts. Sports talk provides a nearly universal basis for male conversations (see chapter 4). Men who have only known each other a short time join with other men in freely evaluating and commenting on the women in the bar. This immediate and dependable camaraderie often spawns the courage and support needed for males to initiate contacts with tables of women.

Interactions between members of the female sex are much more restricted. Women in groups do not meet women in other groups. Such interactions would increase the appearance of female solidarity and thus reduce the possibility of approaches by men. Other groups of women are not seen as comrades but as threats to male-initiated overtures and interest. Women's groups remain isolated from each other and are prohibited from initiating contacts with men. Each group is an island of "good girl" morality.

Women's tables are morally defined groupings, but they are nonetheless subjected to condescension—and sometimes ridicule—by men. Informal male "theories" of reality (Berger and Luckmann, 1966) do not account for the structured morality of women's spatial choices. Common male myths account for the rational, structured pattern of female behavior with explanations such as "women always stick together," or "women are afraid to be independent." Complexly convoluted behavior results. The male-generated structural barriers that prevent women from being in bars alone set the stage for an array of rituals to "get rid of the other girls" at least temporarily so that a meeting can take place.

Alternatively, women sitting together can wait for a male to approach them as a group. This one-to-group meeting is structurally much different than a one-to-one introduction. The women's table furnishes a ready-made audience for the approaching male. If he is initially accepted and a string of small talk develops, he is evaluated by the group as a whole. An imaginative "line" that works in one-to-one meetings may fail miserably when subjected—as sometimes happens—to inquisitional interrogation by a group of justifiably suspicious and mutually supportive women friends. If he is rejected, his humiliation is multiplied by the size of the group. Breaking into women's groups is difficult for men and this barrier may result in entire groups of seated women remaining unapproached during the evening.

I observed that men generally control the area around a bar, and it became evident that it is a violation of social norms in singles bars for "nice girls" to stand alone at or near the bar. Thus I breached this norm by sitting in a male-controlled area and announcing to the men around me that I was looking for someone interesting to talk to. A series of unexpected reactions ensued. Some men were flustered, others sat up straight, and some actually tried to engage in serious conversations. Serious discourse, needless to say, is quite rare in singles bars. I was obviously violating some important rules.

Interestingly, male reactions to my initial breaching demonstrations were strong but not altogether negative. I received invitations for several dates as a result of my experiment in rule breaking. All dates were politely declined, however, as I had made a firm decision to limit my observations, experiments, and personal involvement to the relative safety of the singles bars setting per se. The overall response to my breaching the norms that structure social interaction in singles bars was the judgment by male participants that my actions were acceptable. This positive response to my first breaching experiment led to further exploration of the gendered norms.

The Meat Market Evaluation

The next part of the male meet/meat market ritual I challenged was the "meat market stare." This is the visibly open appraisal of women as commodities that is often exhibited by a group of men who control a particular space. For women, it is often a painful and humiliating experience to walk past long rows of groups of men engaging in this blatant assessment. In bars this may involve a group of men sitting at the bar, standing along passageways to rest rooms, or by cigarette machines. A similar phenomenon occurs at construction sites, although women increasingly claim their right to walk on public streets without this kind of harassment. In singles bars, however, these stares and appraisals are part of the fun for male patrons. Women who protest—a rare event in singles bars since women come there expressly to meet men, not antagonize them—are labeled "uppity," "stuck up," or "teasers." The passive acceptance of this degrading element of the meet/meat market ritual is at least partially responsible for generating depression in women who attend these bars and who come away feeling that everything about singles bars is "superficial" and "antihuman."

As a woman, I reversed the situation by substituting the blatant "boobs and ass" evaluation of women with a "penis" evaluation of men. Other breaching demonstrations analogous to male evaluations include looking over men's heads if the men are shorter (as I am fairly tall this was a ploy I could use frequently, emphasizing my own height while effectively treating shorter men as "not there"). Another analogous evaluation is to openly glance sideways at men's rears. Males generally responded to my open stares by smiling. I completed my reversed evaluation process at this point by not responding to the males' smiles or by making a slight negative shake of the head. I also effectively adopted the male technique of turning one's back immediately following an open evaluative stare. These behaviors—when enacted by women—are not considered tactful and cause men to respond by "flooding out" (Goffman, 1974). Male responses to my rule reversals were strong and visible. For example, several men blushed, some spilled their drinks. They showed signs of anger—immediately followed by displays of calm or nonchalance. When men were obviously embarrassed or angry about my open evaluations, they often looked furtively around to see if anyone had observed our interaction. Males caught in this emotionally compromised situation tried quickly to regain their cool or save face just as Goffman (1967) predicts.

I also engaged in a milder form of female norm breaking: staring back in response to a male's "meat market stare." When a woman discovers that a man is appraising her, the usual female response is to break eye contact. The woman's eye focus shifts, although she may give some indication of nonverbal acceptance, such as a smile. There is often little outward indication that contact has occurred although the participants in the interaction suspect or know that it has. I reversed this pattern by staring and making continued eye contact after discovery of appraisal. Male reactions were numerous, although more subdued than when I engaged in open evaluations. If the male took this as encouragement by the female, but further contact was judged undesirable by the male, he would break eye contact and continue to walk in the same direction but change his goal, thus attempting to save face (Goffman, 1967: 5–47).

Nonhostile eye contact can be used by females to indicate interest in males, but it is not a social norm taught to or learned by many American women (this, despite the "come hither" look popularized in American motion pictures). I found that I could single out a desirable male, look at him, letting him break eye contact as often as he felt necessary, until he responded openly by mouthing "Who me?" or pointing to himself. My positive acknowledgments were received enthusiastically by many males. Involving as it does a reversal of sex code rules, this form of flirting is uncommon due to the social norms generally accepted in singles bars.

These breaching demonstrations reveal the pattern of power and control underlying face-to-face interactions. They clearly show the existence of gendered interaction rituals. Further, they link these rituals to: (1) open commodification, (2) the intrinsic humiliation of rejection, (3) the differential use of tact for each sex, and (4) the association between males and capital that underlies sexual assessments. I have also shown that nonhostile breaking of the rules by a woman researcher can have positive effects, resulting in serious conversations, offers of dates, and enthusiastic responses to unconventional flirting. But rule breaking is an uncommon, reflexive response to the social structure and norms of singles bars. As normative patterns of behavior, the rules guiding social interaction in singles bars are deeply problematic. The contradictions embedded in the meet/ meat market ritual frequently prevent the sexes from meeting, frustrating the ostensible purpose for the ritual.

THE PURPOSE OF SINGLES BARS: MEETING PEOPLE

Singles bars have very poor reputations as places to meet desirable steady dates. Many women say that they do not expect to meet "anybody decent" in a singles bar. Most women deny any interest in meeting a serious dating partner there. These denials are heard so frequently that they are virtually a ritual in themselves. Everyone goes for fun. This announced lack of seriousness, however, projects a false front. Most women admit—with a bit of prodding—that they would like to meet someone serious as a result of going to singles bars.

Some males believe the myth that "nice girls" do not go to these bars. Men, therefore, often present themselves as only interested in "looking over the situation" or getting an "easy lay." This macho display often hides more humane intent. Like the majority of women who patronize singles bars, many men are also interested in meeting members of the opposite sex to date. Both men and women want to have a human exchange of feelings and ideas. Thus, while hoping for human warmth, both sexes are alienated from these intentions by giving ritual expression to expectations that nobody "decent" goes to singles bars.

Denial that meeting people is a genuine reason for going to singles bars neutralizes the threatening interpersonal aspects of attending the bar, but also subverts an authentic goal. As a result of this alienation of intention and action, many people do not meet others at these bars whom they will date. Aggressive males "on the make" appear to predominate because they are interested only in making their mark. They are undaunted by a long string of rebuffs as long as they pick up someone before closing time. More reserved, less predatory, shy or sensitive men find it difficult to initiate interactions, especially if they fear embarrassment and refusal. Therefore, these men and their views are underrepresented in women's overall assessment of the "typical" male and his interests and characteristics (Schutz, 1971a). Conversely, "nice girls" who want to maintain their moral legitimacy have no legitimated conventions or rules for approaching men in the social setting of the singles bar. They have no socially approved rituals available for giving reassurance or support to hesitant men.

Even self-described "liberated" women at these bars rarely ask men to dance first or initiate conversations to meet a man they find interesting. In general, women who frequent singles bars are generally supportive of traditional male-female relationships; these are not women who are liberated in any radical sense. Women uninterested in maintaining these traditional rituals simply do not attend these bars. The result for the essentially traditional women who do go to singles bars is a classic double bind. In order to significantly increase their chances of meeting a "nice guy," they must break the stereotypically feminine, passive, and dependent behaviors that define a "nice girl." Breaking these stereotypes, however, is fundamentally nontraditional and risks the opprobrium of being labeled a "bad girl." As a result, "nice girls" rarely meet "nice guys" at singles bars. The double bind gives rise to a self-fulfilling prophesy.

It is important to note that my analysis of ritual meet/meat market behavior characterizes only one type of bar. Not all bars are characterized by this ritual, nor are singles bars the only social settings in which variations of meet/meat market rituals are found. Family taverns and the proverbial English pub are alternative patterns, although there is little reason to suspect that these settings are any less patriarchal even if less meat market oriented. Sexually integrated health and exercise clubs are often marked by their own meet/meat market rituals as are university-endorsed sorority/fraternity mixers. Other types of events and settings (such as young people's church groups and hobby clubs) are designed for meeting others, but the problematic nature of such encounters is often mentioned in lonely hearts newspaper columns and personal advertisements.[3] Meeting people in present-day American society is more difficult than need be the case, however. Appropriately structured meeting rituals, which eliminate patriarchal sex codes and the moral dichotomizing of women as either "good" or "bad," could alleviate much of the personal pain and alienation now suffered by interactants in public meet/meat market rituals.

A CONTEMPORARY UPDATE

Twenty years have elapsed since the start of my research on singles bars in 1969 and its completion in 1972. The results remain relevant, nonetheless, for a variety of reasons. The continuing validity of meet/meat market rituals in the 1980s is one concern. Another is the enduring significance and meaning of this research for my professional career.

There are several indicators of the timeliness of the meet/meat market ritual. For example, a research note on this project was published initially in 1972 (Deegan, 1972) and was reprinted in an introductory sociology textbook in 1979 and again in 1981. Students in the 1970s and 1980s have studied this research not as a historical document, but as a comment on contemporary everyday life. The findings in this study continue to resonate with their own experiences. The singles bar life and its accompanying meet/meat market ritual remain a component of everyday experience for many young people. Commercial advertising also continues to play on singles bars imagery, including the "Mr. Right" antiperspirant ads in which the "right" deodorant turns ugly "monster" males at a singles bar into handsome "hunks." The popular television series "Moonlighting" recently featured an episode in which Maddie Hays goes to a singles bar purposefully (but unsuccessfully) to "pick up" a sexual partner for the night. The singles bar is becoming institutionalized.

Another indicator of the continuing relevance of my findings was occasioned by my reentry into the singles bars world in the late 1970s and early 1980s.

Although I did not specifically replicate my research, I did frequent a singles bar where I several times asked males to dance with me. My behavior still caused considerable consternation and discussion on the part of many people who observed my actions. This suggests strongly, despite popular journalistic accounts of the "sexual revolution" to the contrary, that there was little change in the traditional sexual meeting rituals during the years between my formal research and my personal experiences more than a decade later.

The breaching demonstration technique used in my project was also used by Warren Farrell (1974), who wrote *The Liberated Man*. Farrell speaks to groups across the country and in the course of his public lectures asks women and men in his audience to play at reversing the ritual of selecting a desired partner. The purpose of this play is to reveal the nature of male domination.

I attended one of Farrell's lectures at the University of Nebraska. I wanted to leave rather than play this reversal. The male with whom I attended the lecture, however, wanted to experience the reversal. Not unexpectedly, the results were similar to those of my study. I selected another male who felt relatively uncomfortable with the game. I inadvertently made up a scenario about myself that in fact mimicked his own lifestyle, a fact I discovered some two months after this breaching demonstration. I began by using lines men have told to me, such as: "I hope you don't mind my saying this but I find you really attractive." Then I proposed going out in my little (mythical!) sports car some evening, and so on. Immediately after I had spieled "my line," I treated it like a stereotypical joke, thereby mocking his lifestyle without intending to do so. My male friend fared even worse. No female selected him and he felt humiliated and angry at me because I did not play the game the way he had expected. The evening as a whole was extremely unpleasant, an outcome that my research and that of Mehan and Wood (1975) clearly predicted.

This research also generated professional interest far beyond what could reasonably be expected, and I interpret this interest as an indication of deep fascination with the sex codes that structure everyday life—for professionals as well as everyone else. Until the publication of this book, my study remained generally unavailable; except for a short, one-page research note published in *Society* (Deegan, 1972) and the two introductory sociology books that reprinted the research note in 1979 and 1981, the details of the project were never published. Thus access to this study through public channels has been very limited. Although I gave copies of my typed report to no more than four friends when I was a graduate student, my unpublished paper was shared and copied by an ever-widening circle of readers. Without any effort on my part, the paper enjoys a lively underground circulation as copies are made and passed from hand to hand. I continue to meet younger sociologists at conferences who have read it because it was given to them by a friend. Despite my publication of more than fifty articles and four books, a significant number of people know of me because of this one, basically unpublished study. A familiar response after an introduction to me is "Oh, *yes*, you're the one who does singles bars!" No doubt this continuing "professional" interest by sociologists reflects, at least in part, their own frequenting of singles bars in the 1980s.

I do not believe that my research on the meet/meat market ritual is inherently more significant than my other work, but I do believe that research on sexual mores is more scintillating than some of my other studies. Despite great professional interest in studies of sexual borderlands, there are very real professional barriers to publishing it. Disapproval by gatekeepers is one problem and the labeling of the researcher is another. The personal consequences of doing research of this type can be profound. James Skipper, for example, published articles on strippers (1970, 1971) with the result that he became professionally stigmatized as a person who researched prurient topics. This led Skipper to write an article (1982) exploring the process that led to his stigmatization for studying a "sexually deviant" area. Thus the research reported in this chapter, and its potential to stigmatize a researcher, remain relevant to contemporary problems in sociology in ways that have little to do with the date of the study or its continuing empirical validity. The study continues to center importantly in my professional recognition and professional interactions.

Sex codes in this society are extremely deep, they are not easily reversed without consequence or reflexive effort. It is not surprising then that media reports of my research entirely missed the point of my findings. Indeed, the most widely circulated account actually reversed my conclusions.

As a result of the short note in *Society*, my study was noted in popular periodicals in the 1980s. Most prominent mention appeared in an article written by Joyce Brothers (1980) for *Cosmopolitan* magazine. In her article, Brothers totally reversed the intent of my study. She advocated the use of male evaluative rituals by women in order to become the "Bold New Women" of the 1980s. Instead of understanding the context of alienation and aggression, Brothers used the research as a model for women to adopt in order to "get" the men they wanted! Whereas I emphasized the degrading consequences of the meat market ritual, she stressed how liberating it was to adopt male scripts, evaluations, and stares. In short, rather than liberate women, Brothers actually reinforced oppressive behavior. While my research shows that *different*, nonhostile rules can liberate women, I nowhere advocate that women (or men) should adopt or employ the commodifying tactics of a meat market.

Each of the responses to this research project illustrates the continuity between this research of the early 1970s and life in the late 1980s. The meet/meat market ritual continues. Popular rhetoric suggests that males and females engage in more equal relations, but the responses to my research suggest that such a popularization is untrue. Meet/meat market rituals are embedded in a series of social constructions that are echoed throughout numerous interactions.

CONCLUSION

This chapter analyzed the meet/meat market ritual in white singles bars. First, I discovered both its male and female patterns, and then proceeded to violate the female pattern to discover and verify the underlying social rules. Specifically, I violated the norms of gendered space and reversed the "male meet/meat market stare." I found that my alterations significantly changed the entire pattern of interaction and could be used positively, in nonhostile variations, for a woman to initiate meetings and conversations with desirable men.[4] The rules generally used by most males, however, are degrading and objectify women as commodities subjected to evaluation and rating. The rules employed by most women are designed to maintain their moral attribution as "good girls" and therefore severely limit their ability to initiate interactions with men in singles bars. Discovering the rules supporting the interaction patterns in singles bars and the convoluted perceptions disguising the primary role of singles bars, that is, to meet members of the opposite sex, led to an explication of the melding of "good times" with the process of commodification. Both sexes participate in the process of sexual alienation, but the female is far more limited in her (1) range of open assessments, (2) access to capital, (3) use of tact, and (4) ability to change her basic commodity (i.e., her physical body).

The rules that structure interaction in the meet/meat market ritual were explored and verified through breaching demonstrations. While I found that alternative, nonhostile rules could be liberating, I also found that strict reversal of male rules generated humiliation and anger in the males who became the unwitting participants in my interactional experiments. For this reason, I conclude that breaching demonstrations that reverse codes of oppression and repression are inherently unethical and potentially cruel research techniques.

Singles bars were chosen for analysis because they are the most open of all bars to women as participants. James P. Spradley and Brenda J. Mann's study (1975) of a more male-defined bar, the cocktail bar, and the gendered division of labor between waitresses, bartenders, and managers affirms the underlying sex codes ordering work and interaction in bars. "For it is here that the ordinary male values of our culture are given ceremonial treatment. It is in such bars as this that the meaning of American masculinity is announced, restated, and underlined for all to know" (1975: 105). Singles bars mute this usual permeation of male control by being considerably more oriented toward sexual meeting.

Despite the emphasis on sexual availability in singles bars, there are other more openly sexual bars for this type of contact and exchange, namely, prostitution bars, strip joints, topless bars, and so on. The singles bars do participate in this sexual mating/swapping/swinging behavior, but to a far smaller degree than is commonly assumed. Despite protestations to the contrary, many people go to singles bars with the hope of meeting a "nice" person, but these hopes are frequently frustrated. Few males and females leave together after meeting in a bar. There are usually large numbers of men and women who never get to meet or talk to members of the opposite sex during the course of the evening.

Self-selection by the patrons of singles bars is common. There are rarely any women who look more than thirty years old. Men tend to be somewhat older, but the proportion of significantly older men is small. People with socially attractive "magazine-type looks" predominate, with the women making a greater effort at grooming than the men (Tuchman, Daniels and Benet, 1978).

Depression and alienation characterize the participation of both sexes: people who openly enjoy going to these bars are in the minority. For any given individual, participation in the singles bars scene is often limited to a year or two. This may be due to having entered a more permanent alliance with a member of the opposite sex, but it may also be due to becoming tired of the game. The level of alienation becomes higher than the achieved fun.

Singles bars casualties, in terms of dropouts and alienated customers, are high. Nonetheless, patrons of these bars remain a significant part of the popular "swinger" image. These images reinforce traditional male and female stereotypes and gendered patterns of behavior. Participation in the singles bars subculture is compatible with idealized modern norms favoring rapid change, instant intimacy, and noncommitment. These "futuristic" norms have now been ritualized to generate a fairly traditional source of—and method for meeting—members of the opposite sex. Fun in these bars occurs within a matrix of meet/meat market rituals that maintain women's subordination in the marketplace and love.

Goffman's analysis of gender display, presentation of self, and alienation closely fits the singles bars meet/meat market ritual. Victor Turner's model of modern leisure as play is too uncritical and superficial, however. Singles bars are "betwixt and between" in a way that Turner never meant; that is, singles bars have both structural and anti-structural elements. They are neither liminal nor liminoid. They are an American ritual embedded in a sexist, capitalist, modern world. T. R. Young's analysis of the dramaturgical society blends Goffman's insights with the more fundamental meaning of alienation from the self in which the person becomes a commodity. The meet/meat market ritual reveals the sex code continuity between everyday and ritual life and its intrinsic role in good times and fun.

NOTES

1. This interpretation of cattle reflects the cultural attitude toward animals, and it is not intended as a value statement concerning their intrinsic worth. Men's penises are called "meat" and the term "meat market" was used by gay men in the 1960s to refer to bars frequented by them. For this latter information, I thank Julia Penelope.

2. The shortening of the phrase to "me/eat market ritual" provides a crude but somewhat correct terminology. A self-centered sexuality orienting toward taking the other as a commodity is one aspect of the setting and interactions. I chose a less harsh and vulgar interpretation, however, because the ritual is not as one-sided as such a term would suggest.

3. The recent changes in personal ads to include information such as age, race, sex, sexual preference, education, and occupation is a new meet/meat market ritual.

4. Risman wrote an extraordinary analysis of the traditional socialization patterns developed through the sorority system today (1982). Spradley and Mann (1975), more-

over, analyzed cocktail bars as major sources of traditional male and female roles, and their setting was populated by college students too. The active socialization of these students for highly traditional sex roles in their everyday life needs further attention. For example, when I discuss this issue with my students in introductory women's courses they insist that "fun" has nothing to do with their serious concerns; i.e., finding employment, getting married, and becoming an independent adult. This kind of split in the self is active training for an alienated adult experience.

3

Having Fun, Killing Time, and Getting a Good Deal

Daily, in hundreds of localities, items are sold to the highest bidders at auctions. Challenging both our fixed-price market economy and our everyday expectations of doing things quickly, auctions are a ritual where people trade their time for a chance to buy goods at a cheap price. The incentive to participate is constructed from the desire to have "fun" and make a "good deal." Many auctions are part of a corporate structure with its attendant bureaucratic underpinnings.[1] The auctions observed in this study, however, are small businesses, often family owned, that are not operated as bureaucracies. Thus bureaucratic codes of repression are not strongly manifested in this study. Where bureaucratic structures are concerned, small auctions are anti-structural.

Sex codes, unlike bureaucratic codes, are deeply embedded in most small, household auctions. Sexism runs blatantly throughout the auction experience and its attendant rituals. Nonetheless, sex codes are systematically excluded from this study by my deliberate focus on a minority of auctions where sexism is greatly muted. My reasons for this methodological and epistemological decision include the following concerns.

The data for this study were obtained by participant observation. Initially I experienced the deeply offensive and continuous sexist barrage of the typical auctioneer's monologue. Most auctioneers are extremely sexist and this is coded into all their actions. For example, sexist jokes about buying objects for an "old girlfriend," or comparing the object to said woman, hiding the object from the "nosy wife," and so on permeate their speech. Sexism is an underlying message in the ongoing spiel of auction "talk." These typical sexist auctioneers, moreover, feel free to comment on women in the buying crowd, for example, "You must have hurried over here before you had time to get fully dressed," or "Let's let this 'little girl' have this one, boys," or "Wouldn't you like to meet me for coffee later, honey?" Women are often physically patted and moved and brought to the front to be auctioned off—all in the spirit of fun. Two auctioneers on different teams referred to all buyers as "boys" and used this term at least once in every chant over a period of hours. My pointing out that we were not all boys in the buying audience was ineffective, and my attempt to remedy the situation only became a point of more humor. Failure to find such behavior amusing is a sign of being a "poor sport."

I could not personally tolerate such auctioneers over an extended period of observation so I systematically excluded them from my sample once they were discovered. The observations here are based on a small number of largely non-sexist auctioneers. This decision allowed me to complete my observations and analyze the auction process without having been further personally assaulted either verbally or physically. While sexism permeates most local auctions, it is clear that auctions need not be sexist.

Rather than focus on pervasive sex codes, a theme already explored in the preceding study of singles bars, I explored a more fundamental, intrinsic, and central characteristic of auctions: exchanging time for money in order to get a good deal. This is a very American way to have fun. Auctions combine structural and anti-structural elements to exchange time for money. Here I examine time and money as commodities that are exchanged by people whose social class outside the auction setting is held relatively constant within the setting. Time and money operate in this closed system as two types of repressive codes that can be traded.[2] I also analyze the way in which auctions are work for some people, while they are more fun for others. This reveals the way in which American rituals variably combine structural and anti-structural characteristics according to the roles people play.

Although auctions are found throughout the world and have a well-established tradition, they are rarely the subject of sociological study.[3] Therefore, I first present an exploratory analysis of their social meaning, structured roles, principal actors, and relation to the community. I conclude that auctions are important rituals that engage us in a barter economy, community assessments, and a way to have fun.

Auctions are conceptually important because they are a good vehicle for understanding how a common American event, on a macrolevel of organization of behavior, is interpreted on a microlevel through the experience of the buyers and the members of the community who attend the sales. Anthony Giddens (1984) correctly rejects the traditional, oppositional dichotomy in sociology between micro- and macrolevels of analysis. He notes: "This sort of confrontation is surely a phoney war if ever there was one. At any rate, I do not think that there can be any question of either having priority over the other" (p. 139). In this chapter, the union of macro- and microlevels of analysis is accomplished through the linkage of Erving Goffman's, Victor Turner's, and T. R. Young's dramaturgical models.

METHODOLOGY

As a participant observer, I attended at least one and often two or more auctions per week from October 1979 to November 1980, observing a total of slightly more than a hundred auctions. These were primarily household and estate auctions. The items for sale in such auctions include a wide assortment of personal and household goods, including: furniture, appliances, bedding, dishes, books, records, jewelry, and a vast array of miscellaneous odds and ends. These auctions are typically occasioned by a death in a family combined with the desire and need of surviving heirs to close the estate and divide the proceeds. In some cases the house itself may also be sold at auction. In addition, I attended three farm auctions and three business auctions. Farm and business auctions contrast strongly with the estate auctions that are the subject of this study. Most of the auctions occurred in a medium-sized city (approximately 150,000 population), but auctions in small towns and rural areas were also observed. This study is based primarily on auctions conducted by two auctioneering firms, although I observed auctions conducted by more than fifteen different, small, family-owned auction companies. The two firms I most frequently observed conducted far less sexist auctions than the other companies.

Following an informal introduction to auctions as an engrossed participant, I began systematic participant observations, taking careful notes, in February 1980. Readers unfamiliar with the details of this approach may wish to consult William J. Filstead (1970) and John Van Maanen (1979) for discussion of participant observation as a research methodology. (Reinharz, 1984, fruitfully explores several limitations to this methodological approach.)

Auction settings are not conducive to formal note-taking during the action, especially if one is participating while observing. Formal note-taking was not only difficult to maintain, it also distracted from the experience of attending to and participating in the bidding. Nonetheless, formal observational recording was completed at ten auctions during the first two months of the study.

The formal observational records reflect specific, detailed focus on selected observational categories rather than everything that happens during the course of an auction. There are several reasons for adopting categorical note-taking. First, while there are many types of interchanges at an auction, these behaviors quickly become repetitive over the course of several hours. No useful purpose is served by repeatedly describing these events in full. Second, the auction itself has a hypnotic effect and this has methodological consequences. The hypnotic effect (which I will discuss more fully) is one of the anti-structural characteristics of the auction, and the observer felt its effect. Participating fully in the rhythm of the auction negates systematic note-taking. Third, the initial familiarization stage, during which no notes were taken, provided me with an introduction to the event and some of the participants. I developed a series of topic issues, which I then articulated more carefully through categorical observation and note-taking. Thus a process of observing, writing, and observing was initiated. There was interaction between the event and its analysis, similar to that suggested by the "grounded theory" approach (Glaser and Strauss, 1967).

I was very much a real participant on many occasions and this is important from an experiential perspective. Shulamit Reinharz (1984) notes:

Although experiential data complement other data, they are unique in that they do not rely on intervening collecting tools, tricks, instruments, tests, or questionnaires; they are completely naturalistic and unobtrusive.... Research that utilizes both the researcher's experience and statements and observed behavior of others enables sociology to be both an experiential and a behavioral discipline. (p. 337)

I not only observed bidding and buying, I engaged in it. I spent my own limited money—(not research funds), carried my goods home with me, and now live with them. I felt both the exhilaration of a good buy and the chagrin of a bad one. My exchanges with other participants concerning the nature of the event were not those of an isolated observer, but of an interested and vested participant. I rely here for my sociological analysis, as Reinharz recommends, on my own experiential insights as well as my systematic observations and theoretical training.

I did not announce myself as a sociologist when I made my observations and thus the ethical dimensions of this research need to be addressed. The ethics of disguised research are properly a concern for all sociologists (Smart, 1988). Public auctions are, as the name suggests, open to the public and I entered the setting as would any member of the public. Indeed, my first appearance at an auction was occasioned by my needing to furnish my house inexpensively. As a researcher, I did not actively engage others in conversations but let them approach me. I am generally reticent in public places and I did not alter the way I behave in this public setting. (Cavan's defense of her similar research behavior in bars is noted in chapter 2.) In Schutzian terms, I participated in the "lived reality" of auctions. My role as actor/sociologist did not differ inherently from the roles of the others who participated in these events. All participants observed, made inquiries, reached conclusions, acted on decisions. The only difference between myself and the others was that my observations were more systematic and were guided by sociological theory. The difference in this case is a matter of degree, not of kind. (Schutz, 1967; 1971a). No private conversations were heard because all conversations were in a public space, available to anyone who cared to listen. When participants obviously intended their communication to be private (for example, by whispering), I made no attempt to eavesdrop. Adult speakers of public statements in public places invest their communications with implied consent; they know their comments may be heard by others and they assume the risks of being overheard. In any event, as most of the participants remain unknown in the observer's everyday life as a professor of sociology, they and their comments are shrouded in a gray haze of anonymity that thickens with each passing year.

In November 1980 as I concluded my observations, a Sunday article in the local newspaper published my photograph with a story revealing my identity as a sociologist. The article focused on my observations of behavior in singles bars (chapter 2). Subsequently, when I was recognized at auctions, several participants spoke to me, commenting on the article and my role as an observer. They were very positive about my research and my observational techniques. This confirmed the acceptability of my role as actor/sociologist in public settings. My role as a systematic observer of everyday life not only became public knowledge, it was well received by participants in the very setting in which I had just concluded a year-long series of observations.

THE RITUAL DRAMA: THE PLOT AND STRUCTURAL CHARACTERISTICS

Auctions are monetary rituals. They are designed to exchange goods for money: this is the contract between buyers and sellers mediated by the auctioneers. The ideal culmination of auction action is to get a "good price" on a desirable item at a "good auction" conducted by a "good auctioneer." Good auctioneers are identified by their ability to sell goods and attract a crowd that buys them. Good auctions have desirable objects for sale. The definition of a good price, however, depends on each actor's role in the ritual. For example, a large sum is good from the auctioneer's point of view since he or she works on commission, whereas a small sum is good from the buyer's point of view. Indeed, the auctioneer may cajole buyers to "make a real good bid" (i.e., a high bid) while buyers obstinately hold out, at least temporarily, for the hope of a "good deal" (i.e., a low price).

The American economy rarely structures bartering into the everyday supply of goods. Most goods purchased in stores have established, fixed prices. Americans rarely negotiate the price of ordinary goods. Thus the auction has a unique status as a common event where the price of goods is open to evaluation. Getting a good deal is a major concern of the buyers, who play parts as both "passive audience" (Goffman, 1959) and active participants. Robert E. Clark and Larry J. Halford's (1978) study of auctions as a "good deal" is an outstanding analysis of this central concern. They provide an ethnographic account of why people go to auctions and how they determine whether they have gotten a good deal or not. Most of the research on this topic explores auctions as competitive, "token economies" (McAffee and McMillan, 1987).

Because money is associated with business and is a profane rather than sacred topic (Durkheim, 1915; Parsons and Smelser, 1956), auctions do not manifest any of the characteristics (such as ingesting drugs, elaborate community myth, transcendent meaning, or worship of society) that Emile Durkheim associates with sacred rituals. Instead, as profane rituals, auctions involve an exchange of time for money, an exchange between two fundamentally important American values. This exchange takes place, however, in a context of "fun" marked by an anti-structural slow pace contrasting sharply with the accelerated pace of everyday life in the commercial world.

It is important to see that auctions have an anti-structure wherein everyday statuses are temporarily lost and new roles are assigned. The major actors are the auctioneers. They mediate the exchange of goods and money and are the source of "fun and entertainment" sufficient to draw an audience.

Buyers are far more numerous. Whatever their social statuses in the community, they all become coparticipants in the drama led by the auctioneers. The wealthy may frequent auctions for good deals on scarce and rare goods, but they must be bidders like everyone else, equalizing their ability to participate in the ritual. Wealthy bidders usually win in the end because they have the monetary resources to outbid competitors, but money alone may not secure a given item. Auction skills are also required. Each bidder must be certain his or her bid has been seen by the auctioneer. There is usually at least one instance, often more, in each auction where a bidder loses to a competitor because the auctioneer literally did not see a bid. It should be noted that the dynamics of auctions are highly visual. I never saw a blind person attend or participate in an estate auction.

Even if the final price on a given item is high, starting bids are often so low that virtually everyone, regardless of class position, can "jump in on the fun" at the start of bidding. Many items at estate auctions are sold at very low prices (for example, fifty cents for an old broom, or a dollar for a box of books). It is not unusual for at least a few items that ordinarily bring moderate to high prices to be sold relatively cheaply due to lack of interest by the buyers or lack of attention by the auctioneer. In short, there are opportunities at auctions for persons from every class position to participate and get a good deal.

In addition to bidding on and purchasing items to be sold, buyers also engage in many other social activities. They may meet old friends, relatives, and acquaintances at auctions. Some buyers just come for the show. Others are primarily interested in learning the current going price for various types of goods. Eating snacks purchased from the ubiquitous "goodie wagon," or a lunch served by a local women's group, is a major activity for some buyers, especially those who try to keep warm on cold days by consuming endless cups of hot coffee.

The goods on the auction block are themselves in a transitional status in terms of ownership. They become liminal, neither owned nor bought once the auction starts. Any attempt by owners to remove items from sale once the auction starts are strongly protested. The bidding process heightens the liminal status of goods sold by the auctioneer. Potential ownership is unstable, slipping quickly from person to person as bid follows bid. At most auctions, a sale is recorded by jotting down the buyer's identification number (usually printed on a card and held up by the successful bidder for the auctioneer to see). Cash does not change hands until much later. In the meantime, the goods remain displayed on the grounds or, if small enough, carried by the buyer. In short, the goods have been purchased but not paid for and cannot be removed until the buyer's account has been settled with the cashier. Meanwhile, the bidding and selling continues at a rapid pace. It is not unusual for large buyers to purchase as many as a hundred items and to have them sitting about the auction site as the sale continues, a situation that sometimes generates disputes over who owns which items. Occasionally, items are sold twice or an item is mistakenly charged to a number other than the buyer's.

Auctions as Gambles

The confrontation of the sale drama is usefully analyzed as a gamble. The stakes are high for all sides in this drama and all play to win. Unlike buyers at fixed-price markets, the buyers and sellers at auctions know the goods go to the highest bidder and one takes one's chances.[4] If no one bids high on a valuable item, the auctioneer loses commissions and the owner(s) of the item can suffer financially. If a buyer bids higher than necessary, then she or he gets "stuck." Everyone accepts the conditions of the gamble and is expected to be a good sport. Hesitant bidders agree to go away satisfied, or at least appearing to be satisfied, even if they lost out on a good deal. Money is at stake here where the auctioneers and buyers engage in a drama of setting the highest bid.

Auction risk taking for the buyer involves placing an initial bid and then determining when to stop making increments in subsequent bidding for an item. Making the first bid reveals the bidder's interest in the item. Some buyers find this public announcement difficult. It is a gamble to make one's tastes and interests known. Opening bids on items of questionable taste (i.e., kitsch such as black velvet paintings) often produce guffaws from other buyers. Occasionally the auctioneer also joins in with good-natured ribbing.

Known buyers of valuable or rare collector's items may not want to alert other buyers of their interest in a particular article. Finding just the right psychological moment to jump into the bidding with just the right bid is an important auction skill. Exercising this skill adds to the gamble of the bidding process.

Another gamble involves the buyer's assessment of the worth of the item for sale. With few exceptions, items are sold "as is" and "as described" with no returns permitted unless the item has clearly been misrepresented. For example, if an auctioneer says a coffee pot is sterling silver but it turns out to be only silver plate, the auctioneer will agree to take it back and sell it again, but only if the error is quickly brought to the auctioneer's attention. Needless to say, auctioneers carefully avoid making claims about the quality or authenticity of items unless they are confident about their claim. Linguistic sidestepping is common: "Boy this *sure looks like gold*, but I can't be sure, these old rings aren't always marked." The auctioneer offers a gamble—perhaps it really is gold!

Auctions usually include an inspection period prior to the sale's start. During this time, buyers can examine items before bidding on them. Poker-faced diplomacy often characterizes these examinations. Bidders usually try to avoid any display of interest, disdainfully handling a "prize" that they "must have" for their collection. Thus, preinspection is itself a gamble in which bidders try not to tip their hands or call attention to some valuable item. Many buyers arrive after the sale starts and may not get a close look at the items. What looks like a priceless heirloom twenty-five feet away may be junk once the new owner takes it home and makes a careful inspection. Less frequently, the gamble pays off and an item that a successful bidder buys as a cheap good turns out to be "a find."

Many odds and ends at estate auctions are sold by the box and bidders might see only the items at or near the top of the box. They may bid high in the hope— a gamble—that there is an unseen treasure at the bottom of the box. Even if the box had been closely inspected, bidders gamble that a dishonest buyer has not switched boxes, placing a particularly desirable item in another box.

Another gamble is estimating the time when a particular item is likely to be sold. Given the hundreds and sometimes thousands of items sold at estate auctions, it may be short minutes or long hours before a buyer will have a chance at a given item. Knowledge of the auctioneer's pacing and preferred order of sale is important in determining when a given item is likely to be sold. I have gambled and misjudged my timing more than once, having left an auction to run an errand, only to learn that the item I wanted was gone when I returned. At other times, however, the timing gamble was successful, allowing an enjoyable lunch at a nearby restaurant, for example, in the midst of a long auction. To be certain of a chance at a particular item, however, one must be willing to wait, exchanging one's time for a good deal.

Once a buyer makes an initial bid, thus advertising interest, it is often difficult to stop bidding, especially if the buyer really wants the item. Since the buyer does not know the value placed on the item by other bidders, the buyer does not know how high the bidding is likely to go. The buyer may stop bidding too soon, losing the item when it could have been had for just a little bit more. Occasionally some bidders appear unable to lose gracefully and keep bidding well beyond the apparent worth of the item. Once the bidding starts, however, it usually comes to a quick, rapid-fire conclusion. If the opening buyer makes the only bid, then the buyer must wonder whether the item was unwanted by others and if it could have been bought with a lower bid. Starting and stopping bids are problematic for buyers; both involve a gamble.

Formula comments on starting and stopping are commonly heard: "I really wanted that, why didn't I bid?" and, from buyers on the verge of bidding who hestitate too long, "That was so quick I didn't have time to think!" Bidders rarely admit publicly that they had trouble stopping, so it is usually others who make the comments: "Boy, what a fool to pay a price like that!" or "They must be crazy to want that old thing," or "I saw the same thing go for half the money last week."

Speaking experientially, I learned to set a ceiling price or limit for each item beyond which I would not bid. Once I began bidding, however, I often found myself—despite all good and rational intentions—going well over my limit before forcing myself to stop bidding. At other times I have bid, stopped, and then wished I'd gone higher. I have also not bid on an item believing it out of my price range only to see it sold very cheaply before I realized I should have jumped in on the bidding. Occasionally I bought an item that I later gazed at in bewilderment, unsuccessfully trying to reconstruct my thinking or rationale at the time I bid for it. Bidding often and easily defies the logic of even sophisticated game-theory analyses.

Nonetheless, the complexities and subtleties of bidding must be learned. Buyers must learn how to bid well or they will not participate at auctions for very long. Repeated hesitancy or other continuing violation of bidding norms brings swift and sometimes merciless ridicule from auctioneers. Foolish bids not only deplete one's financial resources, they result in derision from other participants. Learning how to bid is itself part of the auction gamble. It is a social event to announce oneself as interested, to pay up, and decide if it is a win, lose, or draw situation.

All of these gambles point to the unique character of auctions as commodity markets for everyday goods. There is an established, relatively stable monetary price for objects obtained on the fixed-price market economy. Auctions, however, are characterized by a series of gambles, often social in nature, where the buyer tries his or her hand at getting a good deal.

Auctions as Anti-Structure

I have discussed the ways in which auctions challenge everyday social statuses and assumptions about the nature of economic exchanges. Auctions are public events and often involve more egalitarian play where skill sometimes wins over sheer class advantage. Auctions allow ne'er-do-well schemers and wealthy collectors alike to trade their time for a chance at a good deal. Auctions are more than commodity exchange markets, however. The rules that structure auctions generate more than just good deals; auctions also provide good times.

Auctioneers generate fun by telling jokes, laughing at themselves, or mocking the objects they sell. Sometimes the audience becomes the target of their humor, but with good auctioneers this is infrequent and carefully executed. Such comments are often followed by a statement affirming that the butt of the joke is a friend or someone known to have a good sense of humor. These jokes fulfill an important, overtly recognized function, discussed in greater depth in the next section.

A more subtle and significant process is engendered by auctioneers' typical speech patterns. Utilizing a very rapid, rolling speech in which words are often blurred and repeated, the auctioneer creates a chant, the "auctioneer singsong." This standardized, repetitive speech style and the quick process of buying and selling (an intrinsically fascinating event in our society) allows the audience to be absorbed in the (unreflective) ongoing activities. Although this chant is not technically hypnosis, true fans who frequent auctions commonly remark that they lose all sense of time as they listen to an auctioneer's spiel. People at auctions willingly stand for long periods in any weather, watching all kinds of basically worthless goods being exchanged, while they remain often unaware of their discomfort or the passage of time. The auction becomes another reality with its own set of rules for the use of time and money. For Americans, it is a unique experience.

The audience clearly enters into and leaves this state of absorption fairly easily. A person can make a comment, sight a friend, or focus on an object and thereby withdraw from this dreamlike state. I frequently found myself in such an altered consciousness and would return from an auction amazed that I had stood without eating, eliminating, or being bored for seven hours at a stretch. This same kind of fascination and participation, which could only be extracted under the most extreme circumstances in other settings, has been observed repeatedly. More commonly the absorption itself lasts for only short segments of time, but it is this possibility of withdrawal from everyday life, this kind of flow of time, that is an important underlying anti-structure for the participants (Csikszentmihalyi, 1975a).

Most people who attend auctions infrequently do not experience this. However, one woman (a friend of mine) who attended her first auction reported she was very excited by its pace, the selling, the exchange, and the auctioneers. Nonetheless, I observed that she sat alone apparently doing nothing for long periods of time and she wandered off from the main sale site. She was in fact engrossed in the anti-structural flow of time during much of her experience.

This destructuring of time is important for the participants. Time can be filled by sitting and looking off into space or by poking in old boxes. The memorabilia displayed on tables at estate auctions usually range from junk to personal mementos, nostalgic reminders of past eras, and valuable objects. People can wander in circles about the auction site, buy something to eat, and kibbitz with friends; put succinctly, they can do nothing or kill time by everyday standards while waiting for whatever they want to observe or buy. This sequencing of excitement and relaxation allows the auction audience to become both meditative and tense. This contrast becomes, in and of itself, pleasing. Thus people say they have fun at auctions even if they do not buy anything.

THE AUCTIONEERS AND THEIR TEAMS: THE STARS AND STAGEHANDS

Whereas buyers drift off into an anti-structural flow, auctions are highly structured, everyday events for auctioneers and their co-workers. These laborers have insider knowledge of the backstage. They create the structure of fun for others. Although many auctioneers enjoy their work, it remains work in a mundane sense. A few auctioneers are former buyers who so enjoyed auctions that they got into the business. In the process of shifting from buyer to auctioneer, they gradually adopt more and more of the rules and experiences associated with the structured aspects of auctions as everyday work.

Many auctioneers have a literal backstage area to which they retreat during the auction to take a break from their work while an assistant temporarily handles the sale. These backstage areas are usually located in vans or camper trucks. The private areas are off limits to all but the auction team, although the auctioneer's close friends may be permitted entry. This backstage area separates the buyers from the auctioneers and their teams. It symbolizes a different structural reality.

The auctioneers are the major stars of the drama. They occupy a physically central position and determine the start and end of the sale. They also control the front-stage drama in a series of ways, all pivoting around the rhythm and sound of their voices and management of the crowd. Using microphones, jokes, and the stereotypical auctioneer language and cadence, the auctioneers can be charismatic and powerful. Good auctioneers encourage people to continue bidding by saying things like, "Don't lose it for a dollar," or "Don't stop now," or "It's almost yours," or "This is the best [item for sale] I've seen for a long time." Sometimes they joke about their power and the naïveté of the buyers by saying, "Don't stop until I tell you."

Their rolling, quick, singsong style is difficult to mimic. Bad auctioneers who lack good training or command of the auctioneers' patter and chant quickly lose the crowd's interest and get lower prices for goods. By repeating over and over the desired starting bid or the present bid, auctioneers increase the asking price in relatively small increments. A typical bid goes like this:

Now here we have a piece of Heisey glass with a small piece missing on the edge, but it is still a good piece. Now it's worth at least 25, but who'll give me ten to start?

Do I hear ten, ten to bid, all right a five. I've got five, a five and now a six, a six, a six, who'll bid a six?

Unfortunately, the singsong rhythm is lost in such a literal translation, but the rapidity of speech and changes in bids generate tension and excitement. Recognized, collectible items are the easiest to sell because their prices are standardized. Collectors know this, and business owners (such as antique dealers) know such objects can be easily resold. Much auction work, however, involves selling the mundane and the unwanted. This is a major reason why a good auctioneer is needed, so that large quantities of things that are hard to sell can be sold quickly. Not much money is made on these items individually, so they become the target of jokes to entertain the crowd. Therefore, bed pans become "flower pots," old brushes become "back scrubbers," unidentified objects become "the things you always wanted" or the crowd is asked for their knowledge of what the thing could be. Sexist jokes often provide a quick way to get a laugh—and so the object reminds the auctioneer of his "old girlfriends."

During one estate auction, a relative told the auctioneer to cut out the jokes and get on with the sale. After several comments to this effect, the auctioneer stopped the auction and explained to the owner that this was part of the reason why people came. They wanted to have a good time and that is why the items would be sold. Thus the general aura of household auctions is one of good humor and tolerance. Only a few auctioneers were observed to be humorless, and this was not easily tolerated by the crowd.

For example, I once observed a business auction conducted in a matter-of-fact manner that alienated the buyers. A business auction is designed to sell large quantities of business machines and supplies, which may be surplus materials or the stock and equipment liquidated when a business fails. In the auction observed, the auctioneer in effect used "reserve bids." When the auctioneer's lowest bid was not met, he simply did not sell the item—and moved to a different item. He sold the items rapidly, first citing the market value of the goods and then selling to the high bidder, if there was one. It is common in business auctions for there to be duplicates of many items. For example, there might be hundreds of gallons of industrial paint for sale. The high bidder might offer four dollars per gallon but only wants, say, twenty gallons. Now the auctioneer must dispose of the remaining gallons not purchased by the high bidder. It is typical to start the bidding all over again and usually the high bid will be somewhat lower than the first time around. Again the winner buys what she or he wants at the new price. If more duplicates remain, the process is repeated until the entire stock of a particular item is sold. In the auction at hand, the auctioneer deviated from this practice.

In this auction, the auctioneer offered the remaining stock to other bidders at the first high price established. He did not start the bidding again. If no one bought at the high price, the auctioneer simply did not sell the stock and moved to the next item. There was no joking, just fast-paced, efficient sales. The sale moved quickly and bids were obtained, but the audience grumbled about not returning and asked, with reference to the auctioneer, "Who does he think he is?" The auctioneer was not a local person, causing some to exclaim, "These outsiders sure get high-handed!" This was not an auction to enjoy, good deals were few, and the proceedings were marred by the direct, structural imposition of efficient business practices.

Presumably, these humorless "big city"specialists in business auctions had other outlets for unsold items, but failure to maintain friendly rapport with buyers can be fatal in estate auctions. I observed only one humorless auctioneer conduct a household sale. He immediately began to lose his crowd and only about fifteen buyers remained for the last half of the sale. Prices were exceedingly low, resulting in a small take for the owner and the auctioneer. There were good deals to be had, but this was not an enjoyable auction.

Auctioneers must build established reputations to attract a crowd. This is often accomplished through family ties. The husband/father is the auctioneer; the wife/ mother is the clerk taking money and giving numbers to the buyers. The children are involved with setting up, displaying, and moving the goods. Sons tend to be groomed to become auctioneers while daughters play a more invisible role. Multiple generations of auctioneers and their extended family are not uncommon. This is especially true in rural areas where kinship ties are deeply entrenched.

A reputation for honesty and fair play is crucial for maintaining a good crowd. Since bidders are sometimes difficult to locate—because of the fast pace, "secret" signs, or the size and placement of the crowd—the buyers depend on the auctioneers genuinely having a bidder when they say they do. Otherwise, the auctioneer can "bid up" the buyers. I know of only one auctioneer with an unsavory reputation in this regard. It was rumored that he had stooges place bids or used imaginary bidders. The auctions he ran were sparsely attended due to an informal community boycott by regular buyers. Attending only one of his auctions made me distrust him, because I was involved in a suspicious incident. I bid on an item at a ridiculously low bid and stopped bidding. The auctioneer then tried repeatedly, and unsuccessfully, to have me bid again after a higher bid had been offered. At that point, he should have sold the item to the other person, the higher bidder. Instead, the auctioneer tried to sell it to me at my lower bid. Presumably the higher bidder was fictitious; at least no one stepped forward to claim the item. Since the higher bidder should have the right to buy the object, the auctioneer's behavior was suspicious. I became wary as a result of this and it prompted me to make further inquiries. When I asked others about his reputation, several regulars told me of the community boycott.

More problematic than blatant violations of the rules of the game are the subtle interactions between auctioneers and favorite buyers. These are bidders who attend regularly and are known to be collectors of certain types of items. From the auctioneer's point of view, these buyers guarantee almost certain sale of particular items. Such buyers sometimes start with low bids, usually in an area in which they specialize (such as glassware, jewelry, etc.). Because these initial, expeditious bids help maintain the pace of the auction, auctioneers are quick to recognize these legitimate "helpers" and sometimes their first bid gives them the best deal. They are also singled out as the most likely buyers in their area of specialty and this status gives these buyers an edge over strangers. Such special buyers often have their own, permanently assigned identification numbers. They are thereby spared the need to show their numbers when they win a bid. Conversely, novice, less well known buyers are often scolded repetitively by the auctioneer to "show your number" to the clerk who records the sales. The known buyers are often referred to by name, which makes them feel like insiders while others feel like outsiders. Obviously, frequent buyers are most likely to get such recognition, but frequency and recognizability are only two factors. The auctioneers' personal likes and dislikes also figure in the decision about who gets this kind of recognition, resulting in an informal special group of buyers within the bidding public.

Auctioneers can become charismatic stars: they control the jokes, the singsong bidding, and the movement and order of the sale. They open and close the deals and recognize the bids. Like central directors and major actors they are the focal point of the auction drama. In the process, however, they are aided by a cast of characters, the "auctioneer team."

Each auctioneer needs a variety of workers to help set up the auction. Sales are usually organized out-of-doors on tables surrounding the premises of the estate (otherwise, the goods must be moved to some other location for the sale). Items are ordered as to type of object and sometimes boxed into small units. Especially valuable objects must be identified and are usually segregated from other items, often displayed in a locked case. This sorting may occupy most of the week before a sale while actual setting up for sale day often begins early in the morning of a sale, which then starts in the late morning or early afternoon. For very large sales, the auction may extend over two or three days or last seven to ten hours. Usually, however, estate auctions run from two and a half to five hours. The team starts working early in the morning and continues until late afternoon or early evening.

The head auctioneer (referred to as a "colonel" if they have specific auction training) has one or two assistants who can temporarily fill the auctioneer's role. Sometimes these substitutes are partners or family members, sometimes they are apprentice auctioneers establishing themselves in the field. In general, however, the head auctioneer is the principal star of the show.

The auctioneer's team (Goffman, 1959) helps to spot bidders in the crowd, moves and displays items for sale, gets food and drinks for other team members, takes cash, signs up the buyers, issues identification numbers, and records the sales. The number of members on the team depends not only on the size of the sale but also on the number of employees in each auctioneer's firm. Those with more team members provide quicker, better service but they make less profit on any given sale due to increased overhead. Family teams, obviously, operate with lower overhead costs and make the most money as a group, which is a major reason why this structure continues in our bureaucratic era.

Teams also serve the function of getting to know more buyers. The team has more opportunity to joke, have friendly interactions, and meet members of the crowd than the auctioneer can do alone. Teams help establish and maintain the tone of an auction and provide a large cast for the backstage work of setting up and conducting the sale.

THE INVISIBLE SELLERS

The sellers who own the items offered for sale generate the reason for the auction. Their relationship to the auctioneer is established through an important preritual negotiation, which includes making arrangements for the auction and signing a contract to conduct the auction. During the auction ritual itself, however, the seller's role is largely invisible. The sellers or the sellers' representative usually attends the auction, but they have a very circumspect role. Sellers are asked occasionally by the auctioneer to provide information about an object, such as "Does this appliance work?" or "How old is this object?" or "Are there keys to the locked drawers?" In general, however, sellers are neither referred to openly nor directly addressed.

Sellers have a variety of concerns and interests that the auctioneer tries to satisfy. Sellers are sometimes anxious about the prices being paid. They may decide at the last moment that they do not want a favorite object sold after all. Some sellers are unfamiliar with and unprepared for the events that unfold as the auction proceeds. The auctioneers or their team, therefore, must reassure the sellers that their best interests are being served. The workers might explain why they are going so slowly or getting such low prices and ask them to be patient. Clearly, the sellers have usually been told beforehand about these typical routines but many nonetheless find the actual auction disconcerting.

On one occasion, an elderly woman seller who also appeared to be a friend of the auctioneer was reassured several times throughout a long day of selling that the prices were going well. Once the auctioneer even said in exuberance, "Well, we got you a really good price for that!" This particular seller kept exclaiming about the wonderful prices. Even the buyers joined in. The auctioneer, seller, and buyers all supported each other's perceptions. Such mutual exchange is rare, however. Usually, actors in each ritual category keep their opinions about the commodity exchanges within their own group or team.

A structured exception to the seller's invisible role occurs when houses and land are also sold. Large sums of money are often involved in these transactions. The seller or legal representative (often both) are present. The ritual rules for these large sales are different, with the bidding typically lasting for a period of thirty to sixty minutes marked by short interludes where potential bidders reinspect the premises, ask questions, and ponder their next bids. During this process, the auctioneer confers with the seller on the progress of the bidding. The auctioneer takes care that no bid is overlooked. Buyers are given every encouragement to bolster their courage to make an even higher bid. They are graciously allotted additional time to reexamine the house or make quick telephone calls to consult with investment partners. If bids are low or if a serious bidder needs time to work a deal, the auctioneer may even call a recess in the bidding and announce the exact time that bidding will resume. Once the final bid is accepted, the seller participates in legal ceremonies completing the transaction.

Despite the physical invisibility of the owners, they are structurally significant figures in the sense that all their goods are displayed for public inspection. From this material array, the public discerns many facts about the owners—their lifestyles, taste, family relationships, and habits. An element of voyeurism is present at any auction—poking around boxes, reading old letters, estimating the care given to things, and finding out how the owner lived. This aspect of auctions can be emotionally wrenching for the seller since the auction may be occasioned by the death of a spouse or entry to a nursing home. The seller watches strangers paw through the accumulations and memories of a lifetime. For professional buyers, this element is of minimal interest since they are most likely to look at the objects as commodities. But naïve buyers, friends, and neighbors are more curious. They say things like: "I never knew they were so poor" or "Where did they keep all this junk?" or "I remember when she would use this and talk about her parents." In this way, objects are related to the seller and become focal points of discussion. Less intimately related buyers, however, also speculate. Family items, old Bibles, pictures, photo albums, postcards (see chapter 5), scrapbooks, and letters are especially noteworthy. It is common for people to comment that these are things that "should not be sold." Others may remark, "You know, [the seller's] possessions sure don't amount to much when it comes down to it."

As a result of attending auctions, I am much more impressed that the prized and valued goods of working- and middle-class families are extraordinarily standardized and easily replaceable. For a few hundred dollars at an auction, one can furnish an entire home, including mementos, heirlooms, and "family" portraits. Experientially, I am much less attached to things than before.

Owners' belongings become open to public analysis; this leads to speculation about the owners. People comment on cleanliness, taste, quantity, and quality of items. Everyone is a potential member of a judging community. Auctions provide one of the few occasions in our society that strangers can look over a person's total possessions and make a community judgment. Although sellers are usually conspicuous by their physical absence from the center stage of the auction ritual, their symbolic presence is concretely manifested in the goods for sale.

THE BUYERS: THE NAIVE, THE FAN, THE SEMIPROFESSIONAL, AND THE PROFESSIONAL

Buyers, like auctioneers, have parts to play in the auction script. Unlike auctioneers, however, buyers vary in their relation to auctions as work or play. All buyers are liminal. They occupy a transitional state, deciding whether or not to try to become owners of a particular commodity. The various buyer roles are delineated here as a function of their relation to the structure and anti-structure of the auction.

Every auction operates by a set of formal rules, announced at the beginning of each auction in a short speech by the auctioneer. These include paying for and removing each sale item once it is announced as "Sold!" by the auctioneer. The order of the sale follows a standard pattern and may be announced by the auctioneer, for example, hardware is sold first, then glassware, followed by furniture. There are many informal rules that buyers must also learn. First-time buyers arriving late on the scene, missing the opening announcements, may not know even the formal rules.

Good Bidders

Learning to become a "good bidder" is important for the buyer. Only a good bidder can buy desired objects at a good price. Good bidders, then, must be alert to the objects being sold, bid for what they want, pay only the price (or less) that they want to pay (i.e., set limits and stick to them—at least most of the time), give clear bid signals to the auctioneer, and show their bidding number (or, more rarely, give their name) to recording clerks.[5] These activities occur very rapidly. Failure at any step means that either the buyer loses or the pace of the auction is interrupted, making the auctioneer and other buyers wait. Good bidders also know how to start and end bidding. They keep the auction going when others are not bidding, and they stop their bids clearly and decisively. There is also a category of super good bidders (or favorites) discussed earlier. Members of this select group are known to buy certain objects regularly and are willing to start the bid and willingly take the item if no one else wants it.

It is a standard rule that bidders should not speak to the auctioneer (other than to bid) while objects are being sold. Neither should they try to stop or interrupt the flow of the auction. Bidders need to bid quickly and surely. They need to pay attention to the bidding and not ask too frequently to have the current bid repeated especially for them. Bidders well known to the auctioneer may occasionally ask to examine an object while it is up for sale, but usually such inspections must occur before the bidding begins. The privilege of inspection during bidding is more likely to be extended to professional buyers than to other categories of bidders. Good bidders avoid jostling others, take an appropriate place at the bidding site, and keep their purchased objects well separated from objects being sold. These and many other rules are part of the expectations for good bidding behavior.

Naïve Buyers

"Naïve buyers" are a large component of any auction. Frequently they are friends of the seller, neighbors, or people who are just curious about auctions. Perhaps they have gone to a few auctions, but they do not remember the rules and, even if they did, there are always slightly different rules for each auctioneer team. Sometimes naïve buyers express surprise at the pace of the auction, that it is either too fast or too slow. Some naïve bidders are too afraid to bid; their friends can be heard urging them on: "You know that's what you want," or questioning them, "Why didn't you bid?" (They may answer: "I don't know" or "It was happening too fast" or "I'm not really sure if I want it.") Thus there is some anxiety about or resistance to placing a bid and participating in the bidding process. Frequently I would bring naïve bidders with me and do the bidding for them. Often the first bids, though, lend a sense of excitement to the event for the real buyer, and these naïve bidders will exclaim with excitement about an object that they actually "got." For most people, it is a new experience to bid competitively in this economy, and they marvel that they could do it so quickly and get rewarded immediately with possession of a desired object.

Fans

The "fan" is quite another category. Attending auctions regularly, they go for the fun of it, to get a good deal, see friends, and pass the time. Fans enjoy a good show. An especially memorable event enjoyed and talked about by fans for several months involved an auction gamble called "bidding up." Occasionally, one buyer will bid higher than his or her limit just to see how high the bid can be raised without the buyer getting "stuck," pulling out of the bidding with the penultimate bid. I witnessed an especially amusing instance of this gamble when a well-known and astute collector of fine glassware decided to bid up a rude, naïve professional buyer who was buying everything in sight regardless of price in order to set up an antique business. The object of the bidding in this instance was a tasteless wooden sculpture of little value. As the bidding soared, the community of fans caught on and started to enjoy the show. They enjoyed it so much, with unsuppressed giggles and outright laughter, that the butt of the joke also caught on and stopped bidding, leaving his would-be tormentor stuck with the trashy sculpture at a vastly exaggerated price. The perpetrator took his licks with requisite good grace and was much admired for trying to stick the new professional buyer. He received many "congratulations" on his "fine acquisition."

Fans experience auctions as anti-structural events. Fans watch everybody at the auction and enjoy their observational power. They are generally known to other fans, the auctioneers and their team, the semiprofessionals, and professionals. Fans, therefore, enter a small community to have fun and get good deals. They know how to bid correctly. They enjoy themselves and share this enthusiasm with others, and they provide a regular following for the auctioneers. Fans often eat at auctions. Sometimes they come prepared with thermoses and sandwiches, but they often eat from the local food carriers' vans or tables. They compare the present auction with past sales. They ask questions about the sellers, and they talk with others around them. They are the repository of information on past good deals, good auctions, and good auctioneers. Fans may help naïve bidders learn how to bid. Fans make small talk as they sit on furniture to be sold or stand under shady trees in the summer. They greet each other, talk about recent personal events, and, if all else fails, they talk about the weather. Fans clearly intend to have a good time and they make an effort to share it with others.

Many fans are older, retired persons or housewives. They have the flexible hours needed to attend auctions frequently and have just enough money to be able to buy things cheap. Auctions give pattern to their everyday lives, and in this sense the auctions provide a structure. If auctions were not fun and the people in attendance were not congenial, these fans would not go to auctions.

A few fans are grouchy types. They can be counted on to pronounce gloomily that it "looks like rain" or complain that items are being sold "too high." They may simply scowl at the people around them. These pessimistic fans are well-known regulars and have a small circle of cronies with whom they visit. Grouchy fans, moreover, are likely to be kidded by other fans and auctioneers. Their presence is an occasion for public comment. Thus not all fans are necessarily enthusiastic and friendly.

All fans, whether enthusiastic or grouchy, share a set of characteristics. Fans (1) attend auctions frequently, (2) are not antique dealers or "in business," (3) know and are known by others, and (4) like to get good deals. All fans, even grouches, appear to like auctions.

Semiprofessional Buyers

"Semiprofessionals" are buyers who periodically resell some of their auction buys. They may be collectors who buy too much of one item. They may be people who want to become professional dealers but do not have enough capital. The size of their businesses ranges from annual or semiannual garage sales to regularly kept booths at flea markets. Semiprofessionals often want to buy large quantities of things cheaply, or get a good deal to resell. Auctioneers recognize them as a steady source of income for the sellers. Semiprofessionals form part of the regular crowd. Fans sometimes become semiprofessionals. Many semi-professionals have a serious interest in buying, however, because they are working to increase their capital. They may buy items to sell that they do not like. They may stay at auctions when they are tired or restless, when an auction is no longer fun. Profit becomes a significant motivation for semiprofessionals and this subtly changes the nature of their participation.

Professional Buyers

"Professionals" are even more deeply committed to resale and profit. Frequently, they own and operate antique stores. Auctions become a major business resource and strict accounting of capital outlay is necessary. Professionals are major spenders and they are necessary to an auctioneer's continued success. Professionals are greeted and recognized by auctioneers and by each other. Professionals often congregate together, and talk over past auctions. A frequent topic of conversation is a series of complaints about how badly their businesses are doing: "People don't like to buy good pieces"; "You can't trust them alone in your shops"; "You could really get good deals a few years ago"; or "Things are really moving slow now." The reasons for this pessimistic conversation style are hard to determine. Many of these professionals have had businesses for several years, and they have been observed repeatedly getting good deals. Nonetheless, they frequently depict their businesses as suffering.

Professionals have access to trucks and vans to haul their buys. They are prepared with mats and covers and often arrange to have others help them finish their moving. They often buy in specific areas. If they are known (and liked), professionals may be told by the auctioneers when their specialty will be sold. I observed auctioneers who kept back certain items until professional buyers arrived. I also observed changes in the traditional order of sale to accommodate the needs of professionals who must arrive late or leave early. As a courtesy to professional buyers, auctioneers sometimes accept bids from absent professionals—this service was not announced and was rarely extended to other buyers, myself included.

Professionals provide the most reliable source of capital at auctions. The power to spend money allows them to act in ways that are unacceptable for the other categories of actors. I observed professional buyers push people away from tables and items. They sometimes argue with the auctioneer over bids. I have seen bidding reopened to include them when the sale to another buyer seemed clearly fair and final to me. They may give signs of being bored and "above" others in the crowd. When they move furniture, some professional buyers do not ask others to make a path. They simply push the furniture into the crowd and plow through. Some professional buyers have very loud and irritating voices. Their dissatisfaction with the crowd is made evident through rude comments. None of these behaviors would be tolerated by auctioneers if the buyers were naïve, fans, or possibly even semiprofessionals. The rude behavior of professionals is generally "not seen" by auctioneers, however. This does not mean that the behavior is liked by the auctioneer, only that it is tolerated. Living with these behaviors is part of the work of being an auctioneer and a reason why it is not a playful activity.

Professionals, like auctioneers and their teams, are at work when they attend an auction. Auctions are part of their everyday labor. The work status of semiprofessionals is intermediate, between that of fan and professional. Semiprofessionals tend to enjoy auctions, but they can also get caught up in the everyday structural realities of profit and loss. Auctions, for professionals and auctioneers, are not anti-structural experiences.

Interrelationships

These groups of buyers—the naïve buyer, the fan, the semiprofessional, and the professional—have various interrelationships. The naïve bidder may be helped by the fan to bid right. Fans and naïve bidders may chat. In general, however, fans enjoy each other the most, although they often talk with any other member of the crowd. Semiprofessionals and fans, because they are frequent participants, have a great deal in common. Semiprofessionals and professionals may share a serious concern about resale, capital, and other business concerns. Professionals may give business advice or trade information with semiprofessionals. Professionals clearly speak differently to each type of buyer and appear to enjoy the proceedings less than any other buyer category.

Buyers have different relationships to the structure or anti-structure of the

Table 3.1
The Relationship Between Participants' Roles and Experience at Auctions

<u>Roles</u>

```
Fans <--- Naive Bidders --- Semiprofessionals ----> Professionals

              Seller <---------------> Auctioneers


Anti-structural <--------------------------------------> Structural
```

<u>Experience</u>

same event. The relationships between structure, anti-structure, and the various roles of the auction participants are diagrammed in Table 3.1. For the naïve bidder and the fan, the auction is anti-structural. They attend auctions to have fun and get a good deal. Over time, fans may save considerable sums of money by. buying at auctions or build impressive collections of particular items at reasonable cost. Semiprofessionals are partially at work, partially trying to get into work they enjoy, and partially having fun. Professionals may have fun, but this does not determine their attendance at auctions. They are at work, attempting to generate income by securing as many good deals as possible.

The auctioneers and their team members are hard at work during each auction. Their task is clearly structural. The seller's role is more complex. Sellers are interested in the size of proceeds from the sale (a structural concern), but the sale is for them very far from an everyday event (i.e., it is different, anti-structural). The auction may well symbolize or mark a major life transition. In this sense, the auction may be part of a liminal journey for the seller. This potential, however, is not formally ritualized at auctions—although it certainly could be.

Bad Buyers

Like some bad auctioneers, "bad buyers" sometimes engage in "dirty tricks." Bad buyers add unpleasantly to the risk or gamble of an auction. Stealing, for example, is worrisome for the sellers and auctioneers. Indeed, "buyer" is a misnomer in this particular regard. Theft is a problem for legitimate buyers who have bought items but have not yet paid for them or removed them from the sale grounds. Under the rules of the auction, the buyer is responsible for the item once it is declared "sold" by the auctioneer. With goods strewn about the grounds and buyers frequently removing their wares, ownership of items is often difficult to determine. I sometimes observed people who appeared to be thieves.

On the few occasions when I felt confident that a robbery was in progress, I brought the situation immediately to the attention of a member of the auctioneer team. The auctioneer team is understandably hesitant to act on such information, and often the article at stake is not an expensive one. Rather than responding on the spot to the apparent robbery, the auctioneer team members told me that potential thieves are identified and particularly watched at auctions—and that this is accomplished surreptitiously. Thieves are not viewed as desirable or good buyers by any participant at an auction.

Other bad buyer behavior is more common than thievery. An especially irritating behavior is exhibited by bad buyers who hide objects in boxes or move desirable objects from box to box. This is a problem because many smaller items at auctions are sold by the box rather than by the item. This hiding or moving items is considered unfair but is done regularly by a small number of bad buyers. As a result, other buyers do not obtain desired objects, even if they wait for hours to bid. Not realizing that a bad buyer has rearranged the contents of boxes, a legitimate buyer often bids high for what turns out to be a box of literally worthless junk. Meanwhile, for a low bid, the bad buyer secures the box in which he or she hid the desired item. Even more commonly, bad buyers move objects out of several boxes and assemble a select group of things in a single box. This behavior is often open, however, so it does not have quite the same consequence as surreptitious hiding. Professionals sometimes engage in this behavior but are rarely punished, verbally or nonverbally, as are other buyers when caught. Occasionally, when I observed people engaged in these behaviors, I returned the objects to their original cartons. Persistent bad buyers would then try to sneak the objects back to their "favorite" boxes, and I would again restore the items to their rightful place. Sometimes we faced each other, but words were never exchanged. My restorative persistence, especially when made obvious, was usually sufficient to deter further moves or hiding by the bad buyer.

Bad buyers also try to turn the bidding to their advantage through various techniques considered unfair by other participants. Crooked bidders may make a bid and then claim that they were not bidding, or say that they had a lower bid, or that they were bidding when they in fact were not. Such "misunderstandings" are not tolerated for long, however. The auctioneer and his or her team will force these individuals to make clear, unequivocal bids in the future, even if this means temporarily disrupting the flow of the auction. Poor bidders are likely to receive short, humiliating lectures—often over loudspeakers or bullhorns for all to hear—on how to bid. Thus poor bidders lose face (Goffman, 1967) as a consequence of their actions.

The moral categories of good bidder and bad bidder stand in a hierarchical relationship to the richness of anti-structural experience. Table 3.2 diagrams this relationship. It is a significant observation that the fullest enjoyment of the anti-structural aspects of auctions is accessible only to those bidders who participate on the highest moral plane.

Each buyer group also has moral attributes. Sorting out morality can be com-

Table 3.2
The Relationship Between Moral Categories and Experience at Auctions

Moral Category

```
Good Bidders <-------------- Bad Bidders --------------> Thieves


Anti-structural <------------------------------------> Structural
                        Experience
```

Table 3.3
The Relationship Between Bidders' Roles and Standards for Bidding

Roles

```
Fans <--- Naive Bidders ---- Semiprofessionals ---> Professionals


High <----------------------------------------------------> Low
                        Standards
```

plex, however. A professional buyer might be an astute, attentive bidder while still being rude to other buyers. A bad bidder might sometimes be a regular while not a fan. And a bumbling but polite and scrupulous novice shares some attributes with fans. Despite these crosscutting complexities, it is correct to note that each group has a generally associated standard of ethics and comportment. Table 3.3 summarizes the relationships between bidders' roles and the standards of behavior expected from each. The highest standards are observed by knowledgeable fans who regularly attend auctions and who greatly enjoy the liminal and anti-structural elements of auctions. Naïve bidders, as with children in many cultures, are given some moral leeway, but are soon expected to live up to the standards of older and more experienced participants. Expected standards and good behaviors drop preciptitously as buyers abandon the anti-structural world to engage in work and profit making at auctions. There are limits, however, as theft and chronic bad bidding are not tolerated for very long by auctioneers. The liminal flow and anti-structural good humor of auctions, however, are supported fundamentally by the civility (Goffman, 1959), mutual respect, and community of fans and other good buyers.

CONCLUSION

Auctions exchange time for money, and they are often conducted in a "fun" context. A small, intermittent community is established through regular auctions, and the stagehands for its performance are the auctioneers and their teams. In a capitalist society, auctions are a way to make money and, therefore, they exhibit some of the structural problems characterizing business in America. Thus unfair advantages are given to certain buyers, and their rude behavior is more tolerated. Occupying or maintaining a position outside of the community of favored buyers/bidders mars the pleasure of attending an auction.

The creation of fun is work for auctioneers and their teams. They are onstage in a way similar to other dramatic performers in society. Although such work may be fun for them (making it a good job), it is still a structural part of their everyday life.

Of all the groups of buyers, the fans are most likely to have an anti-structural experience. Their time is well spent even if they do not obtain any goods. They want to be entertained, see friends, observe the goods and lifestyles of the sellers, and enjoy a community experience. The other buyers vary in their relationship to anti-structure. Naïve buyers may have a good time, but they are strangers to each other and to the auction experience itself. They have to learn the rules and try to make a good deal. Semiprofessionals and professionals in varying degrees are at work. Their time is costly and measured. It takes more of a good deal for them to have fun than it does for any other actor.

In this chapter I focused on the variability of ritual experience as a function of the structure and conduct of ritual roles enacted by participants. American auction rituals involve a mixture of both structural and anti-structural elements—and the balance of the mix depends on each participant's role. Auctions to auctioneers, for example, are work and are significantly more tied to everyday life for auctioneers than for fans. American rituals typically have this variable pattern of roles in relation to the structure and anti-structure of the event. This analysis suggests additional questions about auctions as rituals. For example, when, if ever, do auctions become fun or play for auctioneers? When specifically are auctions work or alienating for fans? Is work in anti-structural rituals less onerous than work in other, more mundane settings, like an assembly line? Or is it just different from work in more mundane settings?

Singles bars, examined in the previous chapter, have less flexibility for the workers, such as bartenders and waitresses, who must serve customers. Auctioneers set the dates of sales. They and their teams control the pace and structure of the auction more than workers in singles bars do. Interaction rituals are part of the auction as a ritual, but they are coordinated more by the workers at the auction than they are in a singles bar. The power to define the auction is greater, and the tolerance of unruly conduct is less. Inebriated customers are routinely problematic for workers in bars but would be seen as outrageous by everyone at an auction. Turner's analysis more closely fits the anti-structural experiences of participants at auctions than in bars, but his theory still fails to explicate the complexity of roles, experiences, and the economy intrinsic to modern life. This chapter partially fills the gaps between Goffman and Turner and also shows how a Marxist analysis of auctions is too simplistic; much more transpires at an auction than a simple exchange of material commodities. Time can be made into a commodity that can be exchanged for capital, but time itself is not capital because it cannot be accumulated. Time is intimately rooted in the cycles of life and nature, and exchanging time for money can be fun—perhaps even play. Capital relations structure behaviors, but other, different, anti-structural rules may be enacted simultaneously. This chapter documents the complex internal roles and relations within American rituals. I mapped these roles, at least partially, to show both the complicated nature of modern rituals and the flexibility of critical dramaturgy as a theory.

NOTES

1. Large auction houses, such as Sothebys, have large staffs, multiple offices in several countries, publish expensive and detailed sales catalogs, deal in highly valued, often rare and extraordinarily valuable objects such as paintings by Michelangelo and large, one-of-a-kind diamonds. Unlike bidders at local auctions, bidders in sales conducted by large houses can often remain anonymous. Some auctions, such as the recent disposition of the jewelry owned by the late Duchess of Windsor, are so exclusive that attendance is by invitation only.

2. Money has the capacity to be part of the codes of repression when it is a commodity and part of the codes of oppression when it is associated with a given social class. Labor has this dual commodity/class character in a Marxian analysis. Labor is both capital and the indicator of class.

3. The few social science studies that have been conducted in other disciplines almost always describe auctions as barter exchanges. Thus the economy of auctions becomes the overriding characteristic studied by most social scientists, while the nature of the experience, its community function, and its work aspects for auctioneers are unexamined.

4. A standard technique to limit the gamble in high stakes auctions such as those conducted by Sothebys, wherein highly valued items are put on the block, is to issue or advertise a "reserve price," below which bids will not be accepted. This mechanism protects the seller from collusion by buyers to "steal" an item at a very low price. At household estate auctions, however, reserve prices are rare. All items go to the highest bidder no matter how low this bid may be. Most auctioneers, however, will not accept starting bids (or bid increments) of less than fifty cents or one dollar.

5. Winning bids are almost always written down and then paid at a later point in the auction. On two occasions, however, I went to auctions where payment in cash was demanded on the spot following the sale of each item. Buyers and auctioneer carried large wads of folded money for payments and making change. All bids were in dollar or multiple dollar increments.

4

The Big Red Dream Machine: Nebraska Football

MARY JO DEEGAN and MICHAEL STEIN

Sports are big money-makers in the United States. Unlike singles bars or auctions, they are formal rituals that can involve thousands of people in participatory events and millions more in media-constructed versions telecast around the world. Because of this massive social participation, sports are closer than the other participatory rituals studied here to Victor Turner's nonmodern ritual, which reflects the entire community. Simultaneously, sports are further from Turner's nonmodern ritual because sports are particularly embedded in the everyday structure of American life.

T. R. Young gives us an idea of the size of the audience for sports by giving us statistics for televised events alone:

USA Today lists some 81 hours of commercial sports programming for the weekend of 21–23 April 1984. . . . If we assume that an average 80 million are watching across all sports events, all channels, and all times, we find a total of some 2.1 billion person hours are spent watching individuals and teams deal with the exigencies of scheduled and regulated conflict relations. If each hour of programming has six commercials and if each commercial costs $100,000 (a very modest estimate) then the American economy allocates some 500 million dollars per weekend or 26 billion dollars per year for just television broadcasting of sports. (Young and Walsh, 1984: prologue)

Football is, then, a major media-constructed ritual. In this chapter, however, we emphasize the football game itself and observe participants at the event, not viewers of a televised event. The mass media are briefly considered in light of a particular team's participatory ritual. In the process, we theorize that football is a major sport in the United States because of its dramatic enactment of structural codes concerning the control of time, bureaucratic order, and sex/class relations. Football is, in other words, an "ideal type" of American ritual that institutionally reinforces sexism, class antagonism, and modern orientations toward work and time. (See Schutz, 1967; Weber, 1948; Berger and Luckmann, 1966.) It amplifies these codes by making symbolic competitiveness, male control, time pressures, and bureaucratic order into physical actions. These codes of oppression and repression mesh with anti-structural elements of leisure activities where a large number of Americans act as one: united in support of "their" team and the good times associated with it.

The spectators of this game are particularly enthralled in the state of Nebraska. Here, in a state with a large geographical area and a small, predominantly rural population, the fans have elevated football to a significant ritual and source of identification. As avid supporters they dress in the team colors, red and white; participate in pre- and postgame celebrations; travel great distances; and emotionally express their loyalty and dedication to "Big Red." Studying Nebraska football as a dramatic ritual, then, reveals its creative and destructive roots in American society.

THEORETICAL AND SITUATIONAL BACKGROUND

Erving Goffman's concepts of "audience," "teamwork," "performers" (1959), "gender advertisements" (1976), "stigma" (1963b), and "games" (1967) are all particularly relevant here. With each of these theoretical abstractions we obtain a view of the self in everyday life, presenting appropriate behavior in situations where the individual must guard against possible attacks on this self-presentation. These enacted roles can sometimes ally the actor with others in similar situations who are in opposition to "outsiders" (the audience) judging their performance (1959).

Goffman's view of teamwork as "negative unity," that is, unity in opposition to others, is captured in this passage:

Secret derogation seems to be much more common than secret praise, perhaps because such derogation serves to maintain the solidarity of the team, demonstrating mutual regard at the expense of those absent and compensating, perhaps, for the loss of self-respect that may occur when the audience must be accorded accommodative face-to-face treatment (1959: 171).

Goffman further states: "Games place a 'frame' around a spate of immediate events, determining the type of 'sense' that will be accorded everything within the frame" (1961b: 20).

His analysis of "character contests" also illustrates struggles of honor that are won at the expense of others' loss.

During occasions of this kind of action, not only will character be at stake, mutual fatefulness will prevail in this regard. Each person will be at least incidentally concerned with establishing evidence of strong character, and conditions will be such as to allow this only at the expense of the character of the other participants (1967: 240).

Each of these concepts provides us with abstractions "loaded" with a view of the person as defensive, attacking, and manipulative. (Deegan, 1978; Psathas, 1977). Goffman's value positions are accepted in this chapter when applying his concepts to football games.

Turner's concepts are laden with values opposing those of Goffman; that is, each person searches and finds dignity and community through and with others on specialized occasions. The actor's sense of oneness with others, the sharing of common fate and humanity, is expressed by the concept of "communitas" (Turner, 1969). Situations marked by highly structured events and surrounded by community myths and symbols create a situation where people allow their everyday differences to lapse and new relationships to emerge. A highly structured, or ritualized, special event is marked by changes in statuses, or rites of passage (Van Genepp, 1960). These rites of change are characterized by three stages: preliminal (rites of separation), liminal (rites of transition), and postliminal (rites of incorporation) (Van Genepp, 1960: 11). The liminal stage is characterized by ambiguity, heightened excitement, and danger. Liminality fosters, then, the development of new forms of relationships; new bonds are created between participants joining them in an undefined status that threatens the order of everyday life. Liminality induces them to trust one another, to struggle together, and to see themselves as humans with a common fate and danger.

Extraordinary events—formal rituals—provide the community with an alternate social world to that found in everyday life. Part of the power of these events lies in their ability to evoke symbols and myths relating to the community. They create a setting in which people simultaneously experience their humanity. The feelings expressed at this time and the acknowledgment of common bonds is communitas.[1]

These special, ritual occasions are characterized by a sacred quality and are structured by the major themes and values of a culture. The "Durkheimian" or sacred quality of ritual events was analyzed and elaborated by Michael Stein (1977) in reference to Nebraska football.[2] His analysis examines this event as a ritual in a religious cult: the extreme loyalty of the fans is comparable to that of the religious faithful; tithings are offered, pilgrimages made, and even weddings performed in the Nebraska stadium (the red "cathedral"). Ritual clothing (discussed later) and various interpretations of events and actions are compared to scriptural readings. The extreme allegiance elicited by this ritual is reinforced by the geographic location of Nebraska, its small population, and the dramatic ability to make the sparsely inhabited state "number one" in a national event. All of these factors make Nebraska football a major ritual event enacting American values and themes.

FOOTBALL AND THE AMERICAN DREAM

American structural codes are enacted, displayed, and observed in football. The game itself follows popular social themes: winning, fighting in face-to-face combat, functioning under strict time constraints, and control by arbitrary rules.[3]

Violent sports have, of course, been present in other cultures and times, but the conjunction of violent combat with a closely timed, secular occasion, and a bureaucratic model is uniquely American. The predominance of elaborate rules, interpreted by an arbitrator or referee, demonstrates to the nonspecialized person that one can make decisions only by virtue of holding an appropriate office. Spectators who disagree with the interpretation of the game rules and the resulting situation often feel superior to the referee in their judgment and immediately express this opinion with boos, hisses, and swear words; occasionally they throw objects or make a direct physical attack. The official office of the referee (Weber, 1947) is supported by an even more arbitrary and controlling event—the clock. The division of the game into arbitrary time units, agreed upon beforehand, creates added tension that dominates the game, particularly as it progresses. Basketball, another typical American sport, shares this peculiar relationship of control by the ticking of seconds. Football, though, is more vulnerable to time tension than basketball. Football has fewer time-outs and a pattern of scoring that makes each score more difficult to obtain and numerically more significant than in basketball. Americans reenact in football their daily confrontation with arbitrary rules, official officeholders, rational authority, and the pressures of time. Their lives are structured by these core codes in play as well as in work. In leisure time, however, there is the illusion of control for the fans who choose to be spectators. It is the players after all and not the fans who are physically bashed. The players must "toe the line" and "put themselves on the line." The fans can thereby use players as living symbols of role distance. Every paid worker has to "get in the game" at some point, but during their leisure time everyday actors can pretend to be the victims and victors.

An equally strong American code, the sex code, reinforces the aforementioned codes. Football is a gendered game; men engaged in football are the extreme embodiment of the ideal male, physically big, aggressive, violent, and controlled by arbitrary, efficient, rational authority. While they abuse their bodies in a brutal but often graceful and lyrical manner, the ideal, typical woman—the cheerleader—screams, jumps, and displays her body. Gymnastic talents, which are sometimes included in the basis for selection, are secondary to the woman's presentation of a feminine ideal: the attractive "Miss America" model (Deford, 1971). This sexuality is grotesquely evidenced in the cheerleader—cute, peppy, and petite—in comparison with the football player—a big, muscular brute who can "mow down" other men. Their dress accentuates these extremes. In a search for photographs juxtaposing these ideal types of slender, provocatively and minimally dressed females and large, well-padded and aggressive males, I visited the Department of Photographic Reproductions at the University of Nebraska.

Although over a thousand visual images (including slides, photographs, and negatives) were seen, only two showed the female cheerleaders and the male players "at work" together. Thus the juxtaposed dichotomies are rarely seen in still photographs.

At Nebraska football games the cheerleaders assume a typical stance watching the game by holding two large pom-poms behind their backs. The caricature of two large "cheeks" or, when held in front, of two large breasts, is strikingly apparent. The football equipment of shoulder pads, hip pads, tight pants, and helmets likewise emphasizes male physiognomy and its association with toughness. Goffman's "gender advertisements" similarly depict these "ideal" types as they appear in everyday life (1976). These static images and gestures are embodied, amplified, and dramatized on the field. The football game ritually reenacts the male's battle against other men in a violent, competitive world controlled by arbitrary rules, and tightly structured by the clock. The women, on the sidelines, dressed in sexually provocative clothing, encourage men in this battle, engaging in movements indicating their sexual availability and desirability. The men may be on the field or on the sidelines, but women symbolically encourage both groups to endure.

The class codes of oppression generated by capitalism surround football and are often allied with patriotism, the mass media, and the sales of liquor and Coke (favorite "drugs"). (This pattern also characterizes other sports.) This set of class-related themes is briefly considered here.

Capitalism "storms the gates" of the stadium. The official selling (and unofficial scalping) of tickets occurs immediately outside the entrance, programs are sold along the routes to the game, and a plane flies over the stadium during the game announcing the arrival of new cars (another American value) at local auto dealers. Football is itself a major generator of income for the university, and ticket sales subsidize several other athletic activities. Tickets are sold out long before the season begins. Opportunities to subscribe to season tickets open rarely. Legal transfer of rights to order season tickets is often an important item on a Nebraskan's last will and testament. A successful season also helps raise additional money from alumni and other contributors. A scoreboard, rising above the seats, is capable of producing not only pictures, but also a running commentary of the game and extensive advertisements for local businesses.

Patriotism is enacted with the singing of the national anthem at the start of the game and the accompanying signs of respect and allegiance. The American flag is displayed prominently. For Nebraska, though, reinforcement of patriotism is given a unique opportunity through the team's colors of red and white. Since the fans make a serious effort to appear with at least some item of red clothing, and frequently with an all-red, or red-and-white outfit, and since denims are blue and a favorite apparel for Americans, the crowd of 75,000 people is overwhelmingly red, white, and blue. Although this may be a coincidence based on the popularity of blue denims, at one game among fifty people counted, two were wearing predominantly green clothes (the Astroturf is green), eight were wearing blue, and forty were wearing red. Orange, yellow, brown, black, and purple are so noticeable as to be outstanding in a section with 10,000 or more people. The police, who embody the state and the authority associated with it, also wear blue. Although other teams use other colors, the loyalty of other "Big Red" teams, such as Alabama's "Crimson Tide," is remarkable. Team colors, of course, are only part of a matrix of symbols, but the conjunction of patriotic and team colors is a particularly powerful emotional mix.

Outside commercial enterprises join in this mythmaking. A local bank offered (via a television advertisement) depositors commemorative belt buckles that included representations of an Indian head, the American eagle, the shape of the state of Nebraska, and "of course" the "Big Red *N*" (*Omaha World Herald*, Sept. 27, 1977). One especially enterprising savings and loan offered special savings accounts in 1986 with interest rates keyed to the win/loss record of the Nebraska football team (the more wins, the higher the interest rate).

The media dominate one top section of the stadium taking treasured seating and desirable views. Similarly, the television crews ride in trucks at the sidelines, getting top priority in visual access. This participatory ritual is brought thereby to numerous others who observe a media-constructed ritual. To pursue this aspect in depth is beyond the intent of this chapter (it is discussed more in the concluding chapter), but two examples of this media transformation illustrate the differences between participatory and media-constructed football. In media-constructed football games there are regularly scheduled capitalist commercials, often showing advertisements for the military as well. The technique of "instant replays" is an ideal type of construction in which minutely timed, selected important events are immediately replayed while the real game time is interrupted. In modern society, ritual events are subject to manipulation by the press—particularly by television, with its support of commercialism and arbitrary control—mimicking the bureaucracy, patriarchy, and time structure evinced in the game.

The number of Cokes sold at the game is staggering. Before the half time, one youngster (most sellers are males in their early teens) had sold six full trays of soft drinks with barely enough time to refill. Peanuts, associated more with baseball than football, had few buyers. The open selling of the substance that "brings the world together" and "joins generations" is contrasted with the drinking of liquor, which is legally forbidden but tolerated, in defiance of bureaucratic proscriptions.[4] The attitude that such behavior is illicit but acceptable was evidenced when a policeman took liquor away from one young man and the crowd only watched. When he took liquor away from someone else, crowd members indicated surprise and started to put their liquor out of sight, but when he tried it with a third person, the crowd stood up and started to boo him.[5] The official authority is seen as endowed with the power to bar scalping of tickets and the imbibing of liquor, but not to enforce this authority frequently. Unofficial sanction of these American values of commercialism and booze indicated their high status in the value structure.

Other symbols displayed at the game are unique to Nebraska, the "Cornhusker

State.'' The name of the team, the Cornhuskers; their symbol of a ruddy, rather porky, beaming farmer; a big red neon ''*N*'' on the stadium; and the use of the state name on signs and the football field all point to the uniqueness of the state. ''Cornhuskers'' refers directly to the major commercial enterprise of the state— agriculture. Politically conservative, as evidenced by the voting patterns of government officials on a state and national level, and by the populace in local and national elections, this state emphatically accepts capitalism, traditional sex roles, patriotism, and the ''American Way.''

THE RITES OF PASSAGE: FOOTBALL AS A LIMINAL EVENT

Nebraska football is surrounded by ritual events, forecasts, and reviews. For example, there are pre- and postgame shows with the Nebraska coach and the televised Tom Osborne show Sunday night. Likewise, newspaper coverage is impressive. The Lincoln papers begin daily features of Nebraska football news in mid-August with their annual football review. From this point until the start of the season, the front page of the sports section will feature daily a story on various aspects of the fortunes of Nebraska football (for example, returning stars, new players, and coaches). Once the season begins in September, coverage becomes even more intensive and widespread, including scouting reports on opponents (a column titled ''Know the Foe'' appears each Thursday), and Nebraska depth charts. The Sunday paper devotes several pages to the preceding game. This generally includes at least two pages of photographs of key plays, interviews with both winning and losing coaches and players, and various commentaries on the game. Though this coverage decreases markedly after bowl games have been completed, one may still find occasional stories throughout the year. These would include notes on former Huskers now playing in the professional ranks, and speculations on the previous or forthcoming season. In addition, extensive coverage is given to the annual intersquad scrimmage played in the spring. This event, incidentally, generally draws over 10,000 fans.

Such elaborate systems of preparation and summation are events in themselves with their major focus on the game. On game day, though, there is an analytically complete ''rite of passage.'' Since many people travel great distances,[6] their pilgrimage or preliminal rites are elaborate and expensive, involving the expenditure of two valued commodities: time and money. Parking is at a premium within a five- or six-block radius immediately prior to game time; the streets are filled with fans dressed in red, holding radios next to their ears or even wearing radio ''earmuffs.'' The priority of the event masks to the eyes of the faithful their unusual self-presentation: their illuminated faces anticipating the coming event, their ritual clothing, the streams of like-minded humanity. For example, I was almost paralyzed by laughter and embarrassment when confronted by a very staid-looking couple, both in the traditional red clothing (her dress, his tie and shirt), marching arm in arm to the game with Martian-like earphones commanding his engrossed attention. Their presentation is commonplace on game day in the streets surrounding the stadium, including the downtown area of Lincoln. As noted earlier, the selling of programs and tickets occurs outside the stadium entrance. One's class is evident outside of the stadium, for instance, by one's means of transportation, access to privileged parking space, and participation in elite program events. Such status differentials are largely irrelevant, though, once inside the gate. There, all spectators shed their everyday status and join in "Big Red" status.

Inside the stadium, the fans and players enter a liminal state. Will they win? What is the other team like? How will they play today? Will there be any embarrassing plays? Any upset? Will "we" be elevated or shamed at the end? These and similar questions fill them with an agony of anticipation, expectation, and dread. Although the tests of the game will be sharply visible and enacted by the players, the audience shares this challenge and is the focus of study. This joint sharing in the ritual by the audience is evidenced by their reaction to the game. They move as one, highly knowledgeable of the game and the players, their responses are immediate, facilitated by radios available to approximately one in fifteen fans. (Ear radios are worn by about one in forty—a very rough estimate.) The radios transmit instantly the opinion of media "experts" from their vantage viewing points, showing quite well the overlap between the participatory and media-constructed ritual. This does not mean the fans are passive; they express their opinions in raucous jubilation or heated anger. Jumping up and down, congratulating each other, smiling, clapping, and yelling are all typical expressions of joy. Shaking one's arm in a vengeful fashion, shouting "kill the bastards," and booing are all equally likely displays of anger. This participation in judgment and support is one of the prime factors, in my opinion, for the large expenditures supported by the fans. The challenge to their identity, the heightened sensibility of the crowd, their visible allegiance to the state, the team, and the values embodied there are all motivations to participate.

Other liminal, egalitarian characteristics are present. Anti-structural rules operate when fans share the transitional stage of "trying to win." Thus strangers will talk eagerly and in depth about the team, its players, their skills, the opposing team, and any ritual associated with the event. Often they pound each other on the back or yell obscenities—in other words, they become intimates. They are part of one "team." Their side is "number one." Children, old people, married couples, teens, college kids, farmers—any combination of potential rivals or enemies are "friends" in this setting. Tears and laughter are indeed possible and are often spontaneously shared. The use of liquor prior to, during, and after the game aids in promoting the breaking down of barriers, but during the game liquor becomes secondary to the event. As mentioned earlier, the similar character of the crowd's response is overwhelming: they are engaged in following the game, they usually understand the signals and the plays, and the responses among thousands of people are similar.

The tension induced by the liminal status is evidenced by the crowd movements: the frequent clutching of fists, biting of lips, concentration on the moves, the obliviousness to all other elements of their surroundings unless these have relevance to the game. All of these are signs of possible danger—will we lose? And therefore: will we be shamed? After losing the first game of the season, the audience marched solemnly out of the stadium, disbelief, disappointment, and anger etched in their faces. One athlete said that the halls were "like tombs," and dread filled the players (*Lincoln Journal*, Sept. 19, 1977).

But this same crowd is not necessarily a friendly or joyous one. The aforementioned characteristics and structure follow the expectations of Turner's ritual analysis. A more critical element is established by the application of Goffman's concepts. The audience (i.e. "team") is, indeed, united but it is a solidarity based on opposition. We are "number one" because someone else, and hopefully many others, are losers. Part of the joy is one of triumph and, even better, revenge. A loser is discredited, stigmatized (Goffman, 1963b).

This theme is acted out in a serial cartoon presented on the front page of the *Lincoln Journal* the night before football Saturday. In the Alabama-Baylor confrontation, for example, a huge Husker football player bullies a Baylor Bear while "Journal Johnny" pours salt in the wounds of each touchdown (*Lincoln Journal*, Sept. 23, 1977). On occasion, Nebraska confronts an opponent of even greater stature than itself. This heightens the drama and the subsequent defeat or victory; such was the win over Alabama. "Bear" Bryant, coach of the high-ranking Alabama team brought to an unexpected defeat by low-ranking Nebraska, ate humble pie in an extensive postgame report. The newspaper heading read "Bryant learns another lesson." During the interview, "The 'Bear' wadded a kleenex [sic] as he slowly analyzed the game" and he managed a weak smile. The Bryant interview is further "framed" (Goffman, 1974) by pictures of Nebraska's triumphs and Alabama's defeats. Thus "their" mistakes are embarrassingly evident and "our" unexpected razzle dazzle are highlighted by contrast (*Lincoln Journal*, Sept. 18, 1977, 7-D).

Thus in this setting fans not only express positive emotions, but can also vent hostility. The bitterness of their attacks on the other team is evidenced by the frequent reference to "kill the other side." Although this is metaphorically powerful, it draws upon the most vile of crimes and injustices. The game is indeed a serious one.

The potentially amoral character of the crowd is shown by their response to an ill fan: numerous officials including the Red Cross, the Boy Scouts (who act to control the crowd), and the police were summoned through walkie-talkies to the emergency. The spectators to this new event watched with similar concentration and interest the human drama in the bleachers as they did the game. This parallel was summed up by one member of the audience after the hapless victim was removed: "The show's over."

The turning of the crowd against the police who tried to limit liquor consumption illustrates this same power and response.[7] They come to see blood and shame. They gather to witness the symbols and myths surrounding core codes of American society.

The ritual's participants, then, not only are sharing a liminal state and restoring their beliefs in American society, but they are elaborating these beliefs in a uniquely American ritual. These values and rituals can be evaluated; that is, they are not only interesting indicators of our belief structure and ability to let down our barriers—they are predicated on a system of values, some of which I find questionable. Specifically, I object to the peripheral and limited role of women, the acceptance of bureaucratic control as "fun," the establishment of human contact at the price of losing or winning. Other American values such as patriotism, liquor, and the mass media are not seen as intrinsically oppressive. Violence is a value that is difficult to judge. Random violence does not have a high value but the ritual enactment of violence (with its accompanying real violence) may, in fact, be a value to be defended. The cathartic value of harming a voluntary few within limits may provide some people with an enjoyable release of aggression. Vicarious enjoyment and respect for such values have certainly played a major role in human history and are cautiously acknowledged here. (See Geertz's discussion of the Balinese cock fight, 1973: 412–53.)

CONCLUSION

Goffman's concepts provide a view of human interactions as manipulative and defensive that is characteristic of American core codes of oppression—especially sex and class—and core codes of repression—especially allegiance to arbitrary authority embodied in bureaucracies, the demarcation of controlled time, and the need to "win," to live life as a "zero-sum game." In the example from the Alabama game, the team and their fans were stigmatized as losers, the performers "lost face," they "acted badly." Furthermore, the game is the frame for making these judgments. Thus Goffman's concepts are insightful guides for analyzing the football game. But these concepts, useful in describing everyday life, have a different meaning and enactment at a ritual event, and such community events were never systematically examined by Goffman. The rules are clearer, the drama starker, sex roles are amplified; and themes implicit in American culture are symbolically expressed and embodied. The everyday structure is writ large.

The most positive themes of ritual events evolving out of anti-structure and liminality are more adequately explained by Turner. Most importantly, ritual events are directly tied to culture and social structure. Goffman's frames, then, are embedded in myths, symbols, and institutions that help generate, define, and maintain social behavior. (See Deegan and Stein, 1977, for a discussion of pornographic frames and their relationship to myths, symbols, and institutions.) Goffman's concepts of everyday life provide us with a means to examine the often deep emotions and human renewal possible through ritual participation in

America. The ability to have something in common with strangers, to sing and yell and cry in public, to root for one's team (i.e., community), and to publicly participate and reaffirm one's values, are strong bonds that help us tolerate and give meaning to daily life.

The particularly American nature of this community ritual reflects Young's dramaturgical society. Football games, even at "nonprofit" universities, are large-scale capitalist enterprises. ("Nebraska's football program took in more than $9 million in revenues in the past fiscal year while distributing just over $600,000 in scholarships." *Sports Illustrated* column cited by Babcock, 1988.) By applying my concepts of core codes to these events, the structural continuity between sexism, capitalism, and modernization is made clearer. Unlike traditional Marxist accounts of a repressive society, however, my approach can explain the good times and fun at football games. The coherent symbolic universe of football weds Americans to their everyday oppressions with deeply internalized emotions. Thus millions of Americans spend their spare time having fun by watching football games.

NOTES

1. A long summation of the characteristics of communitas is found in Turner and Turner, 1978. Communitas is:

a relational quality of full unmediated communication, even communion, between definite and determinate identities, which arise spontaneously in all kinds of groups, situations, and circumstances. . . . The bonds of communitas are undifferentiated, egalitarian, direct, extant, nonrational, existential, I-Thou (in Buber's sense). Communitas is spontaneous, immediate, concrete, not abstract. It is part of the "serious life." . . . Communitas strains toward universalism and openness, it is a spring of pure possibility (pp. 250–51).

2. Goffman briefly mentions the possibility of such cultural events and their Durkheimian quality in his writings. See, for example, Goffman 1967, pp. 44–45 and 1959, p. 35.

3. The competitive, violent, stressful environment of American culture is noted in numerous other ways: through types and distribution of stress-related disease (Levine and Scotch, 1970), violent crimes (Quinney, 1975), and an emphasis on winning, even with children at "fun" events (Shostak, 1977).

4. Boy Scout troops are admitted without charge with the understanding that they will pick up the thousands of liquor bottles left by the fans when the crowd goes home. Through this "good turn" hundreds of young Nebraska males annually learn (1) about the association between sports and liquor, (2) that good deeds are rewarded with football tickets, and thus (3) to tolerate widespread drinking.

5. This incident was observed and noted by Theodore Trauernicht, Sept. 17, 1977.

6. The 1976 Hawaii game sent 20,000 fans to Honolulu. Former in-state fans now living in such places as California and Texas make an annual voyage to attend at least one home game.

7. It should be emphasized that the police officers may be fans but they are nonetheless at work. Indeed, there are many paid participants, including coaches, referees, reporters

and television commentators, concession operators, professional gamblers, team physicians, ticket takers, and so on. Several commentators argue pursuasively that the football players are also professionals, they receive scholarships, housing, food, stipends, and a shot at large salaries as fully professional football players.

PART III

MEDIA-CONSTRUCTED RITUALS

5

The Presentation of the City on Fat-Letter Postcards

MARY JO DEEGAN and MICHAEL R. HILL

Media-constructed rituals are cultural products. Unlike participatory rituals, my focus thus far, media-constructed rituals have more stability, higher internal order and consistency, and greater potential to reach people over time. Cultural artifacts from the past can reach people in their own era, the present, and the future, and in this way they provide a source of continuity even for rapidly changing societies. We begin this section of the book by examining a small artifact in an interaction ritual, the presentation of the city on a particular style of postcard.[1]

Cities are complex human environments that are frequently symbolized in the small space of picture postcards measuring a scant three-by-five inches. This small surface area, however, can capture and create an image of a locale, thereby representing its people, ideals and "good times." Postcards of cities are presentations of the city in an analogous way to presentations of the self (Goffman, 1959). In both types of presentations, the most socially desirable front is displayed. Postcard presentations, unlike human presentations, are static and completely controlled by their capitalistic manufacturers.

Considerable decision making occurs in the process of depicting cities on postcards, for cities are often squalid as well as beautiful, treacherous as well as sublime, and fear-inducing as well as spirit-elevating (see Strauss, 1968; Jacobs, 1961; Sandburg, 1970). In other words, cities reflect the whole range of human behavior and action because they are constructed from our dreams and limitations (Berger and Luckmann, 1966; Goffman, 1974). This wide array of human action, however, is rarely depicted on picture postcards of cities. These cultural artifacts are generally designed to portray the city on an idealized dimension, an attractive, desirable, and enjoyable place. They are, in other words, a form of impression management and institutional reflexivity supporting a particular attitude toward cities (Goffman, 1959, 1977). Although each card is oriented toward a specific locale, these cards collectively reveal the core codes for presenting the "ideal" city (Weber, 1948). When interrelated ideas are repeated in cultural artifacts such as novels and motion pictures, John G. Cawelti (1969, 1976) identifies them as a "formula"—a conventional system for structuring cultural products. Any particular formula tends to be closely associated with a specific culture and era. Each is distinguished by a limited repertoire of plots, characters, or, in this case, settings (Cawelti, 1969: 386–88). Formulas employ structural and anti-structural rules to generate a set of interrelated conventions underlying and giving form to cultural products. Formulas are bounded, repetitive, and anchored in experience, emotions, and ideas.

Formulas are more than mere conventional systems giving expression to the status quo. Widely accepted formulas project themselves into the future as prescriptive rules. This is important culturally because, as Erving Goffman (1974: 7) observed, rules organize our experience of the world. Although images of the city are generated by particular, historically grounded objects depicted on the postcard as artifact, such images (or as Goffman called them, "displays") form part of an "order set" of experientially and emotionally charged symbols of the city that we carry with us into the future (Mead, 1936). This emotional attachment, valuation, and concept of the city, in turn, generate the mechanism for perpetuating itself. Thus presentations of the city become established, stable, and greater than their component parts. As a formula, fat-letter postcards provide us with the means to enter and analyze this symbolic universe (Berger and Luckmann, 1966).

Cities, as dynamic social forms, are composed of innumerable people, objects, and interrelationships. Such an array of events, people, places, and things cannot be depicted on one tiny little card nor are all of these objects of equal value and significance. Therefore, certain aspects of the city are singled out for presentation. This selection process is directly associated with the distribution of power in cities. Presentations of the city reveal the nature of social control and power, as well as the type of "fun" associated with the city. Although the city encompasses the rich and the poor, workers and those at leisure, men and women, children and adults, and the young and the aged, the depictions of the idealized city focus on only a narrow range of humans, their activities, and their play. The activities and people that make everyday life meaningful for all people in a city are consistently ignored in favor of the powerful, the wealthy, and the male.

In a similarly incongruous way, fun in the city is often depicted on postcards as occurring in rural-like settings. These notable parklands are frequently not natural areas, but formal entertainment centers, bureaucratically administered public parks, or technologically defined leisure. Thus the seemingly innocent facades of the city found in fat-letter postcards are a hegemonic (Marx and Engels, 1939) message about the beauty of city life and what is to be valued there.[2] The message of power is conveyed to both the sender and receiver of postcards. Fat-letter postcards are part of the process of constructing symbolic universes that alienate people from their experience of the city. By examining the formula for generating fat-letter postcards we can outline and underscore the process of constructing powerful images of oppression while we are having "fun." A study of postcards illustrating city life, therefore, shows us the process of constructing idealized images of the city as well as the final product. It also shows the relationship between the structure and anti-structure of these images, which are part of ritual exchanges accompanying a "fun" vacation to such cities.

The Fat-Letter Format

In this chapter we examine a particular style of postcard that we call "fat-letter postcards" (for lack of a more definitive term). The standard format of the cards provides a good opportunity for analyzing the formula used to select images of the city. Fat-letter postcards (hereafter referred to as FLPs) reached a peak of popularity in the late 1940s and 1950s, although contemporary versions can still be found at some newsstands today. The typical FLP spells out a city's name in large-sized letters and depicts within each letter a local object or subject found in the specific city.

Each card presents an idealized view of a particular city, but since these postcards represent larger cultural symbols and rules for determining city symbols, they exhibit a great deal of homogeneity and repetitiveness. In fact, many of the cards would be interchangeable to a stranger unfamiliar with the cities represented on the cards. Despite the inclusion of multiple visual images from each urban location, the perceptive recipient of FLPs from several cities soon discovers that the specific spelling of the city's name and the number of letters in that name are generally the only unique characteristics of each city. In other words, the cards are overtly intended to be a symbol of a particular city, while in fact they more often depict a generalized formula representing Every City. Postcards are intended to be sent to others and portray an inviting aspect to the receiver. They may become souvenirs to remember something presumably particular and unique. The symbols of the city on FLPs implicitly function very differently. Most city buildings and parks are indistinguishable from one FLP to another. The symbols thought unique to a particular city are often interchangeable with those of another.

Unwilling to wait for friends and colleagues on vacation to mail us FLPs complete with "Wish you were here!" messages from distant urban places while we stayed behind in Nebraska, we were fortunate to quickly compile a collection of 128 FLPs by other means. The cards in our collection were published during the 1940s and 1950s and thus expose this particular era for analysis. Based on the visual images on these cards, we describe the idealized city presentations that were commercially generated and popularly accepted in the recent past. We hold that the system for selecting elements of city life as symbolically important is better understood if we locate it within the broad cultural context of our capitalist and sexist society.

Core Codes and Postcards

In addition to the two core codes of capitalist and sexist oppression, a third is analyzed here: racism. This form of discrimination is blatant on the FLPs. Including racism in the analysis reveals the structural similarity of apparently different forms of oppression. This also allows application of the theory of critical dramaturgy in yet another context, again showing its capacity to account for various forms of oppression and repression in American society.

Since these postcards are associated with vacations (i.e., times away from everyday life and thus potentially anti-structural), bureaucratic values are not centrally represented. Depictions of government offices, department stores, and corporate offices are certainly bureaucratic, but the context of depiction is one of fun, showing places visited on holiday. The activities depicted—and the act of sending postcards—are often associated with leisure time. In these aspects, postcards reveal an anti-structural element. The inclusion of capitalist, sexist, and racist images, however, shows once more that having fun is intimately wedded to oppression.

Our analysis proceeded in two ways. First, we examined the cards to generate categories of frequently found representations. (The details of this methodology are discussed in the next section.) The image classification revealed a formula for depicting the ideal city. Knowing the formula uncovers a set of rules through which the postcard designer routinely identified and featured the "important" and "beautiful" elements of city life. In the process, we discovered that the structure of class elites and white males was institutionally strengthened while, simultaneously and incongruously, the anti-structure of the city was shown as rural and parklike. Communitas and playfulness within the city were less frequently displayed. Second, we critically evaluated these rules by comparing the idealized categories (1) to the everyday life and experience of people who live and work in the city (a more encompassing and egalitarian structure of everyday life), and (2) to the possibilities of playfulness and communitas. In so doing, the dramaturgical rules are seen to produce hegemonic depictions of the capitalist-built environment and its domination by Anglo males (Eisenstein, 1979). The first part of the analysis, then, is a descriptive and enumerative technique for uncovering the pattern on the FLPs, and the second part employs a critical perspective for judging the ideological context of the formula and structure thus revealed.

METHODOLOGY

The source materials for this study consist of 128 FLPs obtained from flea markets and antique dealers in Nebraska during a period of about one month of active searching on weekends. Our ability to accumulate rapidly and easily this number of cards illustrates their continuing availability and status as "collectible" or desired artifacts, underscoring a characteristic of significant cultural artifacts: persistence over time. All regions of the United States are represented in our sample, as well as a wide range of city sizes and types. Since the universe of possible FLPs is unknown, it is assumed for the purpose of analysis that the sample cards are representative and approximate a random distribution, although the sample may be somewhat biased in favor of the Midwest or toward places visited by travelers from the Midwest.

The first analytic step was to devise a scheme for classifying the images depicted in each illustrated letter spelling the name of a city on each FLP. An intuitive classification was constructed for the images presented in our FLPs. The overall classification is a framework for sorting the images. Thus each category in the classification represents a culturally meaningful "typification." This exhaustive classification provides ninety-seven descriptive categories, including subcategories.[3] A second, independently constructed classification was commissioned as a double-check and was found to be remarkably congruent with our initial classificatory system. Although the classification used is culturally situated, so are the artifacts. We conclude that the categories employed provide a descriptive framework that most residents of the United States would find meaningful, workable, and reasonably free of ideological bias. The major categories or typifications in the classification are: (1) nonresidential buildings, (2) residences, (3) transportation, (4) parks, (5) monuments, (6) natural landscapes, (7) rural/agricultural scenes, and (8) people.

The second preparatory phase of the study applied the classification to code or associate each letter on each FLP with the most appropriate typification. A trained coder chose the single best category for each letter and entered his choice on a prepared coding sheet. Mutually exclusive rules were devised to assign category precedence when multiple typifications sometimes appeared in a single letter (e.g., a monument in a park, or a bus parked beside a bus terminal). Sample replications by a second coder demonstrated high levels of intersubjective agreement sufficient for us to place considerable faith in the reliability and reproducibility of the coding. Data from the coding sheets were then entered and stored for machine processing.

EMPIRICAL RESULTS FOR MEASURING THE FORMULA

Given the major category groups and knowledge of the number of letters on each FLP, it is possible to compute the proportion of category types on a typical or ideal FLP. In other words, the formula for generating such cards can be summarized quantitatively. These results are shown in Table 5.1. Review of this table reveals that the great majority of symbols are those of nonresidential buildings. All other major categories in the classification are represented in relatively

Table 5.1
Typifications of the City on Fat-Letter Postcards

Typifications	Proportion
Nonresidential Building	63.1%
Natural Landscapes	8.8
Monuments	7.3
Transportation	6.9
Parks/Recreational	5.1
People	4.0
Rural/Agricultural	2.5
Residences	2.3
	100.0%

small proportions. The predominant image of the city on FLPs is overwhelmingly that of humanly constructed, nonresidential buildings (63 percent).

Identifiability

The images of public buildings on FLPs are frequently not distinctive or easily identifiable as to function (i.e., bank, school, office, etc.). Hotels, public administration buildings, schools, museums, offices, and the like often look so similar that it is not possible for the recipient of the postcards to identify the function of many of these buildings with any confidence. In some instances, lettering on the side of the building such as "Hotel" or "University," or the presence of recognizable symbols such as a crucifix or icon helps the recipient (or the researcher, in our case) to make an informed guess about the building's main use. The identifiability (or, more crucially, *lack* of identifiability) of these buildings is particularly significant to the overall message of FLPs if one remembers that, on average, 63 percent of the images on FLPs in our sample represent nonresidential buildings.

The identifiability of the nonresidential building images was approached empirically in the following way. The coder had available a comprehensive list of twenty-five subcategories in which to place images of buildings. When a structure could not be identified sufficiently using all available information (including printed legends and handwritten notes authored by postcard senders) to place it in one of the available categories, it was considered an "unclassifiable building."

On average, this category was used in classifying 22 percent of the images in the buildings category. This average, however, is somewhat misleading. Approximately 27 percent of all the cards examined included a "key" or printed legend on the reverse side of the card. An example of such a key is reproduced in Example 5.1. Using the key, it is possible to identify the vast majority of buildings, structures, and places shown on the face of the cards.

EXAMPLE 5.1: BOISE (Idaho)

B = Ada County Court House
O = View of Business District
I = Arrow Rock Dam
S = Boise River Bridge
E = Union Pacific Depot

Insight into the identifiability of major buildings is thus provided by looking at the frequency of use of the category "unclassifiable building" for postcards with a key and for those without a legend. For cards without a legend, 29 percent of the building images were categorized as unclassifiable buildings. For cards with a key, the figure drops to below 1 percent. (ANOVA—Analysis of Variance—shows this difference to be statistically significant beyond the .0001 level.) Thus the key provides useful identifying information that cannot be obtained from visual imagery alone. It is not surprising that a key makes the symbols of buildings more identifiable (nearly 100 percent identifiable), but what is surprising is that no key was provided for 73 percent of the cards in the sample. Because buildings comprise such a large proportion of images, the typical recipient of an FLP would be unable to identify the function or purpose of approximately one-fifth of all the symbols on FLPs, unless a key is provided. Each recipient would only be able, at best, to categorize many images as unidentified buildings. Since our coder is an advanced student of urban morphology, it is possible that his skill in identifying building functions is superior to that of the casual recipient of FLPs. Therefore, the suggestion that the typical recipient would be unable to identify approximately one-fifth of the symbols as other than "buildings" is probably a conservative estimate.[4]

Images and City Functions

It might be hypothesized that the symbols on FLPs reflect the underlying individuality of a given city. Generally speaking, this was not the case. Using the appendix provided by Howard J. Nelson (1955), the service classifications for ninety-seven of the cities in our sample were obtained. Nelson's classification used employment data taken from the 1950 U.S. Census (this date is generally contemporaneous with the FLP images analyzed here). A city is placed in a particular classification if its employment in a given employment sector is greater than one standard deviation from the mean or usual level of employment in that sector in other cities around the country. The following categories were devised by Nelson and adopted for our analysis (the percentage of our sample cities in each category follows in parentheses): manufacturing (12 percent), retail trade (5 percent), professional service (4 percent), transportation (11 percent), personal services (4 percent), public administration (9 percent), wholesale trade (6 percent), finance/insurance (16 percent). When no employment sector dominated the employment structure of a city, it was classified as "diversified" (31 percent). Our analysis found that the "real" functions of cities as classified by Nelson are not significantly reflected in the images of the cities found on FLPs. Stated another way, the proportions of images on a typical card devoted to buildings, transportation, residences, parks, monuments, natural landscapes, rural/agricultural scenes, and people cannot be reliably predicted even if one has detailed knowledge of the actual employment structure of the city in question. This conclusion might be reversed by using a larger sample of FLPs, but we doubt it. However, while the fundamental, day-to-day activities of life in cities are not presented in FLP symbols, the formula for the images is partially predictable if one has knowledge of population size, regional location, and whether or not a city is a state capital.

Symbol and Population Size

In our analysis, population size is consistently the most informative dimension. Using 1950 population data, we divided our sample into five population-size categories. The majority of our symbol categories have significant relationships to population size. The specific results are given in Table 5.2. Here one sees that the larger places (Category V) are portrayed as having greater proportions of nonresidential buildings and monuments compared to smaller places. Although large urban areas are not usually known for rustic vistas, they are depicted as having as many parks/recreation facilities and natural landscapes as smaller places. Even more striking are the data on residences. While large cities obviously have large housing and residential areas, this aspect of the metropolis takes a backseat to images of buildings and monuments. Although the following results were not statistically significant, it is interesting to note that images of people were encountered less frequently on the FLPs for the largest cities when compared to smaller cities. Regardless of population size, however, the emphasis on nonresidential buildings is remarkable. In only the smallest places (Category I) is this trend countered with a modest tendency to have more natural landscapes represented (20 percent) and residential structures (4 percent) displayed.

Table 5.2
City Size and Typifications of the City on Fat-Letter Postcards

Typifications

Population Category	Nonresidential Buildings	Transportation	Residences	Parks	Monuments	Natural	(n)
I (LE 10,000)	57%	6%	4%	4%	3%	20%	(24)
II (10,001 - 27,500)	62	4	4	3	6	6	(25)
III (27,501 - 70,000)	59	5	1	8	4	7	(25)
IV (70,001 - 200,000)	67	11	1	6	8	7	(29)
V (GE 200,000)	71	7	1	5	16	7	(25)
Significance	.06	.047	.01	.047	.009	.0000	

Note: Data for nonresidential buildings reaches a level of significance sufficiently close to usually accepted levels to warrant inclusion. Data for Rural/Agricultural Scenes and People did not vary sufficiently at usually accepted levels of significance to warrant presentation.

Table 5.3
Region and Typifications of the City on Fat-Letter Postcards

Typification

Region	Residences	Natural	Rural	People	(n)
Northwest	1%	8%	4%	8%	(34)
Midwest	2	4	4	7	(43)
South	5	11	4	7	(22)
Southwest	1	10	5	25	(17)
Northwest	0	19	11	7	(12)
Significance	.05	.005	.018	.004	

Note: Data for nonresidential buildings, transportation, parks/recreational, and monuments did not vary sufficiently at usually accepted levels of significance to warrant presentation.

Regional Symbols

In addition to size-linked images, some symbols have regional distributions. The data for this discussion are presented in Table 5.3. Here we see that residences are featured somewhat more frequently in the South. Natural (19 percent) and rural/agricultural features (11 percent) are more often projected on postcards from the Northwest. Finally, symbols of people (25 percent) are most characteristic on postcards from the Southwest.

The Symbols of State Capitals

Finally, the empirical findings in our study reveal that state capitals have a slight tendency to differ from other cities on three dimensions (see Table 5.4). No state capitals depicted private residences. Conversely, these cities had twice as many monuments and three times as many images of people when compared to other cities.

Table 5.4
State Capitals and Typifications of the City on Fat-Letter Postcards

Typification

State Capital	Residences	Monuments	People	(n)
No	3%	6%	3%	(106)
Yes	0	15	9	(22)
Significance	.0205	.0095	.03	

Note: Data for nonresidential buildings, transportation, parks/recreational, and monuments did not vary sufficiently at usually accepted levels of significance to warrant presentation. FLPs

THE DEPICTION OF SEX AND CLASS CODES

These categorized empirical data can now be summarized and evaluated. First, it is clear that the most significant ideal image of the city is the nonresidential public building. Such public buildings tend to be expensive, controlled by the elite of a city, and dominated by male personnel. They portray a segment of public life that is dominated by men and displays of their wealth. Thus FLPs are sex- and class-coded artifacts. To many people who live in cities, their everyday life is composed of their residences, their neighbors, their families (particularly children playing in the neighborhood), small businesses, and their places of paid employment. These workplaces, moreover, are often dirty, cramped, old, and undesirable. The places of enjoyment and recreation are often local playgrounds and parks, small restaurants, ethnic and minority businesses, and community buildings. The places, events, and people depicted on FLPs almost entirely negate these elements of city life. A popular argument in support of the hegemonic depictions is that dirty, cramped, old, and undesirable work-places are not "fun" to see, whereas beautiful buildings are. Such an argument, however, ignores the distortion that occurs through these depictions, their support of a certain populace, the control over images and consciousness that results, and the suppression of beauty that is not wealthy, male, or Anglo. The equation of beauty and fun with an elite generates alienation in the general populace who cannot control the presented images of their lives.

A vivid example of how Americans' perceptions are oriented to the elite occurred when we showed a set of slides from Cuba to an American audience. A member of the audience said that the many homes and other buildings with exteriors of peeling paint in Havana were very depressing. When we explained that the Cuban government put primary emphasis on housing for all—empha-sizing the upgrading of rural areas—and that, nonetheless, despite the peeling paint, Havana had no ghettos, the audience member responded that Cuba was better off when it had beautiful facades for the few. For her, workers' homes and peeling paint were shameful and should be hidden, whereas beautiful edifices for the rich were symbolically important for entire nations. When we saw our Cuban photographs we felt warmed by our memories and the social equality symbolized by peeling paint on otherwise remarkably clean and habitable dwell-ings. The audience member, however, was depressed by the contrast with elite, well-painted American homes. This social construction of the presentation of the city is rooted in our core codes and carries over into—and is reinforced by—interpretations of images on FLPs.

In the second most frequent category depicted on FLPs, natural landscapes, the same pattern of atypical urban image is found, but arises from a different context. It exhibits characteristics that are anti-structural, but in a "fun" rather than "playful" context. In fact, if this category is combined with those of monuments and parks/recreational, it is immediately apparent that these aggre-gated images (21.2 percent of all images on FLPs) of the city are opposed to the ever-present built environment that characterizes urban life. But these parklike symbols are often images of large urban parks, which are often inconvenient, if not unsafe, for people to actually use. In this way something desirable is tantalizing but unavailable. Similarly, architectural landmarks and statues of Anglo male leaders are elevated in significance, and these are, in Goffman's sense, institutionally reflexive. Many of the rural and leisure activities require automobiles, gasoline, time, and money to use (what Illich, 1981, calls "shadow work"). Entry fees may also be needed. The image of nature, then, is a sub-version of free space and refers to an embedded use of landscape that is structured into our everyday lives.

As we saw in our empirical analysis, the activities and places presented on FLPs are not unique to each city. They are common elements in an interpretive view of what is considered significant. The lives of women and children are rarely symbolized in the public space of the postcard. The average citizen, of either sex, is rarely portrayed. In the infrequent instances where human groups are shown, they predominantly represent people at leisure, not at work. Thus we see groups of people at the beach or in a park. Formal rituals such as community parades or celebrations are rarely depicted. The city as a living entity built by the many workers who live there is absent.

The skewed typifications on FLPs are ways to advertise certain parts of the city as more desirable, more fun, more beautiful. The traveler on vacation (as well as the recipient of a postcard) interprets these idealized images as the "things to see" or admire in a city. Fun but not playfulness is advertised. Central businesses in downtown areas and recreational facilities benefit directly and indirectly from these formulas. Work in the home, neighborhood, and sweatshop remains unseen; these are not fun. Women and children are not shown. On the other hand, the literally concrete accomplishments of architects, civil engineers, park designers, and urban planners form leading images of the city.

The American city symbolized on FLPs is a static image of male capitalists. It is an institutionally reflexive depiction of the city as a "male landscape" (Hill and Deegan, 1982). By valuing these elements of city life, feelings and emotions tied to the city are transferred, ordered, and made meaningful in relation to these symbols. A woman who loves a particular city now imagines or remembers it through the symbols elaborated on a postcard. She learns to point with pride to events and objects that she rarely uses or controls. They are not images with which she feels at home. These selected, capitalist, male objects and events represent the important events and places of her city. She becomes, thereby, alienated from her own experiences, places, and activities in that city, even during those rare occasions when she enters the male landscape as a tourist (Hill and Deegan, 1982).

The poor know, too, that their homes, neighborhoods, shopping areas, and work are not portrayed as ideal parts of the city. People who control and construct the city are the rich. The poor, then, are alienated from their daily lives and learn to admire the places where they have entrée as menial laborers, if at all. This pattern of alienation is reinforced for minority groups. Furthermore, many minority citizens may also hold multiple minority statuses simultaneously, for example, by being old, black, female, and poor (Deegan, 1985), increasing their distance from the "desirable" way of life.

The FLP presentation of the city is alienating in yet another fundamental way. The city as a lived environment is often depicted as parklike. Some FLPs include illustrations of rural areas actually well outside the city limits. Thus the crowded housing, teeming street life, and the vivacity of city living are abstracted from the idealization of the American city found in FLPs. To enjoy the American city, one is ideally in "natural" settings although these are often rarely enjoyed by its citizens on a continuing or everyday basis.

This is not to say that all images of the city are inherently alienating. Beautiful buildings, important male leaders, and architectural constructions such as bridges, lighthouses, roadways, and fountains are human achievements located in specific places and frequently the focus of important activities shared by many.

Placing such symbols in a formula that eliminates other symbols and inflates the significance of these typical patriarchal constructions of reality is problematic, nonetheless. It is precisely these powerful, if not sacred, communal places that are used to justify a patriarchal and hegemonic social order, thereby generating alienation of a populace from its everyday life and meaning. Thus the popular culture of a city is manipulated to serve the interests of the privileged and makes the life of a city a world of static monuments to the male order.

CONCLUSION

This chapter had two major goals: to discover the core codes underlying the formula for presenting the city on FLPs, a media-constructed ritual; and to evaluate this formula as a component in American interaction rituals. In so doing, we documented that the capitalist, built environment is most highly valued while the work and lives of everyday people are consistently slighted. When natural landscapes are depicted, they too reflect an idealization of everyday life abstracted from the mundane structures of existence. What few images there are of people in FLPs are primarily of Anglo males, reflecting their patriarchal control of the city more overtly than their undepicted domination of public buildings, the most frequent image on FLPs.

Although it could be argued that the formula for depicting the city found on FLPs is tied to a bygone era, such an interpretation cannot be established given our data. Only further research on presentations of the city in contemporary life could resolve this issue. Without concrete evidence to support contrary positions, we should not yield to the easy temptation to wish away the obvious and continuing domination of our society by oppressive codes of sex, class, and race. Those who argue that "things have changed" in the last few years must demonstrate their case, not just respond to the mountains of counterevidence with charges of "old data." In fact, there are clear parallels between our findings and Goffman's (1976) analysis of gender advertisements. He found that these capitalist images of women pervaded popular media and followed sex codes similar to those used on FLPs (Goffman, 1977). We have extended his findings to a more hidden dimension of sexism, the "symbolic annihilation" of women through their lack of portrayal in cultural artifacts (Tuchman, 1975). In any event, we demonstrated the existence of a patriarchal, racist, and capitalist formula in FLPs from the 1940s and 1950s. The theory of critical dramaturgy to which we subscribe holds that such formulas gather momentum once they are established and then project themselves into the future. They become part of the ritual of "having a good time" on one's vacation. They are built into one's memories of that event, memories that are recalled later in the everyday world of work and obligations. Have things changed in the intervening years between the faddish use of these cards and today? We find no serious evidence in the literature or observed behavior patterns to demonstrate that they have.

Core codes are dramatically depicted on FLPs and these images are institutionally reflexive of sex, class, and racial inequalities. We believe, however, that control over urban images belongs to the community as a whole and that such images should represent all interests in the community. Community definitions of shared work, of anti-structure and play, and the potential for communitas should dominate future presentations of the city. We urge more research on past and present formulas displaying our cities and people, but we are more concerned with the development of emancipatory formulas for generating symbols that celebrate urban life and our communal bonds.

NOTES

1. An earlier version of this chapter was presented at the meetings of the Popular Culture Association, April 1984, in Toronto, Canada.

2. In hegemonic systems, oppressed persons participate in their own oppression. By selecting (from a stock of prepared, preselected images), purchasing (a capitalist transaction), and mailing (a bureaucratically organized transaction) fat-letter postcards (FLPs) to friends, postal card correspondents unwittingly reify and strengthen the power of FLP imagery—images that celebrate the wealthy, white world of commercial, cultural, and military success. Thus, in this case, there is an intersection between the Marxist concept of "hegemony" and the Goffmanian construct of "institutional reflexivity."

3. A full listing of the classification scheme is available by writing to the authors.

4. Due to the coder's familiarity with American cityscapes, he was able to identify several buildings that might have otherwise remained unidentified. We encouraged the coder to use his stock of experiential knowledge to identify buildings since a recipient of a postcard may also recognize unnamed buildings. Thus, the coder's typifications are similar to, although not identical with, the everyday knowledge of others in this society.

6

Star Trek *and the Freudian Formula: Feminists Boldly Go Where No Man Has Gone Before*

The television and movie series *Star Trek* is a dramatic fantasy about the adventures of three men traveling in outer space centuries into the future. In this chapter, this sexist and extraordinarily popular, media-constructed science fiction vision is examined (1) as a theatrical, dramaturgical frame both relating to and different from everyday life and (2) as a fantasy formula using the same structural rules for ordering the actors' behaviors as those explicated by Freud in his formal theory of culture and human action. Following a prefatory review of the relevant dramaturgical and Freudian issues, a brief methodological note introduces my empirical findings and subsequent conclusions. Erving Goffman and Victor Turner provide a starting point once more.

THE THEATRICAL FRAME AS RITUAL

Dramaturgists make a direct analogy to the theater, for they explore the theater as the model for everyday life. Theatrical presentations are clearly different in some ways from everyday performances, however. Goffman (1974) defined the theatrical frame as follows:

A performance, in the restricted sense in which I shall now use the term, is that arrangement which transforms an individual into a stage performer, the latter, in turn, being an object that can be looked at in the round and at length without offense, and looked to for engaging behavior, by persons in an "audience" role (p. 124).

While participants in everyday interactions are usefully and insightfully analyzed as "performers" and "audience," staging conventions in theater and everyday life differ. According to Goffman (1974: 139–43), the theater has (1) stage sets with "open" walls and no ceiling, (2) spoken interaction directed toward an audience, (3) one person at a time who tends to be the focus of attention, (4) actors who take turns talking, (5) an audience and new stage performers who are told extensive background information ("disclosive compensation"), (6) utterances that tend to be longer and more grandiloquent than ordinary conversations, and (7) every action and bit of information related to the whole. These ritual conventions are exemplified in the televised episodes of *Star Trek*. Nonetheless, roles and performances on the formal stage are structurally similar in many ways to roles and performances in daily life; this is a fundamental assumption of dramaturgy. These similarities between everyday and theatrical frames are rarely made explicit, however. Thus, by studying the conventions of the theater, Goffman formally explored and documented the illuminating parallels between theatrical and everyday life.

Turner also linked the theater and daily life. The elusive but fundamental difference discussed so analytically by Goffman is beautifully expressed by Turner (1982a): "Neither mutual mirroring, life by art, art by life, is exact, for each is not a planar mirror, but a matricial mirror; at each exchange something new is added, something old is lost or discarded" (p. 108). Turner believed that social dramas found in everyday life and stage dramas found in the theater are both part of life and the discovery of meaning. He wrote (1982a): "There is an interdependent, perhaps dialectic, relationship between social dramas and genres of cultural performance in perhaps all societies. Life, after all, is as much an imitation of art as the reverse" (p. 72).

In Turner's (1982a) view, the most important cultural dramas have complexity and ambiguity: "Paradigms of this type, cultural root paradigms, so to speak, reach down to irreducible life stances of individuals, passing beneath conscious prehension to a fiduciary hold on what they sense to be axiomatic values, matters literally of life and death" (p. 73). For Turner, drama is not simply a metaphor; theater is an integral, creative, innovative component of modern life. Simultaneously, the power of theater lies in giving expression to the complex root metaphors that define and give meaning to each culture.

In my analysis of *Star Trek*, I point to the underlying rules guiding what may appear superficially to be a simplistic science fiction series. I propose that the formula for *Star Trek* is rooted in a deep cultural paradigm, one best explicated by Sigmund Freud. Freud is employed here as a key to understanding the ambiguous, implicit meanings of the actions in *Star Trek*. My task here is more complex than the previous study of fat-letter postcards. I explore a multilayered frame: Freud's set of assumptions concerning human instinct and behavior as a formulaic sex code for analyzing *Star Trek* as a media-constructed ritual. By so doing, I link the Freudian literature to dramaturgy insofar as Freudian theater is a major formal theory frequently used to generate media-constructed rituals.

Each dramatic installment of the *Star Trek* saga begins with the following introductory statement: "Space, the final frontier. These are the voyages of the Starship *Enterprise*, its five-year mission to explore strange new worlds, to seek out new life and new civilizations, to boldly go where no man has gone before."[1] With the above words, the basic formula for *Star Trek* is established.

John G. Cawelti's definition of a "formula" refers to a conventional system for structuring cultural products. As noted and developed in the previous chapter, a formula tends to be particularly close to a specific culture and its era and uses a limited repertoire of plots, characters, or settings (Cawelti, 1969: 386–88). The concept of formula links the present analysis to the previous chapter on postcards and to the following chapter on mythic formulas authored by L. Frank Baum in the *Oz* series. (See "formula frame" in Chapter 1.)

Following the ritual recitation of the programmatic prologue, the audience enters the world of the Starship *Enterprise* and travels in "warp drive" (i.e., faster than the speed of light) to the outer limits of space and human endurance. In this way, the media of television and motion pictures dramatically depict life in the future and explore an anti-structural use of time. Life in the series revolves around the communitas (Turner, 1969) generated between the three major male characters.[2] Although they are agents of a bureaucracy, called the United Federation of Planets, on board their Starship they govern through a combination of rules and friendship, an antibureaucratic fusion of the rationally instrumental and the emotionally expressive.

The anti-structural elements of *Star Trek* are deeply embedded, however, in the transference of traditional and contemporary sex codes into future space and time. The dramatic world of the *Enterprise* is a male world centered on the exploits, loyalties, and friendships of three men. Communitas extends only to the central male characters, not to the crew of the *Enterprise* as a whole, not to the Federation, and not to women, alien beings, and other enemies who threaten the safety and mission of the Starship. Women do not enter as equals; they cannot, under the formula of the show, participate in male communitas. The rules generating the dramatic, staged behavior depicted in *Star Trek* are based on arrangements of structural inequality between the sexes in everyday life (Goffman, 1977).

The Starship *Enterprise* is a male-dominated and male-defined world wherein women are shadowy figures who play two primary roles: to provide romance or to illustrate women's "abnormal" desire for power. The struggle for power is usually defined as control over the Starship and is a constant concern for the men. This "normal" male pursuit of power is a reenactment of the Oedipal myth that provides a major structure of the *Star Trek* stories. Male success in the search for power determines the fate of those dependent on the male leaders: the women who love them, the crew, the "female" Starship and, sometimes, the entire human race.

Star Trek is a significant cultural phenomenon. Although it was cancelled in 1969 after only three televised seasons,[3] the show generated a large cult following. The series continues to be rebroadcast in most major television markets, including "educational" Public Broadcasting System stations in some areas, and is widely available for purchase (approximately fifteen dollars per episode) and rental (typically two dollars per twenty-four-hour rental period) on videotape. Videotapes of the *Star Trek* motion pictures are readily available subsequent to their full run in motion picture theaters. Unlike the typical television serial that fades into oblivion, *Star Trek* spawned a complex network of fans, called "Trekkies," who read and write about their favorite heroes and fantasy in newsletters, magazines, serialized cartoons, and books. They buy T-shirts, videotapes, models of the Starship, dolls, and artifacts associated with the show, and annually hold conventions. Trekkies thus engage in participatory rituals generated by a media-constructed ritual. Four large-scale Hollywood movies based on *Star Trek* have also been released for a mass audience, maintaining interest for old devotees and generating new fans two decades after the first *Star Trek* episode was televised. These movies are included here as part of the complete *Star Trek* series. *Star Trek* has captured the imagination, emotions, and loyalty of thousands—perhaps millions—of people, making it a significant American ritual. This ritual has two primary dimensions, in terms of the audience, including the devoted Trekkies, and in terms of the dramatic, media-constructed scripts for the series itself. This latter dimension is examined here. I make no attempt to articulate the vast literature written by or about the Trekkies and the continuing *Star Trek* audience.

In this chapter, the dramatic scripts of *Star Trek* are examined and their formula revealed. The underlying rules governing behavior in *Star Trek* are explicated by analyzing the roles of men and women depicted in each episode and motion picture. In the process, a specific sex code is revealed whereby the *Star Trek* series depicts life in the future as a Freudian fantasy.

The use of Freudian rules for generating a media frame is called a "Freudian formula." A Freudian formula is a particular sex code deeply embedded in Western art, dating back to the early Greek play *Oedipus Rex*, if not further. In Turner's schema it is a root metaphor. In Goffman's theory it is a frame, a way of making sense of everyday life. Enacted on the stage and in daily life it is a dramaturgical ritual with a long history. Connecting the deep past of ancient Greece with the distant future of *Star Trek* is an innovative cultural loop providing continuity in the present under the veneer of great technological change.

The structural pattern for the Freudian formula is examined more fully in the next section. My subsequent analysis documents the Freudian formula in *Star Trek* and this, in part, explains the power of the *Star Trek* series to maintain and generate structural inequality in everyday life in the modern world.[4] I argue that the "fun" fantasy of space travel by a deeply bonded male group is intrinsically linked to everyday discrimination against women.

THE FREUDIAN FORMULA: SEX CODES IN SPACE

Freud's concept of personal development and its instinctual basis is one of the most powerful interpretations of social behavior and is accepted in many quarters today. However, given its central thesis that men are physiologically, psychologically, and mentally superior to women, Freudian thought has been strongly criticized by many feminists (e.g., Friedan, 1963; Miller, 1975; Firestone, 1971; Barrett and McIntosh, 1982). Their critiques interpret Freud's world view as a legitimation of sexism and, therefore, antithetical to feminism. Juliet Mitchell (1975), however, provides an innovative feminist critique whereby Freud is seen as an accurate observer and reporter of sexist society. Adopting her approach, I show how Freud's ideas illuminate, rather than merely perpetuate, sexism.

Freud described human action as a function of three major instincts: sex (libido), aggression, and the struggle to live or die (eros/thanatos). These drives are enacted differently by each sex. The instincts are often unconscious and masked through symbols associated with the body and major life events; for example, birth, sex, and death. The male body is defined by society as superior to the female's, and it drives him to seek power in the social order. Each male's quest for power conflicts with that of other males', especially threatening each father's control over his sons. The theme of males seeking to overthrow the power of other males is a key scenario in mental life and social behavior. Freudians discuss it as either the "Oedipal myth" or the theory of the "primal horde." In the Oedipal myth, the son overthrows the power of the father. This scenario is reenacted in every father/son relationship; it is the major developmental stage for generating "normal" behavior in men and determines their adult capacity to "love and work." The "primal horde" theory is a larger-scale reenactment of the Oedipal myth, in which control over society is gained when the challengers, usually younger men, overthrow once-powerful older men.[5] Females who "properly" recognize their physical and emotional inferiority to males want to love men and bear their children.[6]

Freudian concepts form a network of ideas, a formula, for organizing action in a dramatic script. This particular, patriarchal formula segregates the world into spheres of "male" and "female" control. However, the female sphere depends on the male sphere for definitions of situations, access to material and emotional resources, and power. The male sphere is governed by rational rules that generate and maintain the social order (e.g., the rules and behaviors enacted in the military, education, bureaucracies, and politics). The female sphere is governed by emotions and relations within the family and home.[7]

Sex, combined in different ways with love, links these separate spheres. For women, sex is defined as an emotional and material connection necessary for establishing paternity as well as financial and emotional security. For men, sex is a physical animal instinct that provides a rational basis for succumbing to love. Women gain power and protection through men. Women's world is mediated through men, thereby explaining the women's need to "capture" men.

Another male instinct is the drive to compete with others. Women enter this competition by becoming desired objects. These objects are characterized by youth, beauty, access to material and social resources, and behavior appropriate to the female sphere. These realms of dominance are symbolized in a variety of ways, but prime among these indicators of control are technological equipment and scientific interests (Habermas, 1970). (This partially explains the audience's fascination with the men of *Star Trek* who control a technologically complex spaceship.)

Finally, both sexes are driven to survive. Again, women depend on men for protection. The male drive for power is a partial explanation for the survival of the fittest, for it is the strongest male leader who enables the group to survive. Male leadership is more sorely tested when the entire group is threatened. There are, therefore, three major variations of this Freudian formula in *Star Trek* (sexuality, competition, and survival), with each variation corresponding to a cultural myth.

The first myth involves the sexual instinct. In this romantic scenario, women want to love *Star Trek* men in order to find meaning and happiness. Romantic involvement for *Star Trek* men, however, is a distorting and threatening emotion. The relationship is attractive, due to men's sexual instincts, but it limits men's freedom to explore new worlds. Men do not need romantic love but their desires are awakened by the female presence. Women, however, need love and must trick men into giving it to them. Therefore, romantic love in this formula is an exploitative device that women use to get some control over specific men. The only exception to this rule occurs when a "perfect," sacrificing female attracts the higher emotions as well. Only one such female is allowed in the series, but she dies at the end of the episode in which she appears.

The second myth concerns the aggressive instinct. In this competitive scenario, men want power over other men, and women are not seen as viable opponents. Women who struggle for power are "unnatural." This presumably bizarre desire for men's power is explored in one episode, "The Turnabout Intruder," which is analyzed in a separate section later.

The third myth concerns the struggle between life and death. In this survival scenario, the *Star Trek* men fight "things" that live but are not sexual. The success of the patriarchal leaders literally determines the life or death of all humans, a potential Armageddon. Each episode has components of each myth and instinctual battle, but the most frequent and powerful scenario is the Oedipal one.

In addition to the assumptions concerning male dominance, there are hierarchical rules of power within the male sphere. As a result, Kirk, Spock, and McCoy, in descending order, have power to define and maintain order within the *Enterprise*. Because each has his own area of expertise, this power varies in different contexts. In general, Kirk is the final authority.

Star Trek dramatizes the sex code of male control over women. As such, it enters into emotional relationships with the audience, who not only relive these dramas but become attached to the characters and roles depicted. The audience identifies with the characters, their struggles, and their definitions of situations. Fans enter into imagined relationships with the stars, generating a sense of belonging with this "other" world. Trekkies and other loyal viewers have what

Turner (1969) calls a communitas experience. This ritualized patriarchy, augmented by films that can be repeatedly viewed, becomes a component of the culture. In this way, the *Star Trek* formula supports other sex-coded formulas, each echoing the other in their submissive roles for women and dominant roles for men. *Star Trek* is institutionally reflexive. *Star Trek*'s ritualized relations between the sexes make it a powerful drama, as we see through application of the following methodology.

METHODOLOGY

This chapter employs a more detailed form of content analysis than used in the preceding examination of fat-letter postcards. Unlike postcard images, televised action dramas are temporarily and visually active. They are complex entities, in this case structured by a series of unfolding, interrelated Freudian formulas. Whereas postcards can be assembled in one place for sorting and comparison, commercial television programs are shown only at scheduled times. This problem is ameliorated today by the wide availability of video cassette recorders (VCRs). Still, a researcher can only watch and record data on one episode at a time.

The data for this chapter were obtained just prior to the low-cost availability of VCRs. I watched every episode in the *Star Trek* series when it was rebroadcast on a local commercial station. This requires some diligence and scheduling and is complicated by the fact that not every episode is rebroadcast as frequently as other episodes. As I watched each weekly installment, I took notes in much the same way that a participant observer formally records data in field settings. During each viewing and data-recording session, I was particularly careful to detail the dramatically scripted relationships between men and women. In this way, I could judge the applicability of the Freudian formula as a master code for the *Star Trek* series.

THE FREUDIAN FORMULA AND THE *STAR TREK* PATRIARCHS

The major factors that structure women's roles are reproduction, sexuality, socialization, and production (Mitchell, 1966). Therefore, it is immediately apparent that the male leaders in *Star Trek* have a structural code different from females in our society. They have no stable sexual relationships, have never knowingly fathered children, and have no role in the socialization of children. Instead, these primary factors shaping women's lives are channeled into the males' mission in the Starship. Production for these men becomes their central, personal, and professional basis for behavior.

The major sources of alienation in our society arising from the division between paid and unpaid labor and the separation of our private lives from our public ones are absent in the *Star Trek* world (Zaretsky, 1976). The crew never engages in any capital exchange or accumulation, and their public and private lives are idealized in the small-town atmosphere of the *Enterprise*. Therefore, their productive labor occurs in a "total institution" (Goffman, 1961a) organized in terms of capital, but not authority, on communistic terms. Thus the series illustrates that communism can maintain a partriarchal structure, and that female oppression is a separate issue from class oppression.

Together the male leaders face the dangerous unknown; they fight for and with each other: they experience fear and excitement; they laugh and cry; they are conquerors of both internal and external challenges. This male bond is the focus for the series. This male group also decides the fate of all dependents. The formula is straightforward: "Patriarchs know best."

Captain James T. Kirk has absolute command of the *Enterprise*. In every episode, Kirk makes crucial decisions affecting the lives of his crew, and he usually seeks the advice of Mr. Spock (the half-human, half-Vulcan first officer and science officer) and Dr. "Bones" McCoy (the chief medical officer). As a Vulcan, Mr. Spock is an intelligent being whose everyday life and decision making are based on logic and rationality. Although half human, Spock identifies with Vulcans, whom he considers vastly superior to humans. On a superficial level, Vulcans physically resemble humans except for their highly pointed ears and arched eyebrows. Vulcans also have unique telepathic powers and a "nerve pinch" that temporarily and usefully disables other intelligent life forms. A particularly important aspect of Spock's character as a Vulcan is that he cannot endure strong emotions without being physically incapacitated. These emotions are fatal to Vulcans if experienced for an extended period of time. Extraordinarily intelligent and logical, he is total rationality incarnate. Spock is the fans' favorite crew member (Marsano, 1977).

Bones, the Starship's physician, is responsible for the crews' "bodies," including their physical and emotional states, as Spock is responsible for the ship's "mind." Dr. McCoy, the voice of concern and nurturance, is Spock's foil. McCoy cares for the humans and is concerned with the effects of Kirk's decisions on the emotional well-being of the crew. Outspokenly opposed to Spock's reliance on logic, Bones repeatedly insists that people are not logical and that the application of only logic to a situation is destructive and shortsighted.

A fourth crew member, who is not part of the ruling trinity, is also noteworthy. This is the chief engineer, Montgomery Scott, known as "Scotty." This "laddie" is often called upon in times of mechanical threat to save the Starship from breakdown or attack.

Symbolically, Spock represents the extreme of desired masculine traits and Bones represents the feminine. They serve respectively as voices for reason and emotionality in the captain's continual battle to decide the fate of the Starship and its crew. These men love each other and the ship. Homosexual overtones, however, would destroy this heterosexual vision of male bonding; so women are constantly introduced as attractive, but denied for a "higher" male mission. In this way, "normal" heterosexuality is constantly reaffirmed. Both "gender poles'' (Broverman et al., 1970) are integrated through the patriarchal leader, Kirk. While in some ways Kirk seems to be androgynous, combining both male and female traits, this attribution would be clearly false. Kirk's decisive masculinity is flaunted through his conspicuous heterosexuality, his frequently displayed chest and biceps, and his general ''macho'' air. Kirk is a ''real'' man. All of these men are distanced from the ''female'' concerns of our culture; sexuality, reproduction, and socialization of children. Instead, they live in a rarefied male sphere dedicated to an abstract, rational ideal that is accomplished through a nurturant ship, the *Enterprise*.

THE U.S.S. *ENTERPRISE*: A RETURN TO THE WOMB

The Starship is home to 430 crew members. Powered by computers and engines, it provides defense as well as a life support system. The bridge is the major source of action. The captain's chair faces a giant view screen. The pilot console is ahead of him, Spock on his right, and engineering and communication functions are around him but in the background. The transporter room allows the crew to descend to planets or rise to the Starship.

All the crews' needs are handled quickly, efficiently, and quietly by the Starship. There are wall slots delivering food and drink; doors slide open when approached, and all rooms are spotless without any human intervention. Instantaneous information on the physiological status of major life functions is provided by equipment in the sick bay. The Starship is a home that supplies all and nurtures all.

The *Enterprise* is emphatically female. She is the target of men's ambitions, greed, lust for power, and love. Usually referred to by feminine pronouns, ''she'' is Kirk's love, his ''mistress.'' No mortal woman can compete successfully with ''her.'' In fact, all the male leaders ''love her,'' but for McCoy this arises from his care of human inhabitants and for Spock this is his duty. Only Kirk admits to his emotional bond and need to deny himself sexually in order to have ''her.''

Scotty plays a special role in relationship to the *Enterprise*. His sexual needs are rarely considered in the scripts. When he gets drunk on vintage Scotch he sings to ''her'' and pats her metal bulwarks. He spends his spare time reading up on technical information to serve her better. When he gets in a fight in ''The Trouble with Tribbles,'' it is not to save the good name of Kirk but rather to protect the besmirched honor of his ship.

The Starship *Enterprise* is an idealized womb. All food and water, air and shelter, friendship and social order, and, most importantly, meaning are supplied through her. She makes no emotional demands on the inhabitants, and all intellectual information is provided by her all-knowing computer. She is the only computer in the script with a female voice. It is truly a situation of ''ask and ye shall receive.'' Trusting her to transcend the speed of light and afford defensive and offensive protection, human beings are basically safe and secure within her. She is served by her male priests, and she is an all encompassing mistress/

goddess. Because she enables men to fulfill their life's mission and mutual obligations for each other, she cannot ask too much. Only human females can do that.

THE ROMANTIC MYTH—WOMEN'S PLACE IN SPACE AND THE SEX DRIVE

Although *Star Trek* is a thoroughly male adventure, its scripts are filled with encounters with women. They provide romantic interest, alien threats, and are sometimes given to an unnatural drive to obtain male power. *Star Trek* also portrays women in stereotypically subservient roles, as nagging, fecund, devious.

There is only one female character who appears with some frequency, Lieutenant Uhuru. This black communications officer is associated with the traditional female role of talking and translating linguistic meaning. She is the dutiful telephone operator of the future. As a character she never appears in a starring role in any episode. She is featured more prominently in some episodes than others, however. One of her major feature appearances occurs when she "adopts" tribbles, who are very affectionate, furry little animals unable to control their reproductive functions. Enough said here!

Women are customarily nagging and deceitful in episodes involving Harry Mudd. In "Mudd's Women," this devious salesman of the future gives women a fountain-of-youth drug, making them temporarily beautiful. This "phony" beauty is enough, however, to fool male miners into wanting them and giving away their valuable dilithium crystals. In another episode, "I Mudd," this sleazy entrepreneur creates an army of female androids to trap the crew of the *Enterprise* and steal their ship. Mudd's punishment is to endure an endless tongue lashing from a platoon of androids copied after his nagging, unattractive wife. Against this background of women as clerical servants and constant nags, women in *Star Trek* typically occupy their most significant—albeit individually short-lived— roles as romantic figures (Table 6.1).

The primary characters, Kirk, McCoy, and Spock, all become temporarily ensnared in romantic entanglements. In the very first episode, "The Man Trap," McCoy is lured into protecting and loving a being that he believes to be an old flame. Unfortunately, she is a disguised salt-eating alien who kills men: she murders her victims by draining their body of salt. Undisguised, she is ugly, her face dominated by a large salt-sucking mouth. She is "correctly" seen by McCoy only when he is no longer in love with her. McCoy also "allows" himself to fall in love in "For the World Is Hollow and I Have Touched the Sky" when he believes himself to be fatally ill. He decides to spend his last year with the high priestess of a doomed planet. When he recovers and the planet is saved, they both return to their duties—McCoy's on the *Enterprise* and the priestess's on her planet. McCoy again falls in love due to the influences of alien spores; when the spores' effects are destroyed, he is returned to "normal."

Kirk is also frequently seduced by women. In his one "true love" affair, in

Table 6.1

Star Trek **Episodes Structured Around Women and the Romantic Myth**

	Episodes Involving Human Females	Episodes Involving Alien Females
First Year	Mudd's Women Miri The City on the Edge of Forever	The Man Trap What Are Little Girls Made Of? The Menagerie, Parts I & II The Devil in the Dark
Second Year		Catspaw Metamorphosis Friday's Child
Third Year	Is There No Truth in Beauty? The Paradise Syndrome	The Enterprise Incident Spock's Brain For the World Is Hollow and I Have Touched the Sky Wink of an Eye The Empath Elaan of Troyius The Mark of Gideon That Which Survives

"The City on the Edge of Forever," Kirk goes back in time with Spock to the Earth world of the 1930s. There, McCoy is drug-maddened and aided by a beautiful social worker. Kirk falls in love with her but must let her die rather than save her and alter the course of history. In "Shore Leave," Kirk imagines the presence of another, earlier love. This illusion is fostered by aliens who can make humans' thoughts appear to be reality. Clearly, she is not a continuing character (even being in the series is illusory). In another episode, Kirk falls hopelessly in love with a warrior princess who is bound to a loveless marriage agreement in order to settle a war between two planets. The title, "Elaan of Troyius," suggests she is like Helen of Troy, the most beautiful woman of all times. In "The Paradise Syndrome," Kirk is "allowed" to marry after he develops amnesia. In this false paradise, Kirk is lured into marriage with yet another high priestess and he is proclaimed a god. Spock destroys the mythical paradise and extricates Kirk from his "dream state."

Spock's romantic situations are life and death struggles, since Vulcans cannot physically survive strong emotions. Thus most of Spock's love experiences occur when "he is not himself." Spock falls in love, for example, when he is transported through time to an ice age in "All Our Yesterdays." In this earlier epoch Vulcans were still able to feel emotions. Although Spock falls passionately in love, his duty is to the captain and the ship, so he abandons this seductive alternative. In "This Side of Paradise," Spock again falls in love due to the infiltration of alien spores into his body. Kirk saves Spock from these dangerous emotions since Spock is helpless to protect himself. Restored to his normal state (one could say his "normal" male self), Spock returns to his work. These are unusual, life-threatening states.

Even rational Vulcans must procreate and thus Spock does have a normal period of sexual arousal, but this strange, atypical state of affairs severely limits his ability to work. This libido-driven period of cosmic itch occurs only once every seven years and is called (appropriately enough for patriarchs) "Amok Time." During this vulnerable, short-lived period, Vulcans are completely driven by their sex drive and it is only then that they marry. To choose his bride, Spock fights Kirk, his "best friend and commander." He believes he kills Kirk (but McCoy has given Kirk an injection that simulates death). Despite Spock's apparent sacrifice, Spock's love rejects him because he is away from "home" too much. Thus Spock's "normal" sexuality is satisfied—for at least another seven years.

In every romantic episode, human women are eventually eliminated from the *Enterprise* by various devices in the script. They can have no permanent role or place in this male world. Human female love interests are tempting, evil and illusionary, or culturally and morally superior but unavailable. They are temptresses: "the other" (Beauvoir, 1953). But, at least as romantic figures, human women have a good side—unlike their alien sisters.

Female aliens are usually portrayed as either stupid or vicious. This extreme depiction of women as limited and despicable reveals a deep hatred of women and is accomplished in the scripts by according alien status to the most vile and threatening women. "The Man Trap," already discussed, is a salt-eating killer. The series' answer to the question "What Are Little Girls Made Of?" is "mechanical bodies and brains." In this episode, a male android controls an army of loyal female androids who try to destroy the *Enterprise* and crew.

In "The Metamorphosis," an alien "Companion" enters the body of an ancient, marooned space pioneer. She rejuvenates him physically, and he can communicate with her. He is so lonely, however, that he has the Companion bring Kirk, Spock, and a female diplomat to this planet. This human woman, a brilliant ambassador, constantly demands and complains. She is dying from a rare disease, and on her death bed says she only wanted to love a man and marry. Subsequently, the pioneer realizes he has had an alien form of intercourse with the Companion, and feels he has been raped. Eternal life given him by his immersion with the Companion is not worth this price. The Companion then enters the dying body of the human woman, relinquishing her alien immortality, in order to love a mortal man.

In one of the most complicated deprecations of women, an alien priestess steals "Spock's Brain." She is able to infiltrate the defenses of the men by momentarily gaining mental powers from a computer that needs Spock's brain to continue functioning. (She installs Spock's brain in the computer, which

Spock, the ultimate rational man, finds "very interesting.") Kirk and McCoy, with Spock's brainless body in tow, follow his "brain tracks" and descend to a planet where the native men are cast out into the harsh environment and enslaved by the strange creatures (i.e., women) who give them both pleasure and pain. The pain arises from a strong electric shock transmitted through bracelets worn by the men. Spock's zombie body is impervious to pain, and this circumstance allows Kirk and McCoy to free themselves and retrieve Spock's brain. The concept of a computer-controlled woman stealing a man's brain is an intricate castration fantasy about the power of mindless women.

"Friday's Child" examines the deep-seated fears of men and women touching each other. In this episode's "primitive" world, a man must die if he touches a woman who is not his wife. Every woman, except a husband's wife, is untouchable and deadly to men. Thus, because Bones touches a pregnant woman when she is delivering a child, the infant becomes his. McCoy's virginal fatherhood amuses Spock and Kirk, but McCoy's active paternity is short-lived, ending as they leave the now-peaceful world.

Three female aliens do have slightly expanded roles. "The Empath" is a female whose species communicates only through the mind. Her race is incapable of acting generously or unselfishly, and she learns this capacity from the men of the *Enterprise*. Although the episode is named after her, the real drama and power are found in another group of male aliens who are testing her altruistic capacity by using the male humans from the *Enterprise* as guinea pigs. In "The *Enterprise* Incident," the female captain of a Romulan vessel captures Spock, thereby displaying a slightly different role for women. Because she loves Spock, however, she loses her command, her Starship, and her legitimacy within her species. Finally, the priestess who loves McCoy in "The World Is Hollow and I Have Touched the Sky" remains in her world when he returns to the Starship.

Human women also frequently fall for male aliens, such as the blind telepath in "Is There in Truth No Beauty?" and the woman who loves a Greek god in "Who Mourns for Adonis?" These women leave human society and prefer their alien lovers to the most basic of all human identifications. For women, love overrides any other bond or commitment.

From episode to episode, women are seductive, stupid, and alien, or loving, threatening, subservient. In some ways, human women may even appear to be more foreign than women of other species. "Good women," a very small minority in the scripts, wish only to serve men. Most women will take body-altering drugs, give up immortality, and practice any deceit necessary to trap a man. Nonetheless, women are always put in their place; Lt. Uhuru remains forever at her post—answering the interstellar phone. Men, whether their love interest is alien or human, have their duty, their Starship, their five-year mission—there is no room for enduring romantic entanglements on the *Enterprise*. The real danger to the men of *Star Trek* is not women, however. Patriarchs in this Freudian formula are deeply endangered by loss of their power—and only a male enemy can take it away.

THE OEDIPAL MYTH: THE MALE ENEMY AND THE AGGRESSIVE DRIVE

All patriarchal authority is open to attack by less powerful men, so Kirk is constantly confronted by this Oedipal threat (see Table 6.2). For example, "Charlie X," a seventeen-year-old boy with superhuman powers who is rescued by the *Enterprise*, tries to gain control of the ship, but is subdued by Kirk after a face-to-face confrontation. In "The Doomsday Machine," a mad Starship captain commands the *Enterprise* while Kirk is stranded aboard another Starship. Again, Kirk defeats this challenger. Likewise, in "Dagger of the Mind," the inmates of a model penal colony lure Kirk into their fortification, only to lose their bid for control.

In "Space Seed," Khan, a selectively bred "superman" who once ruled a quarter of the earth, is routed on earth and flees from it in a spaceship where he and his followers remain in suspended animation. They are reanimated by the *Enterprise* crew and Khan immediately tries to take over the Starship. Khan enlists the aid of a female officer who falls in love with him, but Kirk regains control of his vessel and banishes the "superpeople" to a rough but habitable planet. Khan returns in the movie sequel, *Star Trek II: The Wrath of Khan*, for another battle. This unsuccessful bid for power is fueled by the severe deprivation experienced by the colony when their planet is rendered uninhabitable by a cosmic catastrophe. Khan loses not only the battle but also his colony and life as well.

Male Machines

Kirk is occasionally challenged by "male" computers who have run amok.[8] When a computer is selected to replace Kirk as captain of the *Enterprise* in "The Ultimate Computer," it subsequently refuses to relinquish control (just like a man!). This conflict reveals that the female ship is helpless without a human male to command her. In "By Any Other Name," an altered computer "proves" that Kirk is responsible for the death of a former rival and friend. This false information is planted in the computer by Kirk's enemy, a fact that is discovered before the challenging male and his computer "accomplice" can permanently strip Kirk of his rank at a court-martial.

In "The Changeling" an old-earth space probe collides with some objects in deep space, resulting in a damaged program that destroys all imperfections, including flawed humans. Kirk pretends to be the probe's maker, thereby penetrating to the "prime directive" embedded in the machine and establishing a paradox that requires it logically to destroy itself rather than harm people. *Star Trek: The Motion Picture* borrows "The Changeling" plot: here an ancient space probe is granted near-infinite power by a race of supermachines and returns as a potential threat to "flawed" life. It, too, searches for its maker. In this movie, two female aliens are allowed to be officers on the bridge, but only after the

Table 6.2
Star Trek **Episodes Structured Around Men and the Oedipal Myth**

	Episodes Involving Human Males*	Episodes Involving Alien Males
First Year	Charlie X Where No Man Has Gone Before The Enemy Within Dagger of the Mind The Conscience of the King The Galileo Seven Tomorrow Is Yesterday Court-Martial Space Seed A Taste of Armageddon The Alternative Factor	The Carbomite Maneuver Balance of Terror Shore Leave The Squire of Gothos Arena The Return of the Archons Errand of Mercy
Second Year	Mirror, Mirror The Doomsday Machine I, Mudd A Piece of the Action A Private Little War Patterns of Force The Omega Glory Bread and Circuses Assignment: Earth	Amok Time Who Mourns for Adonis? The Changeling Journey to Babel Wolf in the Fold The Gamesters of Triskelion Return to Tomorrow By Any Other Name The Ultimate Computer
Third Year	Whom Gods Destroy Let That Be Your Last Battlefield Requiem for Methuselah The Way to Eden The Cloud Minders All Our Yesterdays	And the Children Shall Lead Spectre of the Gun The Tholian Web Plato's Stepchildren The Savage Curtain
Movies	Star Trek II:The Wrath of Khan	Star Trek: The Motion Picture

*There is one Oedipal myth episode, "Turnabout Intruder," that
features a human female in the threatening role.

romantic threat they pose is cancelled: Illia has taken a vow of chastity since human males would be fatally harmed by intercourse with her, and Savak is incapable of falling in love due to her Vulcan ancestry. Decker, the new captain of the *Enterprise*, is stripped of his authority by Kirk (who has now advanced through the bureaucracy to become an admiral). The adventure concludes with the "merging of Decker and Illia" through the intervention of the space probe, and the men of *Star Trek* are symbolic midwives to the birth of a new species.

Alien Competition for Power

Male aliens vie for power, too. In "Arena," Kirk successfully fights a lizardlike alien commander to settle a territorial dispute. Another male alien, who is evil incarnate, manipulates the fears of children (who witnessed their parents' dying frenzies) to enter and control the Starship. Kirk, however, revives the children's memories of loving parents and thereby breaks the "evil father's " spell. Kirk is temporarily the wise patriarch who cares for abused and exploited children.

Of course, the major alien antagonists are the Federation's traditional foes: the Romulans and the Klingons. Romulans, in "Balance of Terror" and "The *Enterprise* Incident," play more fairly than Klingons. As long as the Federation representatives stay in their territories, the Romulans do not attack. Klingons, however, are a different sort altogether:

Klingons are professional villains. They are nasty, vicious, brutal and merciless. They don't bathe regularly, they don't use deodorants or brush their teeth. They don't even visit the dentist twice a year. They sharpen their fangs by hand because they think pain is fun. They eat Blue Meanies for breakfast. (Gerrold, 1974: 32)

Klingons do things that evil people do, and in this sense they stand symbolically for a dark side of human nature. The similarity between the human and Klingon races is the theme in their first encounter when the Klingons attack a pacifist planet, Organia. Kirk mistakenly feels it is his duty to protect the Organians, but these people are actually more powerful than either the violent men of the Federation or the Klingon Empire. When Kirk fights the Klingon captain, an equal, alien, male foe, he is stopped by the Organians. Kirk's darker side demands the right to fight and he realizes too late that he is very similar to the vicious Klingons. The Organians establish a treaty between the empires, thereby establishing the precedent for the surreptitious conflict between Klingons and the Federation throughout the remaining episodes. Klingons appear in "The Trouble with Tribbles," where it is discovered that tribbles have the admirable habit of making horrible noises and trembling whenever a Klingon is present. This unnerving behavior leads to the unmasking of Klingon spies who are sabotaging food supplies. In both "A Private Little War" and "Friday's Child," Kirk fights Klingon spies who pretend to help unsophisticated natives on a primitive planet. Again, these despicable liars are foiled by human and Vulcan heroes. In "The Day of the Dove," an alien being that feeds on hatred tries to use the animosity between the Earthmen and Klingons to destroy both species. Kirk blocks this scheme by establishing a temporary truce with the Klingons and together they ward off their mutual enemy.

Internal Treachery

Finally, the most serious threat to the ship is internal treachery. This is a major *Star Trek* theme, and a favorite variation is Kirk's vulnerability to the dark side of his human nature. "The Enemy Within" appears once due to a transporter malfunction that splits Kirk into two personae: one good and one evil. Neither side can survive alone and so Kirk must embrace both sides to continue living. In "Mirror, Mirror," Kirk finds a counterpart universe in which the parallel Kirk and *Enterprise* crew are evil instead of good. Evil doubles replace Kirk, McCoy, Uhuru, and Scotty in our universe while our good guys and gals are placed in the wicked universe. The good Kirk wins the day by convincing the bad Kirk's woman to join forces with him.

Since all men vie for power, the lust for illegitimate power or loyalty to legitimate power defines their lives. Human and alien males share this common bond. In fact, male Klingons and Romulans behave more like human men than human women do. In the entire *Star Trek* series, only the very last televised episode, "The Turnabout Intruder," shows a woman as a serious threat to Kirk's power, and she is mad. The Freudian assumption behind "The Turnabout Intruder" is that a "normal" woman could never desire a Starship captain's power.

A "MAD WOMAN" IN AN OEDIPAL CONFLICT: "THE TURNABOUT INTRUDER"

In this section, before turning to the third major Freudian scenario (the male struggle between life and death), I note an episode that features a significant reversal of the two previous themes, romance and patriarchal competition. The plot of "Turnabout Intruder" centers on the "deranged desire" of Janice Lester to be a Starship captain. This madness began when she and Kirk were young lovers. Her "extreme" jealousy of Kirk's chance to be a Starship captain while she, a mere female, could never attain this position leads to their breakup. Later, during an archeological dig, she discovers a machine that lets her exchange bodies with another human. This provides her with the opportunity to "adopt" a male body—a true Oedipal fantasy for the "inferior" woman. So she murders the members of her expedition, lures Kirk to her excavation site, and swaps bodies with him. After using this fiendish apparatus, Janice lives in Kirk's body (this entity is referred to here as "JK") while he lives in hers (referred to as "KJ").

Once on board the *Enterprise*, JK acts "incorrectly." Despite her taking over a male body, she does not have its psychological and moral superiority. The crew knows that something is gravely wrong and a court-martial is initiated. Spock finally deduces that only a woman in Kirk's body could act so strangely— that is, incompetent, easily angered, and irrational. KJ, however, acts "just like a man" even though he inhabits a female body. Through a powerful personality struggle, KJ overcomes JK and each returns to his or her natural body.

After Janice's unsuccessful bid for power, Spock and Kirk speculate on her behavior:

Kirk looked after them (leading Janice away). "I didn't want to destroy her," he said.
"You had to," Spock said, "How else could you have survived, Captain? To say nothing of the rest of us."
"Her life could have been as rich as any woman's, if only—" he paused and sighed. "If only . . ."
"If only," Spock said, "she had ever been able to take pride in *being* a woman." (Blish, 1972: 338)

This episode portrays the Freudian consequences of "abnormal" desire and the distortion that occurs when women want to be Starship captains. Janice Lester would have been "sane" and "lovable" if she had accepted her place as a lover, not a power. Even nonsexed "things" may legitimately aim for complete power, but not women.

ARMAGEDDON: THE MALE STRUGGLE BETWEEN LIFE AND DEATH

A few episodes concern the possible extinction of all human life, an Armageddon myth, posed by nonsexed things, often chemicals and viruses (see Table 6.3). In "Operation Annihilate!" a batlike "thing" attaches itself to the human body causing excruciating, fatal pain. After it kills an entire planet, it is finally destroyed by massive doses of ultraviolet light. Spock plays a crucial role here, because only his extra Vulcan eyelid saves his eyesight and his life when he is flooded by the ultraviolet light.

Dr. McCoy saves humanity through his medical knowledge. In "The Naked Time," a mutated form of water reduces everyone to their most "animal" nature. Spock, of course, experiences emotions while others exhibit various forms of "madness" stereotypically appropriate for their sex and ethnic groups. McCoy finds the antidote "in the nick of time."

In a similar storyline, when the spores in "This Side of Paradise" infect the body, only Kirk's love of the *Enterprise* helps him to conquer this bodily invasion. In "The Apple," Kirk, Spock, and McCoy successfully battle a snakelike computer that controls humanoids. They disarm it and avert a planetary crash with a comet. Things in space are a constant threat to male control of the *Enterprise*.

Table 6.3
***Star Trek* Episodes Structured Around the Armageddon Myth**

Episodes Involving Nonsexed Things

First Year	The Naked Time (alien water) This Side of Paradise (spores) Operation Annihilate! (single cell that attacks nerves)
Second Year	The Apple (snake-image computer) The Deadly Years (aging virus) The Trouble With Tribbles (affectionate animals who hate Klingons) Obsession (chemical creature) The Immunity Syndrome (mega-amoeba)
Third Year	Day of the Dove (entity that lives off hatred) The Lights of Zetar (energy entity)
Movies	Star Trek III: Genesis (uncontrolled human creation of life) Star Trek IV: The Voyage Home (threatened annihilation of Earth by space probe due to the extinction of sentient whales)

The leading male trio defends against nonsexed things in other episodes. They rid the galaxy of "Zetars," a form of living light. When it takes over the body of Scotty's love, Mira, they speak through her. As an especially susceptible female, Mira can host the Zetars through her openness to new experience. (This female aptitude is also a theme in *Star Trek: The Motion Picture* and "The Empath.") Ultimately, the Zetars are forced out of her body by using air pressure. The malevolent cloud of Kirk's "Obsession" is similarly removed by air pressure and forced out of the *Enterprise*'s conduits. In "The Immunity Syndrome," the dynamic trio fights a mega-amoeba that could eat the whole galaxy. Spock's superior scientific training and physical endurance make him the more logical pilot for an exploratory shuttle trip to examine the "thing." Kirk uses the craft as a hypodermic needle to innoculate the virulent virus with antimatter—just before it is ready to form more little mega-things! Another energy "thing" meddles in space conflicts in "The Day of the Dove," when Klingons and Earthmen form a temporary truce to defeat the entity that feeds on hatred and death. By creating happy "emotional pressure," the merry laughs and feigned friendship of the Klingons and humans force the "thing" to go elsewhere. The aging virus of "The Deadly Years" almost causes the *Enterprise* crew to perish due to the ineptness of a "desk chair" commander who governs in Kirk's absence. This Oedipal competitor violates the space rights of the Romulans and only Kirk, after recovering from the virus, can guide the ship to safety.

The third movie, *Star Trek III: Genesis*, carries forward the Armageddon theme in a context of unleashed disaster. Kirk's son, who was introduced to both the audience and his previously unsuspecting father in *Star Trek II: The Wrath of Khan*, appears to have inherited his father's derring-do but not his ability to carry off risky ventures. Thus the brilliant but impetuous son creates life by using unstable matter. (The son is a tragically flawed god-figure.) A seemingly beautiful planet is created and its unbounded capacity for life regenerates a once-dead Spock. (Kirk's son gives birth to Spock!) The Klingons and Kirk rush to the planet, for different reasons, and the *Enterprise* self-destructs to save the lives of Kirk and his core crew. (The *Enterprise* is "allowed" to die after Kirk, McCoy, and Scotty command it to do so.) Now that the usefulness of the *Enterprise* "womb" is over, it immolates itself to save its "sons and lovers."

Star Trek IV: The Voyage Home continues the Armageddon theme. In this case, humpback whales are needed to "speak to" a space probe that put the whales on earth thousands and thousands of years ago. Because these whales were hunted to extinction by humans, the destructive humans must die because the probe cannot "talk to" anyone on earth. In this conflict, however, the aggressive male instinct is diverted once more from its logical ending—the destruction of everyone. The men of *Star Trek* travel in time back to 1986 and abscond with two whales. The men return to the future just in time to have their friends, the whales, "talk to" the whales' awesome and globally lethal protector. In the process, Spock learns to trust his intuition, Kirk brings a female love from 1986 into his own era, and the audience shares in laughing at the present behavior of people in San Francisco. This time-traveling derring-do was accomplished, however, by breaking bureaucratic rules. For the men's disobedient behavior— which merely saves all humanity from annihilation—Admiral Kirk loses his desk job and is demoted to captain (his secret wish) and given a new *Enterprise* to command. Although the Starship is the most important female symbol, she can be easily replaced with a new model.

The category of nonsexed "things" is intricately woven into the larger theme of Oedipal conflicts and romantic entanglements. This ranking of themes (romance, patriarchal competition, Armageddon) corresponds to Freud's relative emphasis on these three drives (libido, aggression, eros/thanatos). The death wish (thanatos), although not extensively employed in *Star Trek*, corresponds to the "enemy within" theme that is explored in various ways throughout the series.

CONCLUSION

Star Trek was originally conceived as less Freudian, less sexist, and less racist than it appeared in the majority of its televised episodes (Whitfield and Roddenberry, 1968). Yet the Freudian formula is a successful one, emotionally and commercially, because it provides a consistent view of women as "aliens" who know their proper place throughout time and space. Powerless in political, military, and economic spheres, these future women resort to stereotypical feminine wiles and snares to lure unsuspecting men into emotional traps. Whether abnormally powerful because of ignorance or android machinery, women are always subdued by the men of the *Enterprise*. Sexually stimulating, women may temporarily distract these men from their higher duty to the feminized machine, the U.S.S. *Enterprise*. The patriarchal leaders love each other and are, in turn, loved by their crew and fans. Emotional attachment to other men and to a machine are depicted as normal; however, commitment to women is not only pathological but—in the instance of the masculine ideal embodied in Spock—can even be fatal.

The world of the *Enterprise* is an entire, bounded community. In this way, the ritual world is similar to nonmodern ones, despite its association with "modern" life in the future. The communitas generated by the men, their liminal journey, and rites of passage for the crew and Starship closely follow the Turner model of formal rituals. The basically egalitarian and humane society for the men is in many ways a mythological utopia.

The oppressive sex codes of everyday life, however, are extended in *Star Trek* into anti-structural time and space. The Freudian formula taps a deep cultural matrix. Formal Freudian practice is embedded in our cultural understanding of "normality" and abnormality. The make-believe ritual world of *Star Trek* mirrors our everyday world and its image of "normal" male behavior. The seductive entertainment of *Star Trek* tells a fast-paced modern world that the universe is best ordered on the American way. Western values are timeless throughout the universe. The deep bonding of the male heroes in a communistic Starship allows for the appearance of communitas in an all-male group with an acknowledged leader. It is hard to imagine *Star Trek* as entertainment in a feminist world, however. For the men of the *Enterprise* would then be seen for what they are: the aliens within our midst.

ACKNOWLEDGMENT

My thanks to Terry Nygren and the class members who worked with me in the course "Wimmin and the Mass Media." Michael R. Hill also provided numerous editorial comments. Like Captain Kirk, I assume final responsibility for the work I do.

NOTES

1. These are the lines spoken at the beginning of each televised episode. They are read by Captain Kirk. The words were omitted from the first two movies but reappear in the third and fourth movies. In these latter films, they are spoken by Mr. Spock.

2. "Communitas" is severely restricted in *Star Trek* to the three principal male characters. It does not extend to the Starship crew as a whole. This is a very different situation than communitas in Turner's nonmodern world wherein entire villages are bound together in communitas. Restricting communitas, unity, and good feelings to the central male trio results directly from the Freudian formula, a formula that excludes "others" from the communal circle of patriarchal domination.

3. A listing of the episodes and their first televised dates is found in Margaret Bailey (1976).

4. For a dramaturgical analysis of the Freudian formula in *Star Trek*, see Mary Jo Deegan (1983).

5. This patriarchal myth is opposed by archeological evidence supporting the reverse reality; i.e., it was men who bound women and children into homogeneous marriage in order to protect the men's accumulation of capital; see Friedrich Engels (1972), Michelle Barrett and Mary McIntosh (1982).

6. An adequate discussion of Freud is beyond the scope of this chapter. Major works that would be helpful for this particular topic are found in the bibliography. An excellent overview of the Freudian model can be found in Daniel Yankelovich and William Barrett (1971).

7. These dichotomized masculine and feminine roles are discussed by I. K. Broverman et al. (1970). Talcott Parsons, a Freudian sociologist, also discusses the instrumental and expressive functions as male and female respectively (e.g., Parsons and Bales, 1955).

8. The only "naturally female" computer is the one on the *Enterprise*. "Male" computers can sound female when they take over female brains and bodies.

7

The Wonderful Vision of Oz

From the extremes of future time and interstellar space, I now turn to a vision from the recent past, to the land of Oz found "somewhere over the rainbow." The fantasy adventures of Dorothy and her friends in the magical land of Oz employ a formula vastly different from Freud's. It is not surprising to find, therefore, that Victor Turner's nonmodern, ritual model also fits closely. This does not mean that this new formula is non-Western, however. For the stories of Oz have been described as the most American of all popular fairy tales, and the movie *The Wizard of Oz* is televised annually to the delight of Americans of all ages. Once again the complexity of modern life appears, revealing a traditional ritual world in the midst of America's heartland.

From 1902 until 1920, a series of utopian fantasies was woven into a tapestry of wonder and play. The land of Oz was entered on the fairyland map and the American consciousness was altered. In direct contrast to each of the preceding rituals, L. Frank Baum created an extraordinary reality that fits Turner's model of celebrations. A complex set of anti-structural rules governs Oz, and humans who enter this world are liminal characters, betwixt and between the earth and magic. These characters, their adventures, and the dramatic tension generated by their experiences are most vividly drawn in *The Wonderful Wizard of Oz*, the first book in a series of fourteen Oz volumes.

THE MARVELOUS AUTHOR OF OZ

L. Frank Baum was born in 1856 and reached the full height of his talents near the end of the Victorian era. He was born into a wealthy family and was intensely drawn to the theater. He has never been recognized as a major literary figure, and his works suffer from hostility by librarians and other cultural gate-keepers. Fred Erisman (1968), a scholar in children's literature, treats Baum as a minor figure while Raylan Moore (1974) documents the systematic barriers to Baum's work. I suggest that part of this professional gatekeeping opposition arises from Baum's formula for Oz and its challenges to the oppressive and repressive structures of life in America. More specifically, the Baum books are not capitalist, sexist, bureaucratic, or in "ordinary" time. They directly challenge the core codes that are usually supported in popular culture. The Baum formula, therefore, is an innovative way to celebrate American life that renews and en-riches our communal experiences.

METHODOLOGY

This study is a content analysis of published works in the Oz series authored by L. Frank Baum. I read all of Baum's works and systematically viewed the three available Oz motion pictures (*The Wizard of Oz*, *Return to Oz*, and *The Marvelous Land of Oz*—a videotape of the Minneapolis Children's Theater stage play). These materials are now readily available for analysis, as many of the books have been reprinted, including some of the subsequent Oz titles written by authors other than Baum. The original, full-size editions of the Baum volumes are much superior to recent reprints, however, in that their illustrations (many are color plates) are far more playful, detailed, faithful, and imaginative than those included in several of the subsequent editions. The early editions have become collector's items and are now routinely available only from rare-book dealers, usually at elevated prices. During my research on auctions I observed a couple bid extravagantly for a set of original Oz books, apparently to present them to their children. I have been fortunate to find several copies of early editions at reasonable cost, however. It was fortuitous, perhaps, that my most prized volume was purchased in a second-hand store in—where else?—Kansas.

THE BAUM FORMULA

Baum's conception of humans evolves from a loving view. Although humans are often frail and prone to error, they have kind hearts and a will to do good. They can exhibit courage, good humor, and a group consciousness that transcends immediate perils. Both men and women are capable of much goodness, but it is little girls who epitomize it. Little boys are more mischievous than girls, but the former are also quite good in Baum's Weltanschauung. Male father figures are devoted to little girls who are rarely their biological relations. All significant interpersonal relationships in these stories are platonic.

Both good and evil exist, and each struggles for primacy. Good is intrinsically more powerful, but individuals must choose to enact it or evil will triumph. The most powerful battles are waged between magical beings, especially between good and wicked witches. Humans, however, can threaten evil beings, even magical ones, because of the "natural" power of human goodness. Objects can become animate in Oz, but their "living" status is ambiguous. For example, when a grasshopper sitting on the head of the Scarecrow asks the latter if he is alive, the Scarecrow replies:

When my body is properly stuffed I have animation and can move around as well as any live person. The brains in the head you are now occupying as a throne, are of very superior quality and do a lot of very clever thinking. But whether that is being alive, or not, I cannot prove to you; for one who lives is liable to death, while I am only liable to destruction. (Baum, 1915: 199)

With the status of these beings not greatly clarified by this and similar explanations, I shall proceed to call them "animate objects" with the reader's kind understanding. Animate objects lack the intrinsic power to threaten evil unless they are empowered by good magical beings. Animals have this same kind of limited power and retain some of their "biologically given" characteristics as well. Thus the Hungry Tiger wants to eat fat little babies, but does not. He has come to know them as lovable beings, but the temptation is literally a ceaseless "gnawing hunger."

Humans seek adventure and even danger because it makes life enjoyable. Even more importantly, humans learn to face their fears and defend their values, notably friendship and loyalty to kin. The Baum formula emphasizes voluntary relationships more than biological ones. Humans do not seek evil to find adventure, but evil threatens them or their loved ones. Greed, ambition, uncontrolled curiosity, and the temptation to know evil motivate evil beings. Humans are rarely totally evil and it is only a very few magical beings in Oz who are destroyed instead of redeemed.

All of the magical events of the Baum formula take place in a fairyland called Oz. Surrounded by a deadly desert and cut off from earth, Oz fits the traditional *rite de passage* structure. The first stage, on earth, is radically altered by some natural disturbance; tornadoes, whirlpools, earthquakes, and storm-tossed seas are all possible pathways into Oz. Some transitional stage is necessary before entry, however, and this stage varies in length. In *The Wonderful Wizard of Oz* Dorothy rather quickly lands in the Munchkin country while still in her tornado-tossed house from Kansas. In *The Scarecrow of Oz*, the entry into Oz takes a considerable portion of the book with various stops in other "countries" before arriving in Oz.

THE ANTI-STRUCTURE OF OZ

Oz fits Turner's "anti-structure" model for *rite de passage* in nonmodern societies. This is diagrammed in Table 7.1. The first stage is introduced usually by a little girl from earth who undergoes a traumatic change in the transition

Table 7.1
The *Rite de Passage* for Oz Adventures

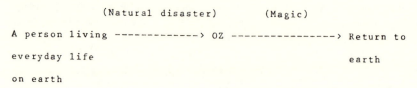

```
                    (Natural disaster)          (Magic)
A person living ------------> OZ ----------------> Return to
everyday life                                    earth
on earth
```

THE RITUAL PROCESS

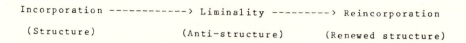

```
Incorporation ------------> Liminality ---------> Reincorporation
 (Structure)                (Anti-structure)       (Renewed structure)
```

from earth to Oz. This magical land then operates by magical rules governing humans, animate objects, and animals. In general, both animate objects and animals think and speak in Oz. Animals retain their animal instincts, however, which causes them to struggle with their ability to reflect on their actions and their powerful unreflective instincts. Good examples of such animals are the Hungry Tiger, and the Cowardly Lion, who is king of the jungle yet subject to fears and doubts about his strength and power. Animate objects have no fixed characters or instincts so they must create a unique place and definition for themselves. The Scarecrow illustrates the need to be intelligent while the Tinman illustrates the need to have a heart. Both of these animate objects already behave with intelligence and empathy, but these abilities must be objectified by the community in order to become real.

In addition to Turner's *rite de passage* model, Erving Goffman's frame analysis can be applied. To use Goffman's analysis, the novel's initial stage of incorporation becomes a "laminated frame." The state of liminality is another lamination occurring through the rekeying of the laminated frame. The reincorporation is marked by a rekeying to the new laminated frame (see Table 7.2). The rites of passage become a certain sequence of frames, "the rite of passage frames," and the ritual process of Goffman and Turner are blended.

Goffman provides us with conceptual links between the contemporary reader, the past author and his publisher, the modern book industry, and its distribution system. These connections are not part of Turner's simplified model of structure in a nonmodern society. The modern response to Oz is based on a traditional *rite de passage* and its possibility for communitas. This modern experience is found through literature and the mass media, however, rather than face-to-face

Table 7.2
A Frame Analysis for Oz Adventures

```
                        (Natural

                     disaster-Key)        (Magic-Key)


A person living  ------------> OZ ----------------> Return to

everyday life                                       earth

on earth



                        FRAME ANALYSIS


Novel as laminated  -------> Another ------------> Return to first

frame of reality            lamination            laminated frame
```

interactions. The written words create the possibility of a ritual process for the audience.

These texts are adventures involving a play on real situations: encountering new species; acting in societies with rules at odds with earth life and perhaps even Oz itself; responding to new situations, rules and others; and depending on others as well as the self. In *The Wonderful Wizard of Oz*, Dorothy takes a liminal journey with the Scarecrow, the Tinman, and the Cowardly Lion to meet the Wizard of Oz. (In contradiction to the other animals, Toto, her earth dog, does not speak in this Oz adventure and retains his earth dog characteristics.) Along the yellow brick road they encounter trees that attack them, a wicked witch, a good witch, little people called Munchkins, and winged monkeys. Each of these encounters follows rules vastly different from those of mundane life. Friendship, bravery, and loyalty are all necessary ingredients for a happy ending. In this first book in the series, this means a return to home, Kansas, Aunt Em, and Uncle Henry.

THE OZ CHARACTERS: HUMANS, MAGICAL BEINGS, ANIMALS AND ANIMATE OBJECTS

There are four major types of beings in Oz. *Humans* are usually from either earth or Oz. *Magical beings* are a very small number of Oz's residents who have fantastic skills. *Animals* can speak in Oz and have the status of humans, while on occasion inanimate objects are given life through some form of magical intervention, thereby becoming *animate objects*. Only humans have an everyday status for "earthlings"; so all the other characters are liminal. The humans are on a liminal journey, however, so they, too, share a liminal status in the stories.

Female humans are central to all of Baum's stories. In twelve of the fourteen Oz adventures, Dorothy is a leading figure. She is sometimes accompanied by the Wizard as a major figure (*The Wizard of Oz; Dorothy and the Wizard of Oz*), but more frequently she is accompanied by male animate objects as friendly companions. In my analysis, I examine the dominant female characters in the Baum formula, especially the human girl, Dorothy, and the magical beings, Ozma and Glinda. The major male characters are the Wizard, a human who becomes a magical being, and the animate objects who have no earthly counterparts. All of the the major characters, and the books in which they appear, are presented in Tables 7.3 and 7.4.

Humans in Oz

Humans in Oz are either born in Oz or enter from other lands. The most important human protagonists are "earthlings," especially little girls who are accompanied by male kin or guardians. The Wizard of Oz is the only male human of any significance in the continuing series of Oz stories, and he is far from an "ideal" male adult. In the first Oz book he admits to being a "humbug"—and an unsuccessful one at that!

Female Humans

In the first adventure, *The Wonderful Wizard of Oz*, Dorothy, a small girl from Kansas, is introduced to the land of Oz and its then-humbug Wizard. Always ready for adventure, calm in the face of danger, and optimistic about the power of good, Dorothy is a powerful protagonist. Her desire to return home to Kansas motivates her first adventure, and her openness to new experiences draws a series of other characters to her and her quest to find the Wizard of Oz. In this book, the reader is introduced to the Cowardly Lion, the Scarecrow, and the Tin Woodman. The Wizard is revealed as an incompetent balloonist who strayed off course and ultimately landed in Oz. The people of Oz are impressed by his balloon landing and declare him a Wizard. Unable to help Dorothy, the Wizard sends her on many more adventures and trials. Finally, Dorothy finds her way home through the magical slippers she wears, and tearfully leaves her new friends.

Dorothy maintains her androgynous mixture of heroism and nurturance in each of the books in which she appears (twelve out of fourteen). These same traits characterize other female humans in the series, namely, Betsy and Trot. These little girls engage in similar adventures and become close friends. Aunt Em, Dorothy's aunt, eventually comes to Oz as well (Baum, 1910). Although she is not as lovable as the little girls, she is as loyal and courageous.

Female humans from Oz exhibit similar, albeit less wholesome and consistent,

Table 7.3
The Female Characters of Oz

BOOKS	FEMALE HUMANS	FEMALE MAGICAL "HUMANS" g/e*	FEMALE NONHUMANS a/o**
WIZARD OF OZ	Dorothy	Glinda (g) Wicked Witchs (e)	Queen of Mice (a)
LAND OF OZ	General Jinjur Jellia Jamb	Mombi (e) Glinda (g) Ozma (g)	Queen of Mice (a)
OZMA OF OZ	Dorothy Queen of Ev	Ozma (g) Princess Langwidere (e?)	Billina (a)
DOROTHY AND THE WIZARD OF OZ	Dorothy	Ozma (g)	Princess of Mangaboos (o) Eureka (a)
ROAD TO OZ	Dorothy	Ozma (g) Queen of Merryland (g) Queen Zixi of Ix (g)	Polychrome (o) Billina (a)
EMERALD CITY OF OZ	Dorothy Aunt Em	Ozma (g) Glinda (g)	
PATCHWORK GIRL		Ozma (g)	Patchwork Girl (o) Glass Cat (o)
TIK-TOK OF OZ	Dorothy Betsy Rose Princess Queen Ann	Queen of Light (g) Ozma (g)	Polychrome (o)
SCARECROW OF OZ	Dorothy Trot Princess Gloria	Glinda (g) Ozma (g) Wicked Witch (e) (Blinkie) (e)	
RINKITINK OF OZ	Zella Island Queens	Glinda (g) Ozma (g)	
LOST PRINCESS OF OZ	Dorothy Jellia Jamb Cayke the Cookie Cook	Ozma (g) Glinda (g)	Patchwork Girl (o)
TIN WOODMAN OF OZ	Dorothy Nimmie Amee Jinjur	Mrs. Yoop (e?) Ozma (g)	Polychrome (o)
MAGIC OF OZ	Dorothy Trot	Glinda (g) Ozma (g)	Patchwork Girl (o)
GLINDA OF OZ	Dorothy Betsy Trot	Glinda (g) Queen Coo-ee-oh (e) 3 Adepts (g) Reera the Red (g?)	Patchwork Girl (o)

* g = good; e = evil
** a = animal; o = animate object

Table 7.4
The Male Characters of Oz

BOOKS	MALE HUMANS	MALE MAGICAL "HUMANS" g/e*	MALE NONHUMANS a/i**
WIZARD OF OZ	Wizard		Scarecrow (o) Tin Woodman (o) Cowardly Lion (a) Toto (a)
LAND OF OZ		Dr. Nikidik Tip (g)	H. M. Wogglebug(a) Jack Pumpkinhead(o Wooden Sawhorse(o) Tin Woodman (o) The Gump (o)
OZMA OF OZ	King Ev	Nome King (e)	Tik-Tok (o) Tin Woodman (o) Scarecrow (o) Hungry Tiger (a) Cowardly Lion (a)
DOROTHY AND WIZARD OF OZ	Wizard	Braided Man (g)	Sorcerer of Mangaboos (o) Jim (a)
ROAD TO OZ	Shaggy Man Button-Bright	Santa Claus (g)	King Dox (a) Tik-Tok (o) Scarecrow (o) Tin Woodman (o) Jack Pumpkinhead,o
EMERALD CITY OF OZ	Uncle Henry Wizard	Nome King (e) General Guph(e)	First and Foremost (o)
PATCHWORK GIRL	Ojo Unc Nunkie Shaggy Man	Crooked Magician (g)	Woozy (a)
TIK-TOK	Shaggy Man Army of Bugaboo	Nome King Great Jin-Jin (g?) Original Dragon (g)	Hank the Mule (a) Quox (a) Tik-Tok (o)
SCARECROW OF OZ	Cap'n Bill Bumpy Man Button-Bright		Ork (a) Scarecrow (o)
RINKITINK OF OZ	Prince Inga King Rinkitink Nikobob Isle Kings	Nome King (e)	Bilbil the Goat (a)
LOST PRINCESS OF OZ	Button-Bright	Wizard (g) Ugu the Shoemaker (e)	Frogman (a) Wogglebug (a) Wozzy (a) Cowardly Lion (a) Toto (a) Lavender Bear (o) Pink Bear (o)
TIN WOOD- MAN OF OZ	Woot the Wanderer Mr. Chopfyt	Ku-Klip (g)	Scarecrow (o) Tin Woodman (o) Capt. Fyter (o)
MAGIC OF OZ	Kiki Aru Cap'n Bill	Bini Aru (e) Nome King (e) Wizard (g)	Kalidah (a) Beasts of the Forest (a) Cowardly Lion (a) Hungry Tiger (a) Li-Mon-Eag (a)
GLINDA OF OZ	Uncle Henry Shaggy Man Button-Bright Ojo	Wizard (g) Su-dic (e)	Tin Woodman (o) Scarecrow (o) Tik-Tok (o) Glass Cat (o) Cowardly Lion (a)

* g = good; e = evil
** a = animal; o = animate object

traits. General Jinjur, for example, tries to conquer Oz, but she does it in a relatively harmless and superficial way. Her first concern is to dress her army in colorful clothing and then arm them with knitting needles for weapons. No one, however, wants to physically hurt anyone. These "conquerors" envision government as a quick way to easily satisfy themselves, but they quickly revert to their everyday roles when they lose control (Baum, 1904). Other women from Oz include Jellia Jamb, a lady-in-waiting to Princess Ozma (Baum, 1904, 1917), and Cayke the Cookie Cook, who bakes marvelous cookies in a diamond-studded pan (Baum, 1917). Nimmie Amee is the patient, downtrodden wife of a man constructed from the old body parts of her two previous lovers (Baum, 1918). (This definitely unusual "birth" resulted from the combination of left-over body parts of two men who were made into tinmen, or animate objects. Their "old human parts" were merged into a new human being.) These female humans from Oz enact much more traditional female roles than their earthly counterparts. These latter girls are free and brave and often help male beings who are not functioning very well.

Male Humans

Male humans are a motley group. Often fakers, like the Wizard of Oz, or retired but financially unsuccessful men, like Cap'n Bill or Uncle Henry, the men are kind, aging, and loyal. Capt'n Bill's description aptly portrays the type. A retired sea captain with a peg leg, he boards with the anonymous mother of an infant girl, Trot.

He loved the baby and often held her on his lap; her first ride was on Cap'n Bill's shoulders, for she had no baby-carriage; and when she began to toddle around, the child and the sailor became close comrades and enjoyed many strange adventures together. (Baum, 1915: 15)

This avuncular role is adopted by all of the human males from earth, so neither sexuality nor patriarchal authority is problematic. These gentle men try to form a protective circle around the little girls, although it is often the little girls who save these inept men.

A number of other males are even more peripheral. For example, Button-Bright is a little boy who is always wandering off and getting lost. He has little native intelligence but he is even-tempered.

This small boy, as perhaps you have discovered, was almost as destitute of nerves as the Scarecrow. Nothing ever astonished him much; nothing ever worried him or made him unhappy. Good fortune or bad fortune he accepted with a quiet smile, never complaining, whatever happened. This was one reason why Button-Bright was a favorite of all who knew him—and perhaps it was the reason why he so often got into difficulties, or found himself lost. (Baum, 1915: 213)

Another example of a human male is the Shaggy Man, a friendly and kindly hobo who enjoys being quite disheveled.

Males from Oz are similar to males from earth, like their female counterparts. Males from Oz, however, are more flawed than any other human type. For example, a small boy, Kiki Aru, wants adventure, even if he must do evil to obtain it (Baum, 1919). Another little boy, Tip, is very unhappy and naughty to his mean guardian, Mombi: "Tip frankly hated her and took no pains to hide his feelings. Indeed, he sometimes showed less respect for the old woman than he should have done, considering she was his guardian" (Baum, 1904: 9). Another adventurous lad, Ojo, has an Uncle, Unc Nunkie, who is silent and sad (Baum, 1913). Ojo's adventures are exciting, like the little girls', but he is never incorporated as a major character in subsequent books.

Summarizing the Human Characteristics

The little girls, especially Dorothy, are key figures in the Oz stories. These girls exhibit traits often found in children's stories about boys: a love for adventure, courage, fortitude, loyalty, intelligence, and good humor. The girls also display traditional feminine traits: they enjoy dressing up; they are affectionate, gentle, and noncompetitive. Little boys from earth are neither as innovative nor exciting as the girls. Older men are kindly and enjoy being with the girls. These men often fail in their brave efforts to protect the little girls, but their intentions and not their success or failure make them lovable. Both male and female humans from earth display more courage and dignity than their "human" Oz counterparts. All humans, regardless of sex and age, nurture and protect each other.

MAGICAL HUMANS

Like the human heroes, magical humans are usually females. Because these magical beings are witches and fairies, it stretches our imagination to call them humans. But they look, act, and speak like humans in Oz, except for their magical powers. Since they are sentient animals and animate objects, "humans" appears to be the most appropriate appellation. The magical humans are clearly liminal and anti-structural.

The Female Magical Humans

Glinda, the Good Witch, appears in all of the stories. She has godlike knowledge and no problem is beyond her powers to resolve. She is introduced in *The Wonderful Wizard of Oz*, and she is the only person who knows how to return Dorothy to Kansas. In this book, Dorothy "washes up" (a rite of purification) to prepare to meet Glinda. When Glinda meets Dorothy and her friends, the Good Witch sits on a throne of rubies. Baum (1902: 254) describes her in this setting: "She was both beautiful and young to their eyes. Her hair was a rich red in color and fell in flowing ringlets over her shoulders. Her dress was pure white; but her eyes were blue, and they looked kindly upon the little girl.''

Glinda has a Magic Book of Records documenting all actions as they occur (no bureaucrats needed here to amass this compendium). She has magic potions, spells, and knowledge. Ultimately, Glinda transforms the Wizard into a magical being. Without her help, he would have remained a humbug (the Wizard is discussed more fully in the next section).

The most important magical being after Glinda is Ozma, the ''rightful'' ruler and princess of Oz. Ozma first appears in the series as a boy, Tip (1904). This gender anomaly occurred when she was an infant and transformed into a male to hide her royal identity. The boy, Tip, is then raised by the Wicked Witch Mombi. Tip is hateful and resentful because of his ''socialization.'' Through the friendship and love of the animate objects around him, he gradually changes his spiteful behavior. By the end of *The Marvelous Land of Oz*, Tip is a generous and loving person, capable of ruling justly over a magical land. It is, of course, Glinda's intervention that makes her gender reversal and royal recognition possible.

Ozma is Dorothy's close friend, but she remains a ruler and authority figure throughout the remaining books. Sweet and demure, Ozma is also wise and magical. She owns the Magic Belt, which has the power to change humans into animals or objects and can take the wearer to any place requested. She also has a Magic Picture, which displays any person or event the viewer wishes to see. (A very magical form of television!) Every day at four o'clock, Ozma watches Dorothy to see if her friend needs her, and in this way many perilous adventures are happily resolved.

The wicked witches are a stark contrast to Ozma and Glinda. Although the two most notorious witches are killed by Dorothy in *The Wizard of Oz*, new ones keep appearing. Mombi, mentioned earlier, was such an evil woman.

There are also morally ''neutral'' beings called Yookoohoos whom Baum describes as ''the cleverest magic-workers in Oz'' (1918: 73). Because they are rarely interested in anyone or anything, Yookoohoos generally keep to themselves. They tend to do harm through their unwillingness to do good. But if their best interests coincide with the right thing to do, they will do it. If their interests are served by evil, however, they will do that, too. These ambiguously moral characters provide an interesting pivotal role in the struggle between good and evil underlying all of the Oz adventures. Rational argument and not justice appeals to these beings, who can act only within their magical human characters.

Despite this array of good, evil, and ambiguous morality, Ozma and Glinda are the most important magical beings. They are a formidable pair. They are traditionally beautiful and demure, but they are also the reigning powers of their realm and strong characters. They rule wisely and lovingly, sitting in judgment on those rare occasions when evil must be halted. These two beings are the public authority in Oz and they reign over a world striving for harmony and peace.

Male Magical Beings

In contrast to the female magical beings, the male magical beings are few in number and limited in power. Only the Wizard is a legitimate male magician, and this status is earned only after considerable training by Glinda. In the first few books, especially in *The Wonderful Wizard of Oz* (Baum, 1902) and *Dorothy and the Wizard in Oz*'' (Baum, 1908), the Wizard is a charlatan. His ability to con others is his only skill. He is not even a very talented con artist! When his sham is uncovered, he dithers a bit—he is lovable but helpless. He originally ''governed'' Oz by scaring the populace through the use of sound, wind, and light effects. They believed he was mighty and powerful and left his ruling claim unchallenged. Later in the series, he fortuitously obtains nine magical pigs who perform tricks, still remaining a somewhat foolish person. The Wizard is not mean-spirited; he tries to help others. His intrinsic goodwill is perceived by Glinda and she rewards him by bestowing upon him some magical skills.

Most of the male magical humans are quite evil. They like having power over others, and whenever they get any power, they misuse it. The Nome King is the most dastardly magical human, appearing in *Ozma of Oz* (Baum, 1907), *The Emerald City of Oz* (Baum, 1910), *Tik-Tok of Oz* (1914) and *The Magic of Oz* (Baum, 1919). In these books he tries to overthrow legitimate power and rules his ''people'' (i.e., the Nomes) and ''allies'' with an iron fist. Like human conquerors and invaders, the Nome King is greedy and ambitious. He is finally pushed into the Fountain of Forgetfulness because there is no other way that he could live in Oz without trying to destroy it. He is also deprived of his magical powers, especially the Magic Belt, and his rule over the Nomes.

Male magical beings range from stupidly harmful to deliberately harmful. Unlike females, male magical beings govern neither wisely nor well. For example, Dr. Pibt, the ''Crooked Magician,'' is patient and good, but he wastes the magical Powder of Life that can make inanimate objects come to life. He is ultimately prevented from using it. Ugu the Shoemaker tries to control Oz and dominate the land and its people. Bini Aru has similar ambitions and flaws. A few men, such as the Braided Man, are relatively harmless but they enjoy living alone and do not desire human friendship.

Summarizing the Magical Beings' Characteristics

Men's drives to dominate, control, and destroy are caricatured in the male magical beings. They are rarely able to use power without being corrupted by it. In contrast, female magical beings draw upon a love for others that consistently tempers their governance. Beautiful, generous, forgiving, loyal, and powerful, female magical beings are the ideal leaders and politicians.[1]

ANIMATE OBJECTS

Objects that are lifeless on earth can live and breathe in Oz. Such "things" can be created with totally new personalities and ways of acting, and Baum made these ways of being with others lovable and amusing. These "living" objects are a major part of the charm of the stories of Oz and reveal ways of being human that are truly anti-structural. In some ways, these living things have sex-linked characteristics, but in other ways, they are androgynous. Each "sex" is presented separately below and then jointly analyzed in a concluding section.

Female Animate Objects

The Patchwork Girl, Scraps, was made by the Crooked Magician's wife to do menial chores. Such prosaic plans, however, were immediately upset when Scraps came to life. Made from a patchwork quilt with red leather shoes and gold-plated fingernails, she is colorful, gay, and silly. Her brains are made of magical liquids for "obedience," "cleverness," "judgment," "courage," "ingenuity," "amiability," "learning," "truth," "Poesy," and "self reliance" (Baum, 1913: 38). Cleverness is the major ingredient taken from the "Brain Furniture," and Scraps turned into an amiable and often witty clown. Scraps "lives" to handspring and joke her way through many a tale. Like all other living objects, she does not need to eat or sleep. This gives her plenty of time to play and investigate the world around her. The Scarecrow thought she was a pleasing and amiable companion with a personality analogous to his own.

The only other female animate object is Polychrome, the Rainbow's daughter. More traditionally feminine in dress and style than Scraps, Polychrome always seeks the end of the rainbow so she can return home. Like the rainbow, Polychrome is a beautiful but fleeting character.

Female living objects are delightful but rarely appear in the stories. Male characters in this liminal status proliferate, however. They are flamboyant, well-developed actors with complex ties to each other, humans, and animals. They are strong foils to the adventures of the little girls who are the major human protagonists.

Male Animate Objects

The male "living" objects are delightful, numerous, and engagingly flawed. The Scarecrow, the Wooden Sawhorse, Jack Pumpkinhead, the Tin Woodman, the Gump, Tik-Tok, the Lavender and Pink Bears, and several other objects were given life in Oz. These beings each deserve a brief introduction to reveal their characters.

The Scarecrow and the Tin Woodman were introduced in *The Wonderful Wizard of Oz* and entered immediately into the American landscape of fairy tales. When Dorothy first saw "the queer, painted face of the Scarecrow, she was surprised to see one of the eyes slowly wink at her" (Baum, 1902: 36–37). She was even more astonished when he spoke to her. This was a particularly difficult feat considering the fact that the Scarecrow was stuffed with straw and did not have any brains. Shortly after meeting each other, they encounter the rusty Tin Woodman in the forest. Together, they go "off to see the Wizard, the Wonderful Wizard of Oz." After the auspicious beginning of their friendship, the Scarecrow and Tin Woodman appear in every subsequent book with varying degrees of importance. Each also has his own book and separate adventure (*The Scarecrow of Oz*, Baum, 1915; *The Tin Woodman of Oz*, Baum, 1918).

As dynamic and colorful as these two characters are, they are soon joined by others who are equally remarkable. Although the origins of the Scarecrow and Tin Woodman are based on the use of magic by humans, the subsequent animate objects were usually given life through an illicit magic powder. Thus Jack Pumpkinhead was fortuitously made from a stick figure that was designed to scare the wicked old witch, Mombi. Instead of being frightened, however, she saw him (it) as a test for the magic powder she had illegally obtained (Baum, 1904). The Wooden Sawhorse also came to life when Tip was escaping from this same witch. The Gump, a wildly improbable melange of a broomstick, sofas, and a "gump" (goatlike) stuffed head, similarly came to life to "save" humans escaping evil (Baum, 1904). Tik-Tok, the marvelous copper clock needing to be wound periodically, was made by highly superior watchmakers. He was a mixture of technology and "being" reminiscent of human robot fantasies (Baum, 1907, 1914).

These characters are mainstays in the stories, and Baum did not invent more living objects for several years. In 1917 he briefly introduced some "living stuffed teddy bears." One was a king, the Lavender Bear, and another was his Seer, the Pink Bear. These cuddly beings never played a major role again, however. Baum also created Captain Fyter, who was designed and animated by the same tinsmith who made the Tin Woodman (Baum, 1918). Again, this animate object plays only a brief role in the soon-to-be-ended series.

As a group, these animate objects play central roles in all of the books. They exhibit male characteristics in speech, dress, and name. They all reveal a playfulness with being male—providing a variegated, if not an innovative, masculine model. The Scarecrow has no brains, and the Tin Woodman wants a heart above all else and frequently weeps over this loss. Tik-Tok is patient and mild. Since he only needs to be wound up (and likes being polished), he can serve others logically and without complaints. Jack Pumpkinhead is vain and silly but very loyal. Always worrying about his potentially vulnerable head, looking ridiculous with his stick arms and legs, he always wears a smile and is helpful. The Gump is such a sorry mixture of objects that he chose to be "dismembered." Only his head remains animate (why the other parts did not remain alive is not explained). Since The Gump is a bit of a grump, he enjoys his continuing role as sarcastic commentator on others' lives. He prefers listening more than doing, a nonstereotypical male trait. Captain Fyter is a soldier and the most "masculine" character of all. But even he does not exhibit male jealousy when he discovers his former lover has married a man composed of his former body parts. Captain Fyter prefers the company of other living objects to that of competitive human males.

Summarizing the Animate Objects' Characteristics

The living objects provide a way to establish asexual characters who exhibit a range of strengths and humorous weaknesses. All of them are loyal and brave, but none need to eat or sleep. Since the majority of the animate objects are males, they provide a male cast of characters with a truly innovative range of natures that contrasts to Baum's heroines. These "men" are not fathers, brothers, husbands, sons, or lovers. Since these traditional male roles have priority in almost all literature or stories on women, Baum invented a way to have women and men relate anti-structurally. The characters themselves are "at play" and the humans play with them.

The strengths exhibited by these animate objects revolve around loyalty, love, friendship, and honesty. The traits that are most useful to capitalists and surely to bureaucrats are all absent. These living objects are liminal and do not intend to be human. Through animate objects, however, humans understand how to be human and most importantly how to love each other and accept differences.

This issue of "differences" is central to an understanding of animate objects. The superiority of animate objects is a frequent subject in the Oz books (1902: 53–54), and their major social claim lies in their uniqueness and right to equal recognition and treatment. In fact, they become rulers and heroes in Oz because of their invaluable, *different* ways of being in the world. The Baum formula clearly honors groups of people who are different. It provides a consistent view of how to value and enjoy these distinctions. The animate objects help humans on their journeys through Oz. They fit a traditional "trickster" role that is found frequently in nonmodern societies.

ANIMALS IN OZ

Animals in Oz speak to humans, and what they say is often funny. They retain their animal traits to the extent that they like to live in their natural habitats and exhibit stereotypical personalities and patterns. Thus the Hungry Tiger always wants to eat fat little babies, but because he has a conscience, he cannot. These animals, moreover, have gender-linked behavior.

Female Animals in Oz

There are only three female animals in Oz: Billina, a chicken, the Queen of the Mice, and Eureka, a cat. Billina squawks often and is very excitable. She is also courageous and it is her eggs that defeat the Nomes. Because a Nome can only be killed by an egg, even the threat of an egg is enough to control them. The Queen of the Mice helps the adventurers in Oz by helping them travel through illusions (Baum, 1902, 1904). Eureka is a well-behaved cat, although she likes to be off by herself. Her character is not well developed and she appears primarily in only one story (Baum, 1907). As a group, then, the female animals are not striking. Only Billina appears with some regularity, and in the majority of books it is only to strut around with her very large brood of chicks. This rather bland set of animals is very different from the male group who are colorful and central to the Land of Oz.

Male Animals in Oz

Two of the most lovable animals in Oz are the Cowardly Lion and the Hungry Tiger. Both are "marginal" animals in that they are always acting against their animal natures. The Cowardly Lion worries about many "unlionly" acts—being afraid, crying, or running away from attack. Since he does act bravely under extreme duress, his worst fears are unfounded. He creates such a fuss before acting, however, that we are convinced that he is afraid. Similarly, the Hungry Tiger is always mourning his lost meals. He looks on many people as tempting morsels but explains quickly that he is too good to actually eat them—although he *really* would like to. Both of these male animals violate not only their animal natures, but also their masculine ones. They moan and complain. Their large size makes them feel that they should be acting differently from what their emotions and ideas tell them is right. Since they always ultimately act correctly, their worries are unfounded but nonetheless tiresome.

H. M. Wogglebug, whose initials stand for "Highly Magnified," is a pretentious but not very intelligent bug. He became highly magnified when he was put under a microscope and his image was thrown on a screen. He walked off the screen at that point and remained in his highly magnified state (Baum, 1904). H. M. Wogglebug is also referred to by the initials "H. E.," which stand for "highly educated." Again the male traits of being authoritative and logical are mocked, for the wogglebug's information is usually wrong and not the least bit helpful.

A similarly pretentious character is the Frogman. He fell into a magical pond and became very large, approximately the size of humans. After eating and thereby "digesting" all the books in a library, he became the wisest being in the region. He caricatures a wise person, however, and tries to act superior to others (Baum, 1917). In the one story in which he figures prominently, he ends up humbled and, in fact, wiser.

Toto is Dorothy's little dog from Kansas, and he acts like a dog from earth in the majority of the books. Finally, Toto speaks in the later books, especially in *The Lost Princess of Oz* (1917), but his speeches are minimal and a bit whiny. His normal behavior is more lovable. He travels everywhere with Dorothy, tries to defend her when necessary, and always comforts her. His role is constant and generally woven into the story in myriad, low-key ways. He is Dorothy's dog and goes where she goes.

The Woozy is an animal found only in Oz. His primary use is as a necessary ingredient for a magical spell. He is good natured, however, and joins in the adventures of finding Ozma when she is lost (Baum, 1917).

All of these animals are humorous, good natured, and loyal. There is only one evil animal, and it is a magical one created by the evil Nome King. Called the Li-Mon-Eag, this creature is composed of parts of a lion, monkey, and eagle. It is designed to lead the animals of the forest in a war against Ozma and the humans. By lying to the animals and telling them they will be enslaved by humans, the wicked leaders twist the limited knowledge and intelligence of the animals. Such evil behavior, however, is not rooted in animal nature, but the human nature that created it.

COMPARING THE BAUM AND FREUD FORMULAS

Baum and Freud depicted two vastly different views of human action and possibility. Baum was optimistic about human growth, flexibility, and relationships, whereas Freud was pessimistic on these points. Baum emphasized the strength and goodness of women, especially little girls, while Freud emphasized the power and inevitable competitiveness of men. Baum's world is populated by people with platonic friendships and loving families while Freud's seethes with sexual drives and cathexes that are enmeshed in the ambivalent atmosphere of family relations. In both world views, men more than women want to rule others, but both sexes participate in this drive for power. Women in Baum's formula, moreover, are more powerful than men in the struggle for power, because goodness and right are on the side of women. This is not explained on the basis of biological goodness, but experienced and lived goodness that is learned through family and friends.

Baum views uniqueness as special, desirable, and certainly possible. Freud presents "the human" as limited within biological boundaries. All boundaries, even the limits of animals and objects, are transcended in Oz. Thus inanimate objects live, animals speak and think, and humans learn to interact with these forms of sentient life. Although the animals and objects can speak with humans only in Oz, the latent skill and right to dignity are present in animals and objects on earth. For Freud, the human is central and selfish in this centrality.

Family relations, too, are vastly dissimilar. For example, Dorothy's Aunt Em and Uncle Henry are loved and cherished, even with their flaws. The strong bonds of human affection are continually emphasized, and the ability to understand the other is central to these relationships. Modern life is often antagonistic to the poor farmer, animals, and children, but Aunt Em and Uncle Henry are exploited by this world even more than children are. For example, "Uncle Henry grew poorer every year, and the crops raised on the farm only bought food for the family. Therefore the mortgage could not be paid. At last the banker who had loaned him the money said that if he did not pay on a certain day, his farm would be taken away from him'' (Baum, 1910: 22). For Freud the family exists as a biological unit, and the pressures of bankers and mortgages are background issues. The family embodies the strength and weakness of the ambivalent human. Family relations are the root of human feelings: desire and repulsiveness, fear and nurturance, hatred and love. The family is the necessary curse of human existence. To the infant, the family becomes its stage for all important later dramas. Civilization is pictured, moreover, as the harsh represser of human drives and a barrier to the individual's attainment of pleasure.

On every central tenet of Freudian thought, Baum poses an alternate view. Clearly relying on both human nature and magic, Baum's utopia is nonetheless recognizable and inviting. Freud's nightmare of the conscious and unconscious is also recognizable and helps to order the chaotic world around us. Neither is seen here as *the* correct formula, but Baum's world does provide a vision for women that is far more enriching and ennobling than Freud's. Baum's formula is also an alternate way of constructing metaphors about life that have tapped the popular consciousness. It reveals the vastly unused potential to generate worlds where fathers and sons do more than vie for power, and women have more strength and dignity than a biological search for the impossible goal of attaining a male anatomy.

THE BAUM AND FREUD FORMULAS COMPARED TO THE DRAMAS OF GOFFMAN AND TURNER

The formulas of Baum and Freud have some parallels to the views of Goffman and Turner. Turner's and Arnold Van Genepp's work on *rite de passage* provides us with a rich theoretical framework for understanding the charismatic charm of the land of Oz and its denizens. Goffman's tactful and defensive vision is compatible with a Freudian view of the surface (i.e., ''performance'') behaviors of the tortured id and ego. The playful and loving vision of Turner fits the everyday and liminal behavior of Baum's land of Oz. This similarity in formulaic structure to the work of the social theorists is deeply embedded in their respective epistemologies. I want to be very clear, however, that I am not equating Goffman and Freud or Turner and Baum. I only point to their compatible frameworks for explaining and interpreting behavior. There is a logical consistency in these perspectives; their analyses, enactment, and dispersion through the mass media. These constructs and the public's way of constructing everyday life are interconnected (see Berger and Luckmann, 1966). From the formulas of Freud and Baum, ways to approach the world, the other, and the self are generated. Each approach has its own power to explain, to motivate, and to suggest solutions to problems. What is vital in my analysis, however, is that one formula emphasizes the process of male control and domination while the other emphasizes the process of human community and enrichment through love and cooperation. Both visions are attractive; both have the power to capture the imagination. Only one has the power to enhance the lives and times of little girls and women.

CONCLUSION

The marvelous land of Oz and its wonderful Wizard, Scarecrow, Tin Woodman, Cowardly Lion, and other characters comprise a beautiful utopia constructed of laughter and adventure. They point to human enjoyment and community that is vastly different from everyday life in America. Although such a magical land cannot exist, its literary and imaginary life have generated part of the everyday life and world view for its millions of readers (and movie, television, and dramatic audiences).[2] The social dramas generated by Baum become part of the ritual anti-structure of literary life in America. In this way, they are part of our celebration of life, community, and being human.

The Baum formula allows me to draw on our collective experience and memory to understand how alternate celebrations and epistemologies are made and enacted. It helps bridge the differences between Goffman's and Freud's pessimistic views of human possibility that are based on modern, Western societies and the optimistic views of Turner and Baum who seem to inhabit such far-away worlds and lands. Within our own world, anti-structure and playfulness are possibilities. These potential playful worlds, moreover, are attractive and charismatic even in a modern age. Such celebrations coexist with the more common "fun" rituals that try to hold communities together by drawing on ties welded through codes of oppression and repression. Rituals that incorporate the everyday inequality of American life into their structure are flawed yet necessary to an anemic community searching for its lifeblood. Baum's world reveals the playful possibilities of loving our homes, families, and friends. Although the vision is a juvenile one, it portrays an American vista of anti-structural communitas and a belief in our ability to understand each other—even if one of us is a human, a magical being, an animal, or a living and loving object. The horizon opened up by the Baum formula has been barely explored. I would like to end this chapter with a few playful suggestions for future adventures in Oz:

Freud Analyzes Ozma

Ozma Analyzes Freud

Captain Kirk in Oz

Ozma and the Federation

The Klingons' Invasion of Oz

Mr. Spock Meets the Cowardly Lion

Captain Dorothy and the Starship *Enterprise*

Glinda Helps Mr. Spock

The Patchwork Girl and the Oedipal Computer

These possibilities turn our attention to the interconnections between the separate rituals studied in this book and the potential to generate more liberating rituals.

NOTES

1. There is an interesting parallel here between Baum's portrayal of women as ideal civic leaders and the sociologist Jane Addams's fictional reversal of the suffrage question in her imaginative essay "If Men Were Seeking the Franchise" (1960). See also Mary Jo Deegan (1988).

2. The recent (1985) movie, *Return to Oz*, has been true to bounded parts of the Oz stories but consistently violates the Baum formula. The Dorothy character in the movie repeatedly screams in fear while the book portrays her as considerably calmer. A wicked witch grovels before the male Nome King in the movie, but the female witches are not portrayed this way in the novels. The friendly ties between the adventurers are loosely integrated in the film but tightly woven and supportive in the novels. Jack Pumpkinhead thought of Tip as "Father" in the book because he was the little boy who brought the pumpkin to life. But the movie version transforms this into Jack Pumpkinhead calling Dorothy his "Mom." These gender violations of the Baum formula result in an unworkable story. The movie is much closer to a Freudian formula, even using a psychologist to "analyze" Dorothy's "fantasies." Viewers unsatisfied with the "Walt Disney treatment" of the Baum formula will, I suspect, be delighted (as I was) by the entertaining, low-budget production of *The Marvelous Land of Oz* staged by the Minneapolis Children's Theater and now available on videotape.

PART IV

CONCLUSION

8

A Theory of Liberating Rituals

Rituals surround us; they are found in small settings for face-to-face encounters in "fun" places like bars and in large formal settings like stadiums that encompass thousands of people. They usually employ structural codes of oppression (e.g., sex and class) and repression (e.g., bureaucratization and the modern use of time) to generate "good times." Sex codes, in particular, are a continuing thread weaving otherwise diverse rituals together. Participatory rituals link rules for action with fun, while media-constructed rituals are more explicitly patterned and repetitious depictions of fun. Both types of rituals mix structural and anti-structural codes, and three examples of each type have been presented. In this chapter these examples are interpreted as components in a ritual landscape, providing new theoretical directions for analyzing American ritual as a phenomenon. I conclude by playing with some modest possibilities for liberating rituals.

RITUALS AND THEIR RELATIONS TO STRUCTURE AND ANTI-STRUCTURE: RITUAL ECHO AND THE CODES OF OPPRESSION AND REPRESSION

Everyday life in America is patterned on systematic codes of oppression and repression. Modern rituals operate in a context reinforcing these structures, notably sexism, capitalism, bureaucracy, and the controlled use of time. This nested hierarchy of power is reinforced by numerous "fun" experiences, and everyday reality is legitimated as "fair" and "inevitable." (The relations between structure and the rituals studied here are diagrammed in Table 8.1.) This ritual support of structural inequalities and limitations creates a community com-

Table 8.1

Participatory and Media-Constructed Rituals and Their Relations to Core Codes—The Ritual Echo

Type of Ritual	Ritual	Support Core Codes *
Participatory Ritual		
Singles bars	structure and anti-structure mix for face-to-face norms to meet the opposite sex	sex
Auctions	structure and anti-structure mix according to roles of buyers and sellers	class
Football	structure and anti-structure for large crowds of fans	sex class bureaucracy modern time
Media-Constructed Ritual		
Star Trek	structure and anti-structure according to Freudian Formula	sex
Fat-Letter Postcards	structure and anti-structure mix	sex class
Oz	anti-structure Baum Formula	none

* The core codes examined here are sex, class, bureaucracy, and the modern use of time. Each core code was not examined in each participatory ritual due to different foci of the original research. All core codes are examined, however, in the media-constructed rituals.

posed of alienated yet partially satisfied members, and this process of ritual enforcement of structure is called here "ritual echo."

An uneasy social and individual equilibrium is maintained. Cynicism; a continual pressure to display the "correct front"; and a distance between the self, the other, and the community are three ways of being in the world that are incorporated into the construction of the self. The ability to be "in the know" and have "good times" whenever possible provides individualistic opportunities to survive in a world that is structurally unjust.

All human societies fail to meet their ideal standards for action. This gap between the real and the ideal is part of the human condition. Herbert Marcuse called this the "repression" of civilization (1956). Modern society also generates what he calls "surplus repression," the social creation and maintenance of unnecessary suffering. Victor Turner's nonmodern societies are seen here as dealing with the repressions generated by all societies. In this way, ritual events provide meaning for the group, a mechanism to reincorporate the alienated and confused into a cohesive whole with the capacity to be flexible and sympathetic to the self and others. Modern society, however, creates many forms of surplus repressions. These inequities and limitations usually are abetted, not challenged, by ritual life. Our ritual structure is corrupted in a "surplus" way that mirrors our mundane existence. Thus women are placed at a ritual disadvantage in bars, auctions, and football games. They are depicted as weak and passive on *Star Trek* and they are invisible in FLPs. Each of these ritual contexts mirrors the others.

Variations abound, but a strong continuity exists. Thus "flirting" and (in a few episodes) bar scenes are found in *Star Trek* episodes; men in "real" bars mimic the strong, masculine models of the men of *Star Trek*; and women copy the self-presentations of mysterious and beautiful women in *Star Trek* who must fight to "get and keep" their men. (It should be noted that women who vie for the leaders of *Star Trek* always lose. The continuation of such a masochistic pattern is assumed by Freud to be normal behavior for women.) As mentioned in chapter 3, these same sexist behaviors are the norm at auctions, but because this lived experience was so oppressive for this researcher, such events could not be lived and repeatedly enacted for this study. Football games create a living drama of male aggression and social support for physically battering and "destroying" others. Thousands of times each year these football encounters are repeated and echo throughout our everyday lives.

Gaye Tuchman (1978) discussed the power of invisibility to annihilate women. This is amply displayed by FLPs, which seem to suggest that women are a very small minority of urban populations, less common than male native Americans or Hispanics. Rituals can, therefore, "echo" an absence of women as well as their typical presence. Rituals augment, build, reinforce, and maintain inequality, and they do so in a way that other forms of everyday life cannot.

Repressive codes are less frequently incorporated into ritual structure than oppressive ones. Only football blatantly includes hierarchical roles and the controlled time pressures of everyday life in its ritual structure. The repressive codes, nevertheless, structure many participatory rituals. For example, bars are closely timed from start to finish. "Closing time" and "last calls" change the pace of action and alter behaviors. Bureaucratic roles in everyday life enter into the meet/ meat market appraisal of the "other." Similarly, the ability to "spend time" at an auction is related to one's control over time and hierarchical roles in the wider society. FLPs represent the entrenched power structure but appear unchanged throughout time. Only the land of Oz is free from modern repressive structures. The men of *Star Trek*, however, often keep their hierarchical bosses distanced by time and space, and in many ways they act like independent agents with the ability and need to make decisions of their own. As pioneers on the frontiers of space and civilization, the men of *Star Trek* are "on their own."

The oppressive codes stand out as more entrenched in rituals as a set than the repressive codes. "Throwing off" repressive codes, or at least putting them in a less prominent position to order action, becomes part of the anti-structure of American rituals. The exceptional case of football merits attention.

Football is an especially male-identified sport. Although many women are fans, many other women work at being fans in order to "share the good times" with their male kin and friends. The football game is the everyday work life of men written large. The replaying of contests and conflicts on the football field particularly attracts men who identify with the battles. This does not mean that women are not engaged in the marketplace battlefield. I am noting only that the emotional bonds generated by repressive codes and football games are more attenuated for women than for men. Televised football games also serve different functions for men at home than for women. The home has a different relation to structure and anti-structure for each sex. Watching TV is leisure entertainment off the job for men whereas it is entertainment at the workplace for women. The need to attend closely to depicted action on the screen competes for women's attention and time that "should be" directed toward child care and housework. Men at home have "time to spend" while women at home have tasks that loom from "dawn to dusk." This analysis of football and its relation to the sexes moves the argument in a new direction—the linkages between participatory and media-constructed rituals, which are examined next.

THE RITUAL COLLAGE: CONNECTIONS BETWEEN PARTICIPATORY AND MEDIA-CONSTRUCTED RITUALS

Rituals exist within a world of rituals wherein the relationships between rituals create changing and unpredictable patterns. I call this the "ritual collage." Part of this collage is evident in the forgoing football analysis. I now extend this analysis by turning to *Star Trek*, one of the most powerful examples of the construction of the ritual collage. *Star Trek* started as a media-constructed ritual in 1963. Since then it has generated a participatory ritual, the *Star Trek* convention. Some fans at these conventions even dress and speak like their favorite fantasy figures and stories. Another *Star Trek* participatory ritual is the "trekkie club" that meets periodically, in small face-to-face groups, and in large gatherings across the country and around the world. A large number of related media-constructed rituals have been generated also in fanzines; paperback books; and commercial products like T-shirts, coffee mugs, and comic books. There are so many collectibles that there is a published catalog listing the prices of each *Star Trek* artifact. The power of *Star Trek* to create behavior is seen most dramatically with trekkies, but a more hidden impact on the social construction of reality coexists with this overt pattern. This subtle power is located in the augmentation of the ritual world provided by the series' formulaic action.

Each ritual is located in an array of ritual and mundane relations that can only be suggested here. The impact of football on American life, for example, is profound. Sex role socialization, the high school experience, and the social construction of the work world are a few potential areas that are directly affected by football ritual. As a faculty member at the University of Nebraska and a resident in Lincoln, Nebraska, for over a decade, I could write a separate chapter on just my experiences as a professor and resident that have been shaped by the Big Red ritual and its impact on my mundane life.[1] This tempting possibility, however, would turn my focus away from the work to be concluded, the analysis of rituals as extraordinary reality and experiences.

THE SYMBOLIC UNIVERSE AND RITUAL WORLD AS EMOTIONAL ANCHORS

The role of emotions in social life appears generally invisible to sociologists (Hochschild, 1979; 1983). Emotions have been defined as "irrational" and, therefore, outside the realm of legitimate scientific study. With this patriarchal logic, the common cement and reason for community and interpersonal action have been eliminated from sociological study. Erving Goffman is one of the few American sociologists to analyze emotion, but he has done so in a negative way. That is, Goffman has shown us the continual experience of cynicism: distance from the self, distance between the self and the other, and alienation. Although these are pervasive, problematic feelings and emotions in our society, they are not the only ones. These are the emotions generated by "surplus repressions and oppressions" and are not intrinsic to the human experience.

Rituals allow us to experience the other in a shared context of good times. They are social mechanisms to organize experiences in a group context (what Goffman calls "frames"). All of the rituals studied here exhibit anti-structure (see Table 8.2). If societies have no release from mundane reality, then their populace becomes systematically limited and stunted. There is a human need to celebrate and renew the community. This social need, a group as well as an individual one, is subverted and corrupted in America so that rules of repression and oppression form a background for "good times." The needs for love,

Table 8.2

Participatory and Media-Constructed Rituals and Their Relations to Core Codes—The Ritual Collage

Type of Ritual	Ritual	Challenges to Core Codes *
Participatory Ritual		
Singles bars	structure and anti-structure mix for face-to-face norms to meet the opposite sex	differential use of measured time, drugs and lighting: often includes music.
Auctions	structure and anti-structure mix according to roles of buyers and sellers	different use of time: "hypnotic" chant of auctioneer: barter economy: community event
Football	structure and anti-structure for large crowds of fans	communal/community event: pride of team/community
Media-Constructed Ritual		
Star Trek	structure and anti-structure according to Freudian Formula	anti-bureaucratic on ship (Federation is bureaucratic): non-capital economy
Fat-Letter Postcards	structure and anti-structure mix	pride of city: sign of travel
Oz	anti-structure Baum Formula	feminist, anti-bureaucratic: outside everyday time and space

* The core codes examined here are sex, class, bureaucracy, and the use of modern time. Anti-structure challenges these everyday values as well as other elements of everyday life.

communication, play, laughter, and a change of pace are channeled in such a way that they are linked to social inequality (see the relationship outlined in Tables 8.1 and 8.2). Generally, rituals in America use structural codes of sex, race, class, age, able-bodiedness, bureaucratization, and control of time in partially anti-structural contexts. This union of structure and anti-structure emotionally anchors us to inequality. As a people, we cannot imagine how we could transcend everyday life without being unfair and controlling. These emotional associations and patterns of meaning are beyond "rational" discussion. They point to what cannot be said but must be lived. Few people can point to times of playfulness, times when they have had fun without inequity as a part of the ritual process. Rituals as emotional anchors are not defined here as unconscious ties. This is not a Freudian explanation of behavior.

On the contrary, I posit that playful experiences and rules generate community bonds. Rituals cannot undo all social injustice or learned experience, but they can point the way to such new forms of being in the world. The process of creating a liberating and just society is predicated on the belief that the "other" can be understood; that the other can act in good faith, that self-presentation can reflect what can be and not merely a defense of what is. Rituals can provide a way to act with good faith toward the self and the other. Without a ritual basis of trust there is no everyday basis for instituting it. For all people, modern and nonmodern alike, to trust the other in everyday life is a daring leap from the real to the ideal. In modern society, such leaps are often foolhardy, stupid, and bound to fail. There are few others there to catch the acrobat who leaps across the distance of inequality and injustice. It is only by holding hands in a literal and metaphorical sense that liberation can occur.

Communitas provides a bridge to reality or lived experience that transcends the illusion of everyday life and the other as always corrupt. Communitas provides the individual with an emotional knowledge that allows trust to be built. The community becomes part of the self in a way that is incorporated and not segregated. The alienated individual who is always separated from the self and the other cannot move to another way of being in the world. The experience of communitas becomes a desirable, rewarding experience. It is a lived possibility of transcendence that is patterned by the group and lived by the individual (Durkheim, 1915).

THE FREUDIAN FORMULA AS A RITUAL ECHO AND EMOTIONAL BRIDGE

The Freudian formula is a peculiar ritual tool. Because it assumes that behaviors emanate from an unconscious, at least partially biological, realm, the Freudian world view is immune from direct attack. It is a "formal theory of the world" (Berger and Luckmann, 1966), legitimated through the practice of psychiatrists, psychoanalysts, and professors in universities. It is embedded in more informal theories in popular psychology, everyday language, and the mass media.

The Freudian formula as a formal theory is popular because it is one of the few systematic explanations of emotions. As noted earlier, social scientists, especially sociologists, rarely describe emotions as logical patterns. Only Freud has become a preeminent social scientist who explains emotions in such a way that his assumptions are incorporated as "informal" knowledge (Berger and Luckmann, 1966). Freudian assumptions are seen here as rules for organizing experience, story lines, and reality (Goffman, 1974). Freudian assumptions fit our everyday family life, social constructions of mental illness, and antipathy to others. No other popular social theory in America is so hostile toward the community and others. In Freudian theory, civilization is designed to thwart the desires of the individual. Each individual would be willing to make all others slaves. This extreme hostility to others is echoed in our rituals. The liberating potential of rituals to provide a key to understanding the other as similar to the self, a partner in social life, and part of a creative experience is thereby systematically truncated when Freudian formulas structure our rituals. The Freudian fear of the self and the other is incorporated in our rituals so that the "sexist ritual echo" is particularly strong. By linking the emotional tie associated with early family experiences to the sacred center of the posited unconscious, sexism is both desirable and repulsive; this ambivalence is legitimated as normal.

Criticisms of rituals are thereby ensnared in a system of logic and emotion similar to criticisms of Freudian thought. The critic is seen as hostile to others and "normally neurotic" at best, and the social creation of positive community is doomed to failure. Indeed, one reader of this manuscript responded that my analysis was "un-American." The compatibility between capitalism, sexism, and Freudianism has been dealt with in depth in a variety of books and analyses. What is important here is not a repetition of these critiques but an emphasis on the peculiar linkages between inequality, Freudian thought, and ritual patterns. The echoing process and emotional bridges to everyday life, formal epistemologies, and experiences are amplified to a towering height. Freudian thought can be structured as a popular formula, a continuity in the ritual collage, and mundane "common sense" in modern life. The outrage Freud called forth around the turn of the twentieth century appears today as a quiet echo of a few opposing rules and experiences in American rituals.

A CAUTIONARY LOOK AT COMMUNITAS

Communitas can limit the community if it stops at the level of ritual life. I posit here that the power to create a communal bond can be a source of momentum against inequality in everyday life. In a society controlled and governed by the community, this is a reasonable proposition. The power of modern society to manipulate the self and experience, however, is little understood. The communitas experience could potentially be controlled and manipulated in such a way that its liberating force is undermined. The ways that genuine playfulness could be subverted to a hegemonic goal are unknown at this time, but caution about its potential to be manipulated in a new way should be exercised. Popular culture is often seen to function in this way in Marxist critiques, but the argument advanced here is that popular culture in America generates fun, rarely play, and even more rarely (if ever) communitas. But my skepticism of modern society runs deep, and the potential to manipulate communitas for oppressive and repressive ends needs to be considered. We must wait, however, for more communitas experiences to be realities before we can document their subversion.

CONNECTING THE RITUAL ECHO AND COLLAGE AS EMOTIONAL ANCHORS TO INEQUALITY

American rituals are structural patterns to reinforce and not transcend everyday life. Inequalities are echoed in our rituals and become wedded to our emotional understanding of ourselves and community. Fun fundamentally draws us to inequality in ways that are difficult to understand given the brutal consequences of injustice. Everyday life and the community are seen as naturally a part of a game, competitive, strange, and always a bit alien. This community of strangers is incorporated in the self through ritual and thereby becomes understandable. Our communities are as untrustworthy as we are. As *Star Trek* repeatedly tells us, it is the alien in ourselves who is most treacherous.[2] The Freudian and Goffmanian view tells us we must embrace cruelty, sneakiness, and injustice. We must incorporate this "reality" and protect our selves by presenting fronts that are kind and benign. The appearance of kindness is socially exchanged, and this appearance is the biggest joke. In this distorted ritual world we feel that if we lose inequality we lose our paths to good times. Our emotional anchors to meaning—which are themselves suspect—provide order for a world of disorder and inequality.

Our present rituals are not alien to inequality but keys to understanding it on an emotional level. Moments of transcending human differences are linked to a particular individual or a particular community and not to a generalized, non-specific other. The other is seen as the threat to meaning and its source, and the difference between inauthenticity and authenticity cannot be seen. Thus many people do not find it incongruous to enjoy *Star Trek*, football, and *The Wonderful Wizard of Oz*—despite the contradictory rules underlying these rituals. They are parts of the American ritual collage and embedded in our experience. Pointing out the existence of degrees of anti-structural rituals, the different experiences associated with them, and the possibility to move in directions that do not echo old experiences but speak to new ones can reveal the liberating potential of rituals. Examples of such new ways of acting can now be considered.

Rituals as Celebration and Liberation: Playful Possibility

Rituals and everyday life stand in a multilectical relation (Deegan, 1984). By this I mean that rituals both support and conflict with everyday life. Different rituals have different relationships to the mundane world, and the ritual world itself can reinforce echoes or challenge patterns within the ritual collage. Because of this range of relationships, structures, and anti-structures, a variety of experiences and ends are possible. Ordinary and extraordinary realities can lead to emancipation and communitas or to repression and alienation. T. R. Young articulates these choices well when he writes that: "Language systems can be organized to create a rich information and interactional field within which the uniquely human labor of reality constitution may transpire or the media may be organized to exclude, restrict and produce patterned activity in non-human modalities" (1982: 2).

This does not mean that these are always dichotomous choices. It is this ambiguity of ritual life that continues to sustain it even when it generates alienation and fun rather than communitas and play. The healing of communal life that is needed to generate modern, emancipatory rituals is considerable. Our communities need to elaborate on our heritage while ruthlessly discarding our cherished rituals of oppression. As Young has explained, such a change requires that "an entire society must be involved—a public sphere must be created" (1982: 10). This creative process is the final focus of my exploration of American drama and ritual.

Emancipatory Rituals as Enacted Liberation

Turner (1967) allows us a peek into ritual worlds filled with "forests of symbols," communal bonds that enrich daily life, and the dramatic production of extraordinary reality. From his elaborated understanding of positive anti-structures, a model for modern society can be generated. We can begin our journey toward new forms of community life by drawing upon our own heritage, experience, and understanding of oppression and repression. Our understanding of everyday structure illuminates the alternate structures that play with our human potential.

Many of the rituals examined in this text depend on modern technology and communication systems to create worlds of fun. This technology is frequently used for hegemonic messages linking systems of inequality to communal experiences, thereby subverting the goal of emancipatory rituals. Therefore a key step in undoing this system of control is to engage in collective, democratic control over rituals.

The forms of authentic social knowledge, in this view, do not arise from objective methods of social science disseminated by lecture, books, documentaries, and journals but rather by intersubjective participation in creating social life worlds. One can learn a bit about Eskimo life or about bureaucratic life from print or from film but creative participation in the production process is necessary for authentic knowledge. (Young, 1982: 7)

Emancipatory rituals must be controlled, defined, and enacted by the participants. They articulate their experience and generate the meaning of their lives in the process.

Rituals that generate communitas must play with everyday structure. We need to laugh at ourselves, disregard our divisions, and enact topsy-turvy rules. Anti-structure can be spun off and woven from its direction against everyday life. Rituals need to be recognized as significant events that are responsive to human needs and demands.

Following the work of Ivan Illich (1973), we can redefine our alienating technology to enhance daily life. Celebrations can be guided by playfulness toward technology as well as toward each other. The orientation of the creative process toward "tools of conviviality" reveals the true emancipatory relation between humans and their products. Ideas controlled by the people and enriched by their creative energy and technological skills can yield new forms of celebration that learn from the past, build a meaningful present, and generate anticipation of a joyful future.

Emancipatory Society

Emancipatory rituals are only one step toward a liberated society. The description and enactment of celebrations that create playful experiences for all members of the community is only a beginning. Such emancipatory rituals must be connected to the larger society and not be bounded by the limited context that they generate. Communitas, therefore, must be related to alienation in everyday life in order to generate a liberating society. Human emancipation in everyday life "is oriented to the reunification of production and distribution; to the reunification of self and society; as well as the reunification of subjective and objective knowledge" (Young, 1980: 3).

The core codes of everyday life fit a tightly woven and powerful pattern of control by males and capitalists who govern a social order that is bureaucratized and inhumanly timed. This pattern generates systematic inequalities and deep divisions between people in American life. These abysses are accentuated within the self and relations to others, so a cycle of alienation and inauthenticity is institutionally reinforced and maintained. "Good times" generated by modern rituals are emotional resources that are connected with the draining effect of hegemonic control over technology and work. Communitas, however, is a potential lever to move the disenfranchised into positions of true democratic control. We need to move out of the present situation that uses hegemony to spin a deceitful web of images and experience that link our emotions to oppression and repression. Emancipatory experiences can be generated by anti-structural rituals, which in turn allow the individual to believe that the community represents the self, and the self represents the community.

I reanalyze some of the strengths of the enacted rituals examined earlier and propose some possibilities of emancipatory rituals arising from Turner's model and my analysis. Such suggestions can only be offered as possibilities for communities and participants to consider, in order to turn around from where we are to where we could be.

The Emancipatory Possibilities of Bars, Sports, and Auctions

Anti-structural elements have existed in each of the popular events examined here. These patterns have been noted in passing, but here this creative potential is stressed, examined, and elaborated.

Bars

Pubs, inns, and the local tavern have long been settings for communal talk and relaxation. Traditionally male worlds, they have nonetheless provided a haven that is often dimly lit, conducive to experiential changes through the use of alcohol, and centers for music and dancing. Entry into a bar can be a step into this extraordinary reality that is loosely oriented toward the control of time (during licensed hours!) and bureaucratic decision making and authority.

My analysis of the meat/meet market ritual stressed its male bias, its inauthentic evaluations of the other as sex object, and the stress on anonymity and interchangeability of the other. To turn this inauthenticity around, it is necessary that the meeting occur in a situation of equality. Commodization must be seen as an alien and alienating process so that evaluation of the self and the other shifts to more authentic "keys" or ritual transformations of everyday life to introduce people to sexually desirable others. Mystery, music, and tension are creative environments for sexuality. The desire to be seen and to see within a sexual perspective are human ways of being that celebrate life. Rituals of polite disinterest are needed, and all such rituals of meeting and avoiding a meeting must be available to all who participate. Patterned discrimination must be defined as a violation of trust. The group needs to disapprove of such ritual violations of the other. Their actions need to be tied to the possibilities of communitas while they are loosened from the bonds of alienation. Sexual encounters create tension, vulnerability, and playfulness. The attempt to meet the other sexually is in itself a liminal passage and the generation of meeting places can be part of the community process of celebration.

Sports

The word "sports" is substituted here for the specific sport of football. This particular sport so idealizes the core codes of present American life that it is hard to imagine its return to the community and to playfulness. The elaboration of football as a big money-maker and a corporate symbol of male power under bureaucratic management has enmeshed it in a male world of elite control. Touch football is the football style that appears to be available to the general community and avoids many of the violent physical confrontations that are intrinsic to the rules of the more violent game.

Sports, however, have a vast resource of celebratory energy and creativity. The popularity of many sports such as jogging, marathons, tennis, and racquetball exhibits this potential to use the body in extraordinary ways, to experience physical and mental changes, and to relate to others in a playful context. Recent popular elaboration of celebratory running is particularly creative and liberating. The large number of runners, the development of short, "fun" runs, the easily accessible "award" of T-shirts that proclaim the person as participant, the easy entry requirements that allow many people to enter, the frequent lack of bureaucratic management, and the development of goals of "running the course" instead of "winning against the enemy" are excellent examples of liberating, anti-structural components. The elaboration of sports for both sexes to celebrate is a crucial aspect of emancipatory sports.

The search for excellence in skill and art is part of the sport ritual. Entry in contests and public events allows for the generation of rituals. Amateur status is not the only way to generate emancipatory sports, but the linkage of sports to the corporate world, nationalism, and elite control over technology has led to a peculiar kind of control over sports that generates an alienated spectator and athlete. Emancipatory sports return control over the events to the community and participants and divest sports from their association with patriarchal power and female passivity.

Auctions

In many ways, auctions do provide members of the community with ways to exchange goods that violate everyday norms of doing business. They also allow the participants to peek into private lives, be entertained, and be lulled by the voice of the auctioneer. These aspects of auctions are part of their present attraction. The avarice of the crowd and occasionally the auctioneers, however, flaws these events. The ability to attend auctions to get "good deals" is directly tied to our labor structure. Those who control their time can afford to exchange it for good deals at auctions. Auctions are intrinsically part of a capitalist society because they are rooted in the desire to obtain goods at less than market value through an unusal "spending" of time.

Auctions also have a negative possibility in terms of scarce community objects. I am referring here to the big art auctions that create a "highest bidder" owner who represents more than an individual interest. Thus an entire country may find that it cannot afford its finest cultural artifacts. European art, in particular, is being systematically bought by rich private collectors who hoard beautiful visions as private commodities. The tradition of a people becomes a commodity to show the good taste of rich capitalists.

Communities based on closer ties and commitments to communal and not private property do not enter into these forms of exchange. A capitalist, modern society makes such community integrity and control untenable. People must choose between material goods to physically survive versus idealistic riches that enable them to live as people of honor. Personal gift-giving ceremonies, such as the Potlach ceremony in some Native American communities, generate more of a sense of community than auctions do. If there were no capitalistic markets, there would be no auctions.[3]

Emancipation and Media-Constructed Rituals

A modern public depends on "experts" in popular culture. Though the public has some control over popular artists through the public's use of money and the occasional appearance of a folk leader, in a much larger sense the public is controlled through the vast cultural industry that markets popular culture.

I have analyzed three types of American media-constructed rituals. Each media-constructed ritual involves the time, money, and talents of many people. Architects, planners, directors, producers, authors, publishers, salespeople, illustrators, actors, agents, and a host of others are employed in the "creation" of these rituals (Becker, 1982; Hill, 1984). Clearly, the role of the public in a democracy is primary to a liberating society. The creative process is both part of a people and distinct from it. It articulates the dreams and fantasies of a group and it forms them. It emerges from leaders and followers. Critiques of the culture industry and the artistic process have not been the focus of this book. These tantalizing issues would only lead me away from the study of the community and its ritual life. So I will return to my empirical analyses of media-constructed rituals to examine our multilectical relation between rituals and everyday life.

The development of anti-structural fantasies is part of the creative process. The community has a role in this process by demanding that stereotypical images of the disenfranchised be excised from times of celebration. Exploring the social process of generating oppression and repression through good times is another creative way to examine who we are as a people and why we defend community hostilities with such vehemence. A conscious understanding of the power of media formulas, such as the Freudian formula, can aid creators and audiences to interpret the message more creatively and reflexively. Knowledge about the generation of emotions and experiences within a community becomes a tool of liberation. The community becomes an active participant through such knowledge, as well as having the more traditional, albeit limited, powers of spending individual capital to have fun. Examples of how the public can enter the creative process for liberating rituals are presented below.

Postcards

New codes for depicting the city would celebrate the activities of all participants. The depiction of unique characteristics of each urban place, playful views of the populace and area, and the generation of fantasies of the city allow for a wide repertoire of vital images of urban life and experience. These playful images could vary considerably for each city. One select group of people or things need not be used. Variety in the categories and images provides an element of playfulness to counteract the tendency to have certain images gain disproportionate power and thereby suppress minority images.

Photographic techniques give us a "tool of conviviality" that opens the horizon of possibilities. Some of the fantasy photographs found on expensive stationery and postcards reveal this playfulness. Depictions of New York City as a large spaceship or Chicago being stalked by large pink flamingos are excellent images of anti-structural celebrations. Many of these "contemporary" cards, however, repeat the same old formulas, especially sexist ones, and the cost of these artifacts is often high. But these images and technology point to a liberating potential and its contemporary enactment.

Star Trek

Playful trekkies have already generated myriad visions of alternate worlds. This body of cultural lore and artifacts needs to be examined in light of its emancipatory potential. It is quite possible that a large anti-structural world has already been generated but not mass produced. The liberating potential of the *Star Trek* fantasy has been carried on by a public who has led the culture industry back to this previously discarded series. The trekkies are an excellent example of a group who wants more than the "experts" thought they should have. This laudatory view of the power of the people in reference to the series should be noted cautiously. For the latest movies produced by the massive culture industry have repeated the Freudian formula underlying the series as a whole.

The exploration of "bold new worlds" has barely begun. Females who struggle for power, men who search for love, the possibility of emancipatory relations within the same sex, between opposite sexes, and within gender-mixed groups could all be explored. There is no end to human imagination that traverses the universe and our experience of space and time. *Star Trek* has the anti-structural potential to be anything, anywhere, anytime. The extension of communitas to women in the series would break through the sexist barriers that have kept it restricted to the core codes of a patriarchal society. The exploration of new myths of creation; the trickster figure, who plays jokes on a populace (this was briefly and tentatively explored in "Shore Leave"); and the various forms of power and the struggle for a community to be vital and emancipatory are all avenues open to the crew of the *Enterprise*.

A critical examination of the Freudian formula is particularly needed. Although this is clearly an economically successful formula, it denotes a creative dead end for the series. The sexist vision that is incorporated in the rules limits the series. An emancipatory public would see such repetitive scenarios as tedious. A key to the power of the series lies in the characters and their relationships to each other. It would be easy to extend these relationships into other dimensions to provide new sources of vitality and authenticity. An attempt to portray the issue of aging space explorers has been timidly added to the movies. This suggests the more daring idea that even the old can take risks and successfully meet them.

A public that is organized, like the trekkies, can demand and create more creativity.

The Baum Formula: Oz Is Everywhere in Fantasy

The Baum formula transcends Oz. It is a powerful American folktale in opposition to the culture industry and its entrepreneurial "experts." The Baum formula emerges from an American tradition, is accepted by the common people, and is playful. It immediately comes to mind as an alternate formula for the *Star Trek* series. Dorothy and Toto also provide an identifiable and positive image of Kansas. (There are now playful license plates characterizing the state as the "Land of Ahhhs," an obvious transpositional play on "Oz.") For example, a picture of this pair could be used on fat-letter postcards of Kansas to show a female, a dog, a child, and the love of Kansas as a home. This is a symbol unique to the state and could be commemorated in statues and parks. Baum has provided a kind of "lever for emancipation" that is a part of our heritage.

The Baum formula has been a loved component of American life for decades. It was greatly augmented by the successful movie portrayal starring Judy Garland, among others, that has been shown annually on television for many years. There is no need to see this formula as rooted in Oz. It is a cultural innovation and has the potential of being a formula that crosses the genres of Westerns and romances. The use of a female heroine, who exhibits powerful behavior while she is both moral and gentle, is a clear alternate to the Oedipal myth permeating our cultural life. Dorothy's friendships with others who are different, her development of a personal world independent of men, and the desire to have a zesty and adventurous life are all components of the Baum formula. The formula could be expanded and elaborated in cultural artifacts and ritual events. It could point the way to an egalitarian everyday life and new formulas that have yet to be discovered.

Emancipatory Knowledge and Critical Dramaturgy

Critical dramaturgy is a way to approach the problems and the creativity of human life. This book is an analysis of the complex way in which oppression and repression are generated by our ways of having fun. Modern life uses new forms of technologies that are channeled through traditional forms of control by men and the economic elites. Since we are often alienated and exploited in everyday life, our good times are increasingly significant forms of control. This control is disguised through fun that alienates while partially easing the pain of everyday life. This interaction between the celebratory and the structurally limiting has created powerful emotional ties to ways of being that are relatively impervious to social critique and change.

Critical dramaturgy reveals hegemonic control and the experiences of healing and renewal that are the bases for human loyalty and meaning. American rituals are part of our heritage and historical location that reflect our unique way of thinking about the world and everyday life. The subversion of this uniqueness, the failure to generate democratically controlled rituals, and the disconnection between everyday life and a healing ritual life divides us as a people.

New rituals of celebration require critical analysis to avoid generation forms of control with even more sophisticated disguises and more powerful methods to alienate and destroy the community. Critical analysis is part of an emancipatory society, but it is part of everyday life and not extraordinary reality. Emancipatory rituals and celebrations require the suspension of critical reflection and immersion of the self with the other in a playful world.

We are a creative people with the potential to control our play and work. Barriers to authenticity can be dismantled by a liberated society that understands its dreams and its everyday life. But we are presently caught in a world that is not liberating, and we live with rituals that capture our hearts and emotions in nets woven from hatred and division. There is no easy way to achieve an emancipatory society, but the generation of rituals becomes a playful way to start.

Let the play begin!

NOTES

1. I was surprised to find my experiences with Nebraska football echoed in the lives of my sociological predecessors at the University of Nebraska who worked there eighty years before me: George Howard (Williams, 1929: 230) and Edward Ross. Ross's insights are particularly relevant here:

In those days we played baseball and football *for fun*; we did not testify to our ardor for sport by sitting inert on the bleachers in the fall afternoons watching the 'varsity football eleven practice again the "scrub" team, while not one person showed up on the tennis courts! When, years later, at the University of Nebraska, I discovered what a farce "student interest in athletics" and " 'varsity spirit" had come to be, I turned my back contemptuously on the whole business. In thirty-five years I have not witnessed a football game. When I quit work I *play* rather than *watch others play*. (Ross, 1936: 14; italics in the original)

2. On the "Oprah Winfrey Show," a television talk show (April 28, 1987), a male guest (a financial management consultant) exemplified this point when he asserted in reference to how to get ahead in the business world: "The real enemy you must face every day is the one you see in the mirror when you are shaving." His sexist assumption about shaving—and who it is that really gets ahead—no doubt follows from his fundamentally deeper Freudian premise about the enemy within.

3. See also my analysis of surrogate mothering, ritual, and the gift relation in "The Gift Mother" (1987b).

Bibliography

Addams, Jane.
1960   If men were seeking the franchise. In *Jane Addams: A Centennial Reader*, edited by Emily C. Johnson. New York: Macmillan, pp. 107–13.

Babcock, Mike.
1988   Formula isn't simple for NU athletic budget. *Lincoln Star* (19 April): 11.

Bailey, Margaret.
1976   *Live Long and Prosper*. New Brunswick, NJ: Graduate School Library Service.

Barrett, Michelle, and Mary McIntosh.
1982   *The Anti-Social Family*. London: Verso.

Baum, L. Frank.
1902   *The Wonderful Wizard of Oz*. Chicago: The Reilly and Lee Co.
1904   *The Marvelous Land of Oz*. Chicago: The Reilly and Lee Co.
1907   *Ozma of Oz*. Chicago: The Reilly and Lee Co.
1908   *Dorothy and the Wizard in Oz*. Chicago: The Reilly and Lee Co.
1909   *The Road to Oz*. Chicago: The Reilly and Lee Co.
1910   *The Emerald City of Oz*. Chicago: The Reilly and Lee Co.
1913   *The Patchwork Girl of Oz*. Chicago: The Reilly and Lee Co.
1914   *Tik-Tok of Oz*. Chicago: The Reilly and Lee Co.
1915   *The Scarecrow of Oz*. Chicago: The Reilly and Lee Co.
1916   *Rinkitink of Oz*. Chicago: The Reilly and Lee Co.
1917   *The Lost Princess of Oz*. Chicago: The Reilly and Lee Co.
1918   *The Tin Woodman of Oz*. Chicago: The Reilly and Lee Co.
1919   *The Magic of Oz*. Chicago: The Reilly and Lee Co.
1920   *Glinda of Oz*. Chicago: The Reilly and Lee Co.

Beauvoir, Simone de.
1953   *The Second Sex*. Trans. and edited by H. M. Parshley. New York: Knopf.

Becker, Howard.
1982   *Art Worlds*. Berkeley: University of California Press.

Berger, Peter L., Bridgette Berger, and Hans Kellner.
1973   *The Homeless Mind*. New York: Vintage Books.

Berger, Peter L., and Thomas Luckmann.
1966   *The Social Construction of Reality*. New York: Doubleday.

Bird, Frederick.
1980   The contemporary ritual milieu. In *Rituals and Ceremonies in Popular Culture*, edited by Ray B. Browne. Bowling Green, OH: Popular Culture Press, pp. 19–35.

Blish, James.
1972   *Star Trek 5*. New York: Bantam Books.
1976   *The Star Trek Reader*. New York: E. P. Dutton.

Brisset, Dennis, and Charles Edgley.
1975   *Life as Theater: A Dramaturgical Sourcebook*. Chicago: Aldine.

Brothers, Joyce.
1980   Can men find happiness as sex objects? *Cosmopolitan* 189 (November): 92, 94, 98, 188.

Broverman, I. K., S. R. Vogel, D. Broverman, F. Clarkson, and P. S. Rosenkrantz.
1970   Sex role stereotypes and clinical judgements of mental health. *Journal of Consulting and Clinical Psychology* 34:1–7.

Browne, Ray B.
1980   Ritual one. In *Rituals and Ceremonies in Popular Culture*, edited by Ray B. Browne. Bowling Green, OH: Popular Culture Press, pp. 1–18.

Cavan, Sherri.
1966   *Liquor License: An Ethnography of Bar Behavior*. Chicago: Aldine.

Cawelti, John G.
1969   The concept of formula in the study of popular literature. *The Journal of Popular Culture* 3(Winter): 381–90.
1976   *Adventure, Mystery and Romance*. Chicago: University of Chicago Press.

Clark, Robert E., and Larry J. Halfard.
1978   Going . . . going . . . gone: Some preliminary observations on deals at auctions. *Urban Life* 7(October): 285–307.

Combs, James E., and Michael W. Mansfield.
1976   *Drama in Life*. New York: Hastings House.

Czikzentmihalyi, Mihaly.
1975a   Play and intrinsic rewards. *Journal of Humanistic Psychology* 15(Summer): 41–63.

1975b   *Beyond Boredom and Anxiety: The Experience of Play in Work and Games.*
         San Francisco: Jossey-Bass.

Deegan, Mary Jo.
1972   The meat market ritual. *Society* 2(November/December): 11.
1978   The social dramas of Erving Goffman and Victor Turner. *Humanity and Society*
         2(February): 33–46.
1983   Feminists frame *Star Trek. Free Inquiry in Creative Sociology* 11(November):
         182–88. (See also a longer version in *Contribution to the Sociology of the Arts.*
         Sofia, Bulgaria: ISA Research Committee, Research Institute for Culture, 1983,
         pp. 486–504.)
1984   Feminist epistemology. Paper presented at the Midwest Sociological Society,
         Chicago, April.
1985   Multiple minority groups. In *Women and Disability: The Double Handicap,*
         edited by Mary Jo Deegan and Nancy Brooks. New Brunswick, NJ: Transaction
         Books, pp. 37–55.
1987a   Symbolic interaction and the study of women. In *Women and Symbolic Inter-
         action,* edited by Mary Jo Deegan and Michael R. Hill. Winchester, MA: Allen
         and Unwin, pp. 3–15.
1987b   The Gift Mother. In *On the Problem of Surrogate Parenthood: Analyzing the
         Baby M Case,* edited by Herbert Richardson. Lewiston, NY: Edwin Mellen
         Press, pp. 91–105.
1988   *Jane Addams and the Men of the Chicago School, 1892–1918.* New Brunswick,
         NJ: Transaction Books.
Forthcoming. The female pedestrian: The dramaturgy of structural and experiential bar-
         riers in the street. Man-Environment Systems.

Deegan, Mary Jo, and Michael R. Hill.
1983   The symbol of the city on fat-letter postcards. Paper presented at the Popular
         Culture Meetings, Toronto, Canada, April.
1987   *Women and Symbolic Interaction.* Boston: Allen & Unwin.

Deegan, Mary Jo, and Valeria Malhotra.
1977   Symbols in the thought of Alfred Schutz and George Herbert Mead. *Interna-
         tional Journal of Symbology* 8(March): 34–45.

Deegan, Mary Jo, and Michael Stein.
1977   Pornography as a strip and a frame. *Sociological Symposium* 20(Fall): 27–44.
1978   American drama and ritual: Nebraska football. *International Review of Sport
         Sociology* 13(December): 31–44.

Deford, Frank.
1971   *There She Is: The Life and Times of Miss America.* New York: Viking Press.

Denzin, Norman K.
1970   *The Research Act.* Chicago: Aldine.

Durkheim, Emile.
1915   *The Elementary Forms of the Religious Life.* Trans. by J. W. Swain. London:
         George Allen and Unwin.

Eisenstein, Zillah R., ed.
1979   *Socialist Feminism and the Case for Capitalist Patriarchy*. New York: Monthly Review Press.

Engels, Friedrich.
1972   *The Origin of the Family, Private Property and the State*. Intro. and notes by Eleanor B. Leacock. New York: International Publishers.

Erisman, Fred.
1968   L. Frank Baum and the Progressive Dilemma. *American Quarterly* 20(Fall): 616–23.

Farrell, Warren.
1974   *The Liberated Man*. New York: Random House.

Ferguson, Kathy E.
1984   *The Feminist Case Against Bureaucracy*. Philadelphia: Temple University Press.

Filstead, William J., ed.
1970   *Qualitative Sociology: Firsthand Involvement with the Social World*. Chicago: Markham.

Fine, Gary Alan.
1980   Frames and fantasy games. Paper presented at the American Sociological Association Meetings, August, New York City.

Firestone, Shulamith.
1971   *The Dialectic of Sex: The Case for Feminist Revolution*. New York: Morrow.

Fox, Greer L.
1977   Nice girl. *Signs* 2(4): 805–17.

Freud, Sigmund.
1905   Three essays on the theory of sexuality. Standard edition of the *Complete Psychological Works* (hereafter, SE), vol. 7, pp. 125–245.
1913   *Totem and Taboo*. SE, vol. 13, pp. 1–61.
1917   Introductory Lectures on Psycho-analysis. SE, vol. 14, pp. 69–102.
1925   Some Psychical Consequences of the Anatomical Distinction Between the Sexes. SE, vol. 19, pp. 243–58.
1930   *Civilization and Its Discontents*. SE, vol. 21, pp. 59–145.
1939   *Moses and Monotheism*. SE, vol. 23, pp. 3–182.

Friedan, Betty.
1963   *The Feminine Mystique*. New York: Norton.

Garfinkle, Harold.
1963   A conception of, and experiments with, "trust" as a condition of stable concerted actions. In *Motivation and Social Interaction*, edited by O. J. Harvey. New York: The Ronald Press, pp. 187–238.
1967   *Studies in Ethnomethodology*. Englewood Cliffs, NJ: Prentice-Hall.

Geertz, Clifford.
1973   *Interpretation of Cultures*. New York: Basic Books.

Gerrold, David.
1974   *The World of* Star Trek. New York: Ballantine Books.

Giddens, Anthony.
1973   *The Class Structure of Advanced Societies*. New York: Harper and Row.
1984   *The Constitution of Society*. Berkeley: University of California Press.
1985   *The Nation-State and Violence*. Berkeley: University of California Press.
1987   *Social Theory and Modern Sociology*. Stanford: Stanford University Press.

Glaser, Barney G., and Anselm L. Strauss.
1967   *The Discovery of Grounded Theory: Strategies for Qualitative Research*. Chicago: Aldine.

Goffman, Erving.
1959   *The Presentation of Self in Everyday Life*. New York: Doubleday.
1961a   *Asylums: Essays on the Social Situation of Mental Patients and Other Inmates*. Garden City, NY: Doubleday.
1961b   *Encounters: Two Studies in the Sociology of Interaction*. New York: Bobbs-Merrill.
1963a   *Behavior in Public Places: Notes on the Social Organization of Gatherings*. New York: Macmillan.
1963b   *Stigma: Notes on the Management of Spoiled Identity*. Englewood Cliffs, NJ: Prentice-Hall.
1967   *Interaction Ritual: Essays on Face-to-Face Behavior*. New York: Anchor Books.
1969   *Strategic Interaction*. Philadelphia: University of Pennsylvania Press.
1974   *Frame Analysis: An Essay on the Organization of Experience*. New York: Harper and Row.
1976   "Gender Advertisements." *Studies in the Anthropology of Visual Communication* 3, no. 2 (Fall). "Gender Display," "Picture Frames," and "Gender Commercials," pp. 69–95.
1977   The arrangement between the sexes. *Theory and Society* 4 (Fall):301–31. Reprinted in *Women and Symbolic Interaction*, edited by Mary Jo Deegan and Michael R. Hill. Boston: Allen and Unwin, 1987, pp. 51–78.
1981   *Forms of Talk*. Philadelphia: University of Pennsylvania Press.

Gouldner, Alvin.
1970   *The Coming Crisis of Western Sociology*. New York: Basic Books.
1976   *The Dialectic of Ideology and Technology*. New York: Continuum.

Gregory, Stanford W., Jr.
1977   The grammar of motives as elicited by bracketing experiments. Paper presented at the American Sociology Association, Chicago, September.

Habermas, Jurgen.
1970   *Toward a Rational Society*. Boston: Beacon Press.
1974   *Theory and Practice*. Boston: Beacon Press.

Hare, A. Paul, and Herbert H. Blumberg.
1988   *Dramaturgical Analysis of Social Interaction*. New York: Praeger.

Harre, Rom, and Paul F. Secord.
1972   *Explanation of Social Behaviour*. Oxford: Basil Blackwell.

Hill, Michael R.
1984   *Exploring Visual Sociology and the Sociology of the Visual Arts: An Introduction and Selected Bibliography*. Architecture Series, No. A–1271. Monticello, IL: Vance Bibliographies.

Hill, Michael R., and Mary Jo Deegan.
1982   The female tourist in a male landscape. *CELA Forum* 1(Summer): 25–29.

Hill, Michael R., Valerie Malhotra, and Mary Jo Deegan, eds.
Forthcoming. *Images of Women in the Arts and Mass Media*. Lewiston, NY: Edwin Mellen Press.

Hochschild, Arlie Russell.
1979   Emotion work, feeling rules and social structure. *American Journal of Sociology* 85 (November): 551–75.
1983   *The Managed Heart: Commercialism of Human Feeling*. Berkeley: University of California Press.

Illich, Ivan.
1973   *Tools of Conviviality*. New York: Harper and Row.
1981   *Gender*. New York: Harper and Row.

Jacobs, Jane.
1961   *The Death and Life of Great American Cities*. New York: Random House.

Kanter, Rosabeth Moss.
1977   *Men and Women of the Corporation*. New York: Basic Books.

Kaplan, Abraham.
1964   *The Conduct of Inquiry*. San Francisco: Chandler.

Lane, Christel.
1981   *The Rites of Rulers: Ritual in Industrial Society—The Soviet Case*. Cambridge: Cambridge University Press.

Lavenda, Robert H.
1983   Family and Corporation. In *The Celebration of Society*, edited by Frank E. Manning. Bowling Green, OH: Popular Culture Press, pp. 51–64.

Lehman, Timothy, and T. R. Young.
1972   From conflict theory to conflict methodology: An emerging paradigm for sociology. *Sociological Inquiry* 44(1): 15–28.

Lemon, Thomas A.
1972   *The Rites of Passage in a Student Culture*. New York: Teachers College Press, Columbia University.

Levine, S., and D. Scotch.
1970   *Social Stress*. Chicago: Aldine.

Lincoln Journal.
1977   September 18.

1977   September 19.
1977   September 23.

Lincoln Journal and *Star*.
1977   September 11.

Littlefield, Henry.
1964   The Wizard of Oz: Parable on populism. *American Quarterly* 16(1): 47–58.

Lyman, Stanford, and Marvin B. Scott.
1975   *The Drama of Social Reality*. New York: Oxford University Press.

McAfee, R. P., and J. McMillan.
1987   Auction and biddings. *Journal of Economic Literature* 25(June): 699–738.

Malhotra, Valerie.
1977   A dramatistical analysis of power in relation to women. Paper presented at the
        Midwest Sociological Society, April 14–16, Minneapolis, Minnesota.

Manning, Frank E.
1983   Cosmos and chaos. In *The Celebration of Society*, edited by Frank E. Manning.
        Bowling Green, OH: Popular Culture Press, pp. 3–30.

Marcuse, Herbert.
1956   *Eros and Civilization*. Boston: Beacon Press.

Marsano, William.
1977   Groking Mr. Spock. *TV Guide* (March 25, 1976), quoted in Jean Winston, *The
        Making of the Trek Convention*. Garden City, NY: Doubleday.

Martin, Susan.
1980   *Breaking and Entering: Policewomen on Patrol*. Berkeley: University of Cal-
        ifornia Press.

Marx, Karl.
1936   *Capital, A Critique of Political Economy*. New York: Modern Library.

Marx, Karl, and Friedrich Engels.
1939   *The German Ideology*. Edited and introduced by R. Pascal. New York: Inter-
        national Publishers.

Mead, George H.
1936   *The Philosophy of the Present*. Chicago: University of Chicago Press.
1972   *Mind, Self and Society*. Edited and introduced by Charles W. Morris. Chicago:
        University of Chicago Press.

Mehan, H., and H. Wood.
1975   *The Reality of Ethnomethodology*. New York: John Wiley and Sons.

Miller, Jean Baker, ed.
1973   *Psychoanalysis and Women*. New York: Penguin Books.

Mitchell, Julliet.
1966   Women: The longest revolution. *New Left Review* 40(November): 11–37.
1975   *Psychoanalysis and Feminism*. New York: Vintage Books.

Moore, Rayland.
1974   *Wonderful Wizard, Marvelous Land*. Bowling Green, OH: Popular Culture
        Press.

Nebraska Sociological Feminist Collective, eds.
1988   *A Feminist Ethic for Social Science Research*. Lewiston, NY: Edwin Mellen
        Press.

Nelson, Howard J.
1955   A service classification of American cities. *Economic Geography* 31:189–210.

Omaha World Herald
1977   September 27.

Overington, Michael.
1976   Policy research and the future. *Sociological Focus* 9(August): 239–50.
1977a   Kenneth Burke and the method of dramaturgy. *Theory and Society* 4(Spring):
        131–56.
1977b   Kenneth Burke as social theorist. *Sociological Inquiry* 47, no. 2: 133–41.

Parsons, Talcott, and Robert Bales.
1955   *Family, Socialization and Interaction Process*. Glencoe, IL: The Free Press.

Parsons, Talcott, and Neil J. Smelser.
1956   *The Economy and Society*. Glencoe, IL: The Free Press.

Partridge, William L.
1973   *The Hippie Ghetto: The Natural History of a Subculture*. New York: Holt,
        Rinehart and Winston.

Penelope, Julia (Stanley).
1970   Homosexual slang. *American Speech* 45(Spring/Summer): 45–59.

Psathas, George.
1977   Self and society: Human nature and symbolic interactionist perspectives. *Hu-
        manity and Society* 1(Summer): 84–94.

Quinney, Richard.
1975   *Criminology: Analysis and Critique of Crime in America*. Boston: Little, Brown.

Rader, Victoria.
1977   Dramaturgy and social life: First steps towards a theory of authentic social
        performances. Transforming sociology series of the Red Feather Institute, Red
        Feather, Colorado.

Reinharz, Shulamit.
1984   *On Becoming a Social Scientist: From Survey Research and Participant Ob-
        servation to Experiential Analysis*. New Brunswick, NJ: Transaction Books.

Risman, Barbara.
1982   College women and sororities: The social construction and reaffirmation of
        gender roles. *Urban Life* 11(July): 231–52.

Ross, Edward A.
1936   *Seventy Years of It*. New York: D. Appleton-Century.

Sandburg, Carl.
1970   *The Complete Poems of Carl Sandburg*. New York: Harcourt, Brace, Jova-
        novich.

Schutz, Alfred.
1967   *The Phenomenology of the Social World*. Translated by George Walsh and
        Frederick Lehnert, and introduced by George Walsh. Evanston, IL: North-
        western University Press.
1970   *Collected Papers 3: Studies in Phenomenological Philosophy*. Edited by I.
        Schutz. The Hague: Martinus Nijhoff.
1971a   *Collected Papers 1: The Problem of Social Reality*. Edited by Maurice Natanson.
        The Hague: Martinus Nijhoff.
1971b   *Collected Papers 2: Studies in Social Theory*. Edited by Arvid Broderson. The
        Hague: Martinus Nijhoff.

Shostak, Arthur B., ed.
1977   *Our Sociological Eye: Personal Essays on Society and Culture*. New York:
        Alfred Publishing.

Skipper, James K., Jr.
1982   Public reactions to a popular study: The case of stripteasers. In *Sociology of
        the Offbeat*. Washington, DC: University Press of America, pp. 25–41.

Skipper, James K., Jr., and Charles McCaghy.
1970   Stripteasers: The anatomy and career contingencies of a deviant occupation.
        Social Problems 17: 391–405.
1971   Stripteasing: A sex-oriented occupation. In *Studies in the Sociology of Sex*,
        edited by James Henslin. New York: Appleton-Century-Crofts, pp. 275–96.

Smart, Carol.
1988   Researching prostitution: Some problems for feminist research. In *A Feminist
        Ethics and Social Science Research*, edited by Nebraska Sociological Feminist
        Collective. Lewiston, NY: Edwin Mellen Press, pp. 37–46.

Spradley, James P., and Brenda J. Mann.
1975   *The Cocktail Waitress: Woman's Work in a Man's World*. New York: John
        Wiley and Sons.

Stein, Michael.
1977   Cult and sport: The case of Big Red. *Mid-American Review of Sociology* 11,
        no. 2 (Winter): 29–42.

Strauss, Anselm.
1959   *Mirrors and Masks: The Search for Identity*. New York: Free Press.
———, ed.
1968   *The American City*. Chicago: Aldine.

Swartz, Marc, Victor W. Turner, and Arthur Tuden, eds.
1966   *Political Anthropology*. Chicago: Aldine.

Tuchman, Gaye.
1975   Introduction: The symbolic annihilation of women by the mass media. In *Hearth*

and Home: Images of Women in the Mass Media, edited by Gaye Tuchman, Arlene Kaplan Daniels, and James Benet. New York: Oxford University Press, pp. 3–38.

Tuchman, Gaye, Arlene Kaplan Daniels, and James Benet, eds.
1978   *Hearth and Home: Images of Women in the Mass Media*. New York: Oxford University Press.

Turner, Victor.
1957   *Schism and Continuity in an African Society: A Study of Ndembu Village Life*. Manchester, England: Manchester University Press.
1966   Ritual aspects of conflict control in African micropolitics. In *Political Anthropology*, edited by Marc Swartz, Victor Turner, and Arthur Tuden. Chicago: Aldine, pp. 239–46.
1967   *The Forest of Symbols*. Ithaca, NY: Cornell University Press.
1968   *The Drums of Affliction*. Oxford: Clarendon.
1969   *The Ritual Process: Structure and Anti-Structure*. Chicago: Aldine.
1974   *Dramas, Fields, and Metaphors: Symbolic Action in Human Society*. Ithaca, NY: Cornell University Press.
1975   *Revelation and Divination in Ndembu Ritual*. Ithaca, NY: Cornell University Press.
1982a   *From Ritual to Theatre: The Human Seriousness of Play*. New York: Performing Arts Journal Publications.
1982b   (ed.) *Celebration: Studies in Festivity and Ritual*. Washington, DC: Smithsonian Institution Press.
1983a   CARNAVAL in Rio. In *The Celebration of Society*, edited by Frank E. Manning. Bowling Green, OH: Popular Culture Press, pp. 103–24.
1983b   The spirit of celebration. In *The Celebration of Society*, edited by Frank E. Manning. Bowling Green, OH: Popular Culture Press, pp. 187–91.

Turner, Victor, and Edith Turner.
1978   *Image and Pilgrimage in Christian Culture: Anthropological Perspectives*. New York: Columbia University Press.

Tyreel, William Blake.
1977   *Star Trek* as myth and television as mythmaker. *Journal of Popular Culture* 10(Spring): 711–19.

Van Genepp, Arnold.
1960   *The Rites of Passage*. Chicago: The University of Chicago Press.

Van Mannen, John.
1979   Qualitative Methodology. Special issue of *Administrative Science Quarterly*, vol. 24, no. 4 (December): 515–683.

Webb, Eugene J., Donald T. Campbell, Richard D. Schwarz, Lee Sechrest, and Janet Below Grovel.
1981   *Nonreactive Measures in the Social Sciences*. 2nd edition. Boston: Houghton Mifflin.

Weber, Max.
1947   *The Theory of Social and Economic Organization*. Edited and introduced by

Talcott Parsons, and translated by A. M. Henderson and Talcott Parsons. New York: The Free Press.

Wedel, Janet M.
1978   Ladies, we've been framed! *Theory and Society* 5(Spring): 113–25.

Whitfield, Stephen E., and Gene Roddenberry.
1968   *The Making of* Star Trek. New York: Ballantine Books.

Williams, Hattie Plum.
1929   Social philosophy of George Elliott Howard. *Sociology and Social Research* 8(January–February): 229–33.

Wolff, Janet.
1981   *The Social Production of Art*. New York: St. Martin's Press.
1983   *Aesthetics and the Sociology of Art*. Controversies in Sociology, No. 14. London: George Allen and Unwin.

Yankelovich, Daniel, and William Barrett.
1970   *Ego and Instinct: The Psychoanalytic View of Human Nature—Revised*. New York: Random House.

Young, T. R.
1972   The politics of sociology: Goffman, Garfinkel and Gouldner. *The American Sociologist* 6(November): 276–81.
1975   *Critical Dimensions in Dramaturgical Analysis*. Red Feather, CO: The Red Feather Institute.
1976a   *Critical Dimensions in Dramaturgical Analysis: Part 1*. Red Feather, CO: Red Feather Institute.
1976b   *Critical Dimensions in Dramaturgical Analysis: Part 2*. Red Feather, CO: Red Feather Institute.
1976c   Theoretical foundations of conflict methodology. *Sociological Inquiry* 46, no. 1: 23–30.
1977   Research in the land of Oz: The yellow brick road to success in American sociology. *Sociological Inquiry* 47, no. 1: 65–71.
1978a   The division of labor in the construction of social reality. Red Feather, CO: Red Feather Institute, Transforming Sociology Series.
1978b   The need for an American critical sociology. Red Feather, CO: Red Feather Institute, Transforming Sociology Series.
1978c   Values and epistemology in dramaturgical analysis. Red Feather, CO: Red Feather Institute, Transforming Sociology Series.
1979   A theory of underground structures. Red Feather, CO: Red Feather Institute, Transforming Sociology Series.
1980   The structure of self in mass society. Red Feather, CO: Red Feather Institute, Transforming Sociology Series.
1982   The structure of democratic communications. Red Feather, CO: Red Feather Institute.

Young, T. R., and Garth Massey.
1978   The dramaturgical society. *Qualitative Sociology* 1 (September): 78–98.

Young, T. R., and John F. Walsh, eds.
1984   Critical Dramaturgy: Change and Renewal in Social Psychology. Red Feather, CO: Red Feather Institute.

Zaretsky, Eli.
1976   *Capitalism, the Family and Personal Life*. New York: Harper Colophon Books.

Subject Index

Abandonment, 13; passive, 55

Alienation, 14, 24–25, 27–28, 162; cyclical, 161; definitions of (Goffman, 13; Marx, 25; new, 25; Young, 25); general, 35–36, 47, 50, 62, 155, 157, 161; postcard image, 103; sex-linked, 36, 113

Anti-structure: and auctions, 53, 56, 59–60, 68, 71, 74; blurred, 10; definitions of (new, 14, 25; Turner, 8, 11); and football, 84; in Oz, 131; playfulness of, 25, 28 n.2; postcards, 92, 102, 164–65; in singles bars, 31; and *Star Trek*, 109

Auctioneer: bad, 63; charismatic stars as, 61, 64; family team, 63; and generating fun, 59; good, 55, 61; head, 64, 74; humorless, 62; reputation, 62–63; sexist, 51–52; sing-song, 59–61; team, 60, 64, 67–68, 74; *See also* Auctions

Auctions, 4, 51–57, 130, 163–64; bidding process, 54, 56–57; (bid up, 68; estimating time, 58; as a gamble, 57–59, 75; learning, 58–59; "show your number," 56, 63; starting, 56; stopping, 63; super bidders in, 67); business, 53, 62; buyers, bad (crooked bidders, 72; fans, 68–71; hiding objects, 71; naive, 67–68, 70, 73; professional, 69–73; semi-professional, 69–70, 73; thieves, 71–72); farm, 53; good, 55; as monetary ritual, 55; nonsexist, 52; as public events, 59; and sellers, 64–66; sexist, 51–52; as token economies, 55; *See also* Auctioneer

Audience, 12, 41, 60, 78, 84–85, 107–108. *See also* Football, fans; *Star Trek*, fans

Backstage, 12; at auctions, 61

Bars: "bar-hopping," 39; cocktail, 48, 50; and sex, 44. *See also* Singles bars

Bartering, 55, 75

Baum formula frame, 130, 132, 166; animals (female, 143–44; male, 144–45); animate objects (definition, 131–32; female, 141; male, 141–43); and Freudian formula frame, 145, 147; and Goffman and Turner, 146–47; human beings, 130; (female, 130, 135; male, 136–37; from Oz, 133); magical beings

Name Index

About the Author

MARY JO DEEGAN is Associate Professor of Sociology at the University of Nebraska-Lincoln. She is the author of *Jane Addams and the Men of the Chicago School, 1892–1918* and coeditor of two volumes: *Women and Symbolic Interpretation* and *Women and Physical Disability*.